About the Author

Nobuko Albery is Japanese, but studied and worked in New York for several years, and is married to an Englishman. She is the author of *The House of Kanze,* a widely praised novel about the great Zeami who created the theatre of Noh, and *Balloon Top,* an enchanting story about a girl growing up in the post-war chaos of Japan.

ABSURD COURAGE

Nobuko Albery

CENTURY

LONDON   MELBOURNE   AUCKLAND   JOHANNESBURG

First published in Great Britain in 1987
(simultaneously in paperback and hardcover)
by Century Hutchinson Ltd, Brookmount House, 62-65 Chandos Place,
London WC2N 4NW

Century Hutchinson South Africa (Pty) Ltd
PO Box 337, Bergvlei 2012, South Africa

Century Hutchinson Australia Pty Ltd
PO Box 496, 16-22 Church Street, Hawthorn, Victoria 3122, Australia

Century Hutchinson New Zealand Limited
PO Box 40-086, Glenfield, Auckland 10, New Zealand

ISBN 0 7126 1894 5

Printed in Great Britain by
Anchor Brendon Ltd, Tiptree, Essex

'Parmi les courages hors de saison, la bravoure des jeunes filles est insigne. Mais, sans elle, on verrait moins de mariages.' Colette *Mes Apprentissages*

– Amongst the most audacious forms of courage, that of young girls is quite astounding, without which one would see fewer marriages – Colette *Mes Apprentissages*

To Una, Lady Albery, my late mother-in-law with
much affection.

1

'Tristram, tell me about you more please,' I said in English, minding my 'l's, 'what make you happiest, what your parents like, why they live in France . . .'

'Darling Asako, not so much noise. I have told you enough.' Tristram patted my anxious warm hand on an aluminium armrest rather like indulging a pet animal, which reminded me that he had a dog called Sido, either in England or in France; that much I knew.

'But, I want to know more, I am your wife.'

'You're *adorable*,' he pronounced the adjective in French, looking exquisitely bored, and shut his eyes.

And our aeroplane was already 35,000 feet above ground, halfway between Tokyo and Anchorage, Alaska.

I sat up as tense and mistrustful as a thistle, not even daring to let down the back of my seat, lest it should provoke the aircraft to more unnerving jerks and jolts; and with such pain and alarm I thought of Father, Mother, Big Brother, Sister Fumi, and Brother Kenji to whom I had said goodbye at Haneda Airport only a few hours earlier but already a thousand miles away to the east.

'Don't cry, Asako, not in front of your foreigner,' had whispered Mother. 'Your foreigner' was how she described her son-in-law whom I had well-nigh jammed down my parents' throats as a *fait accompli*. 'You'll make him think you don't want to go with him and that's rude. Buddha knows how hard we are trying not to cry!'

Mother, then, quickly turned her back on us and took a long time blowing her nose, while Tristram, desperate to get away from the icky family scene, kept expectantly eyeing the flight announcement board, he who had already made his view clear on the subject of family: 'Family is an affliction, an injustice as well, when you think you didn't choose them.'

'I want to give you a piece of advice,' began Big Brother, grave and solicitous, just the way he was with his patients who suffered from pituitary gland disorders. He had spent a year in Germany studying endoctrinology. 'When you get there and enter a room or a bus, full of, naturally, foreigners, people might suddenly burst into laughter. For no reason whatever to do with you, it just so happens. Don't ever imagine that it's you they are laughing at. I want you to remember this. They are not laughing because you are Japanese.'

'What a damn paranoiacal advice that is! What inferiority complex!' Kenji stamped on his cigarette butt with virulence. 'My advice to you is this: if a blue-eyed-red-haired *gaijin** shows you but two front teeth, kick him in the crotch and a karate bang in the pit of his stomach. That'll teach him.'

'Don't listen to him, Asako. He is jealous.' Mother snarled, then smiling like a full-blown peony, made a sinuous bow to Tristram, the significance of which eluded us all.

Suddenly Tristram revived: our flight was now ready for boarding. As he held out his hand to bid farewell to his affliction of in-laws, Father and Mother plunged their heads down to their knees, mumbling again and again their entreaties that Tristram should be patient and be good enough to put up with me, the unworthy, inadequate, scum of a girl, etc. In the end even Kenji bent low before the man who was taking away from him his best friend and sister. Tristram stood amidst the low tide of bouncing heads, looking so foreign, so handsome, so stylish in his British horror of the gushy. I looked at him, melting inside with pride and thrill, then at my family . . .

Oh, my family! They were not only twenty-two years of my life but my continuity, my beginning and end and

*gaijin: a foreigner

10

the whole lot in between them. What little good, if any, there was in me, I owed it entirely to these five people I loved more than anything in the world. And I was leaving them, leaving Japan, on my own headstrong initiative and militant volition.

Two reasons why I was leaving: First, I was Japanese. Second, my brother Kenji was getting married when I met the *gaijin*. My favourite poet, Hagihara, sang:

I yearn to go to France
But France being so very far
I'll content myself with taking a train
In my new blue suit somewhere in the dawn of May

Every time I read this, I cry, choked with such yearning. Who, if alive and sentient and Japanese, would not? Would one be Japanese and not long to go away, go out into the world, the world that begins beyond the high seas that encircle our handful of islands? A frog in a well that does not dream of oceans, is he worthy of being a frog? I was a frog with a dream of unknown horizons wreathed round its inquisitive head. Whenever I read in foreign literature such a phrase as 'the train crossed the frontier and the Countess heaved a sigh of relief,' I could not go on. So overcome was I by envy and longing.

Kenji and I were conceived as our parents' patriotic response to the warring government's February 1939 decree to 'breed and expand' and our first memory on this earth was that of an oil lamp inside an air-raid shelter; whereas Big Brother and Fumiko, born in 1933 and 36, belonged to the generation of children who could remember eating chocolate and bananas. After the War, Big Brother called Kenji and me *après* as opposed to *avant* which, they claimed, applied to Father, Mother and themselves.

'Why are you *avant?* You're not many years older than us.' Kenji and I asked.

'Generation gap, stupid!' replied Big Brother, so proud to be using a phrase borrowed from adults' conversation. The *avant* brother and sister adored each other. It was

Fumiko's skin allergy that made Big Brother decide to specialise in endocrinology rather than dentistry like Father, having been throughout his childhood revolted by Fumiko's lovely porcelain face erupting in red spots and pustules, with adults helplessly repeating: 'Only way to cure her allergy will be to change her parents, grandparents, great grandparents . . .'

Naturally, Kenji and I, the two *après* in the family bound ourselves together in friendship tenaciously loyal and close. We felt ourselves so much one that when we developed a method of making precious pieces of chewing gum go further by keeping them in a glass of water with diluted saccharin as we went to school or to bed, then continuing to chew the tasteless but still chewable gum upon returning home or waking, we did not find it at all disgusting if one was chewing the gum previously chewed by the other.

I cannot exaggerate how much I adored Kenji: quite early I had determined to liquidate any woman, should she one day be so unpardonable as to try to become his wife, by mixing a small quantity of chopped hair and powdered glass into her food. But, a year after Kenji graduated from Keio University, things happened so quickly that my mortal concoction had no chance to intervene: a distant branch of my father's family had no male heir. In order to keep the old family name intact, as is common practice, Kenji was chosen to be adopted into this family, inheriting not only the obligation to marry their only daughter but also the name and a considerable fortune in land and property. Being the second son in our family and having neither a clearly defined future nor a markedly outstanding ability in any particular field, he could not have hoped for anything more opportune. Whatever reluctance he may have felt at suddenly having to call 'Father' and 'Mother' those who had hitherto been some vaguely recognisable relatives was dispelled more quickly that *I* thought seemly or loyal. I was stunned.

'I hate events overtaking us like this. I like to be prepared so that I can turn round and cock a snook,' I said to Kenji as I helped him pack to go to Tokyo. '*Les jours s'en vont, je demeure*. Apolinaire,' I said and quickly stretched out my arm against a revolting grimace I had expected him to make. When he did, I could not help whining with pain: to think that I was losing someone whose kinks and habits had been so much a part of me.

Kenji went on smoking, sitting on the window sill, his white smoke rings rising and collapsing in the over-perfumed spring breeze. I saw how blue his jaws glowed in the late afternoon; on his neck where I used to press my teeth, pretending to suck blood as Dracula, stood Adam's apple.

'Between twenty-two and death,' I groaned.

'What?'

'Talking about you, and myself.'

I was about to graduate from the cosseting hothouse of Sacred Heart University and face the pressing danger of my parents hustling me into an arranged marriage, when I met Tristram, caught in a monsoon downpour, outside the Imperial Hotel in Tokyo.

He was staying there and I had just slipped away from Kenji's engagement reception. My brother's fiancée, a year younger than myself, was quite pretty, affable, easy of address in an insincere Tokyo manner and together they presented a very attractive picture of a young engaged couple. As I joined the long queue for taxis and stared at the rain that ricocheted from the pavement on to trousers, kimono hems and bare ankles, my thoughts dwelt grue-somely on the effects of chopped hair and crushed glass inside my future sister-in-law's intestines.

'Yes, I found you altogether very fetching, for which reason when the over-zealous porter began speeding things up by making everyone in the queue share taxis, I tried to get in to the same taxi as you,' Tristram later told me. 'The tipsy businessman with a foul-smelling pomade on his flat head almost wrecked my plan by tumbling into the taxi after you, but the porter was so intent on getting rid of the cumbersome *gaijin* that he pushed me in as well. I'd been for some days in and out of nasty black moods, depression, if you like. As we sat cramped in the back of the taxi, taking at least three green lights to pass each sodden crossing, I was more convinced than ever that my past was a failure, my future a bore, my present a mess. You could say I was recklessly ready for anything new, mad, diverting . . .' So, there we were, Tristram ready for any mad diversion and I, ready to murder my brother's fiancée and hang the consequence!

I had not taken full notice of the American co-passenger – in the eyes of Japanese at that time all Westerners risked being taken for granted as being Americans, unless otherwise identified – till the man who sat between us, no doubt over-indulged on a business expense dinner, woke up with a belch and on hearing where we were heading, scrambled out in a pitiable panic into an orgy of rain and honking cars. The American was still young with his lean jawline not yet slackened, but fine long-fibred wrinkles ran horizontally below his eyes and gave his face, very regular and handsome, a texture of a weathered beam. Recognisably a gentleman, his high forehead bore an alabaster luminosity as if there were a lamp lit inside his skull. The narrow high ridge of his nose landed on the nostrils shaped like Gothic cathedral windows. I was quite moved by the not-of-this-world aspect of his profile and hazarded that he must be odourless, a compliment I do not squander on foreigners.

'What impressed me most vividly about you was your unobtrusiveness,' Tristram on his part said about me later. 'Maybe it's an inherent racial discipline or something to do with religion or diet, I don't know, but it would have been impossible to imagine Felicity, my ex-wife, for example, in a similar situation and not making her bulk and personality resoundingly known. I loved your bulk-lessness, being there but not overly there.'

As we approached the Marunouchi Hotel and I began feeling for my purse, he asked, 'Do you speak English?'

'Gladuated English Literacha,' I replied, over-anxious not to get my 'l's wrong.

He then said something with such speed and agitation that I did not understand; so I coped with it with what is known as a Japanese grin, which made him even more agitated, pointing urgently at me. Surmising he wanted

14

to know my name, I said loud and clear: 'Asako Katagiri!' shoved two hundred yen for my share of the fare into the ashtray half-covered with a sign 'NO SMOKING' and jumped out of the taxi.

When my parents returned to the hotel they scolded me: 'Unspeakable behaviour, stealing away like that! You're jealous, very selfish and ungenerous,' fumed Mother. 'When it's your turn, Kenji will be the first to congratulate you and respect your husband.'

The next morning, feeling generally rebellious, I was browsing through the 'Waitress and Hostess Wanted' section in the morning paper, when the American telephoned me.

'L-l-look he-he-here,' he began and even on those two most elementary English words he stammered and faltered, making his subsequent proposition: 'Have lunch or dinner or tea' sound so pressing as if his whole life depended on it that I blurted out:

'Tea!'

He chose the hour of five the same afternoon and I chose the place, Fugetsudo in Ginza.

Mr Tristram Harder was not American. He was British and was born and lived in London although his parents lived in France. After the usual preparatory and public school education he went up to Magdalen College, Oxford, where, said he with his irresistible chic of understatement which never failed to give me a ticklish delight, he had *read* history. After graduating with honours, being so full of promise, cocksure but not knowing what to do next, he stayed on, I presume, to go on *reading*, went to the Sorbonne in Paris as well, then obtained a doctorate.

Nanny Binn from Edinburgh who had watched over him from the day he was born, a true Scot, solid as a rock throughout his trials and tribulations, died on the night of Queen Elizabeth's coronation, November 1952, thence began his insomnia. This was about all I could ferret out of him.

'That's all. You're like my dog, Sido-Basta, so curious; her wet black nose poking about everywhere. I'll call

15

you Asako Basta unless you stop interrogating me. Very American, this mania to know all and reveal all.'

The startling first time for me, one of General McArthur's children, to hear 'American' used as a pejorative. I was profoundly impressed. Of course, I thought, he is English and after all what was America but an ex-colony of the great Empire!

As to his profession, too, he was exceedingly chic, almost dismissive, about it and unlike all superior Japanese males carried no visiting cards on him. Aside from writing art books, he apparently half-owned a gallery. 'Not contemporary, mainly nineteenth-century European. My mother paints abstracts, but that's her choice. From time to time I indulge in frivolities such as coming here to organise an exhibition of William Blake's drawings at Mitsukoshi Department Store. The dottiest, the most incongruous affair I've ever let myself get involved in: with the smell of fried shrimp wafting up from the restaurant below, loudspeakers blaring out the week's bargain items, escalator girls bowing and warning you all day long not to miss the step, the British Ambassador officiating at the vernissage, press photographers popping flash bulbs at the Emperor's art-loving brother or uncle, and the swarm of celebrities bowing everywhere, and no one's pulling anyone's leg, no, dead serious. Quite, quite unbelievable!'

How delightfully iconoclastic and original was this *gaijin*, I squealed and giggled, for up till that moment, to me Mitsukoshi had been a paradise on earth.

On the train journey home with my parents, I sat in a trance with my English-Japanese dictionary against my breast, reliving my conversation with the Englishman: I should have said it this way; had I known, I could have replied that way . . .

Four days after our tea at Fugetsudo in Tokyo, Tristram took the train for Kobe as we lived nearer to Kobe than to Osaka and after a long stroll along the deserted wharves and hilly streets of the port town, I found myself in his arms behind a telegraph pole, a few streets downhill a dog barking in the warm voluptuous

16

dusk after a shower. Feeling my lips burn wet as if blood kept pouring over them, I shut my eyes and lifted my chin and everything was suspended and dead still. As our lips parted reluctantly, like hot caramel being pulled apart, he said very softly:

'I wish I could take you with me.'

'You mean wedding, you wish it?' I asked.

'Well!' He quickly removed his lips from the tip of my nose, gazed down at the harbour and at the acupuncture clinic signboard, looking rather dull-eyed with all his blood rushing up to his brain in panic. That absurdly naive interrogative sentence of mine had quite undone him.

'You're really rather sweet,' he hugged me 'Well, suppose we get married..?'

Now it was he who uttered the word and my turn to go dull-eyed with a storm in my brain. He took my hand and kissed it on the knuckle. My fairy-tale infatuation turned to something much more serious, hardier as I peered up at that frowning grave look on his alabaster forehead.

I told Mother who tended to lose her nerve less readily than Father. She listened as she sipped her green tea. So pensive and steady was she that I almost began suspecting her to be mentally composing a haiku poem: nubile daughter, spring rain, bitter tea, and so on into seventeen syllables.

'So, I had it in mind, Mother . . . to marry him.' On this, Mother stretched out her right hand, grabbed my head, crept her fingers into my hair, ruffled it and all the while tears welled up in her eyes.

Is she going to be embarrassing? I panicked. To have rattled my cool, valiant mother! I burst out crying myself, then heard her say, far from being soppy.

'This is beyond me, you know that. I have seen *Waterloo Bridge* and *Brief Encounter* but what do I know about England, how can I tell whether you'll be happy over there? Twenty-two, look at you!'

She looked at me, taking stock of me and all my twenty-two years.

'Let's see your *gaijin*, there are foreigners and foreigners.' Mother sipped the lukewarm tea and stared in front of her.

That evening she spoke to Father, many of whose ancestors had perished in their fanatic resistance to opening up the country to the Western powers.

'She was not born for nothing on a new year's eve, Father. She is impetuous, headstrong, leaps before looking. It's in her karma. Who are we to thwart it? Besides, I must confess I am very curious, aren't you, Father?'

'You shock me. How frivolous could you be?' growled Father, arching his back. 'To rush a daughter into matrimony just to satisfy your own curiosity!'

'Think of her curiosity,' Mother retorted. 'Besides, they have sworn themselves to each other.'

'With no regard to parents and ancestors. This is *après* inconsiderateness,' Father raged and Big Brother who always took his cue from Father heaped on me how-could-you disdain. Sister Fumi, a much praised type of Japanese beauty with droopy shoulders and slanted long eyes, who at the drop of a pine needle would fall into a sentimental fluster, asked to see me alone and shutting the sliding paper doors of my room with melodramatic caution, began whispering urgently:

'So, you're off to the other side of the world! And, tell me on whose shoulders will the entire burden of looking after the ageing parents descend? When it gets to the stage of bedpan and incontinence, sons and their wives can't be relied on, you know that! In the final analysis, it's us, daughters of the house, you and I.'

Father was fifty-five and Mother not yet fifty and Fumi was talking of bedpans! With the self-righteous persistence of a rain drop that will dig a hole in a rock, Fumiko went on: 'How do you suppose my children will communicate with yours, their mixed-blood cousins? Their schooling, their language, eating habit, have you thought of all these consequences? Poor Father, to have to suffer this at his age!'

By imagining the joy of shoving her out of my low

18

window into a bed of iris I somehow managed to overcome the excrutiating irritation of having to listen to her worry aloud.

Tristram said he would brave my family. For tea. I had heard and read about xenophilism, but never before had I seen it put into such a spectacular action till Tristram crossed our threshold. That day, I had lunch with him in Kobe and took him home at four. A Saturday, not the new year's day or the Emperor's birthday, but just an ordinary Saturday, yet I found my father in his formal set of kimono, having closed the surgery hours earlier than normal; Mother resplendent as if about to attend a wedding for which she was the matchmaker. Big Brother, in his new mohair suit, sat on his folded knees behind Father in the entrance hall and I could see Fumiko had been to the coiffeur. Before Tristram's embarrassed eyes, their four heads went down in the direction of their hands placed flat on the tatami mats.

'This is Mr Harder. And there, my father, mother, big brother and sister Fumiko. *Shoes!*' I yelled just in time. Tristram with a jolt bent his five-feet-eleven in half and began untying his shoelaces. Mother and Fumiko burst out giggling behind their tea-ceremony-trained curled hands, whilst Father and Big Brother laughed and repeated: 'Ho-ho!' or 'A-a-ah-ha!' in amicable sympathy with the foreigner who, having obediently removed his outdoor shoes, was now clumsily stepping about in socks in the area which to us was a continuation of the filthy outdoors. Mother with charming alacrity offered him a pair of large felt slippers studded with absurd mauve woollen grapes. Tristram had no alternative but to put them on and follow Mother on wobbly steps into the receiving room, the only room in the house with Western legged furniture.

Father, Big Brother and Fumiko suddenly in unison raised an urgent shriek, pointing at the low beam and at Tristram's head, although I could see there was a clearance of at least five centimetres. Tristram, too, infected by my family's inexplicable hilarity, mimed a man whose head was in dire danger of being attacked by a beam. A general jocularity and childishness ensued and I simply could not fathom why everyone had suddenly to behave like subnormal drunkards.

In this frivolous mood everything went considerably better than I had expected. Father and Big Brother spoke haltingly in English with many German words mixed in. Mother and Fumiko fussed over tea, glared at Sawa, our maid, as she gawked at the visitor, cricking and cracking her false teeth, a hideous habit of hers to express astonishment.

Father, choosing the odd moment when Tristram was just about to tackle his three-tiered strawberry shortcake, drew himself up to his maximum height, corrected the folds of his kimono sleeves and, looking as grave as custom on such occasions demanded, boldly spoke out:

'My daughter no good. You want her wedding. Grateful.'

Tristram relinquished his strawberry temptation, clasped his hands together. Mother searched for a handkerchief inside her obi in readiness for the emotion of the scene.

'Yes, you take my daughter far away. I worry. Mother worry. Too far. *Zu verschieden und meine Trotter nicht genug. Zu junger.*' My father squared his shoulders and bowed very low. 'Take care, please, my daughter no good and too green.'

Mother in unison bowed her head with her handkerchief squashed between her eyes. Fumiko's boneless warm hand flumped on mine as she drew a sharp breath with a noise like a train whistle. I was flabbergasted and totally unprepared for this. A fluke, a divine fluke of parents. Father, thank you. Mother, thank you! As I dissolved into a shameless slobber, Mother and Fumiko simultaneously passed me handkerchiefs.

As for Tristram, he looked like an inexperienced actor who had just come on stage to find he was in the wrong play and did not know how to get off the stage.

'What is one to make of it all?' Tristram was more than a little bewildered as I walked with him to the Mikage station. 'In and out of *zu verschieden* and *meine Trotter nein gut*, was your father sure he wanted me to marry you?'

'He was, he was!'

'I see, well, here we are then. I am thrilled; in fact, overjoyed, if that is the correct reading of what he said. But, tell me, my pet, why in his view are you so positively no good?'

'Oh, he didn't mean I am no good,' I smiled, shaking my head indulgently. 'He was saying I love my daughter, she is precious, please accept and cherish her as she is.'

'He didn't, he did *not* say that. He said, in a nut shell, she's no good, you can have her.'

'The same thing.'

'It is *not* the same thing!' Tristram raised his voice, violently scratching his hair. I have since learnt that illogicality and contradiction can arouse such passionate irritation in a Westerner; unlike us who take pleasure in flitting over them with the wing of sentimental licence or whatever. So, taking a sledgehammer to crack a pearl oyster, I explained in my poor English that a Japanese father would consider it unpardonable bad taste to praise his own daughter to anyone; the more savagely he derogates his daughter, the greater esteem and affection, it must be reckoned, he holds her in.

'Darling madcap, before your father can tell me any more about you, let us get married.'

Accordingly, as soon as all the necessary papers were ready we were married at the British Consulate in Tokyo without pomp and cermony, about which Fumiko was scathing: 'What an anticlimax. Like giving away a puppy!'

Mother had the unenviable task of informing brother Kenji by telephone as he had been staying in Matsumoto with his adoptive parents-in-law-to-be, arranging his own resplendent wedding ceremony due in a month's time. He was outraged, laid the blame, as most of our relations and friends did, exclusively on my parents:

'How long have they known each other, a week, two weeks? Who is he, what is he? None of us have the slightest idea. And what does my idiot sister know of men, marriage, life? Nothing. You are there to protect her, not

21

to offer her to the first stranger who comes along: yes, sir, yes, sir, only too anxious to please you, sir!'

Mother was taken aback. I think she sincerely believed that both Father and she had acted in admirable accordance with the spirit of our *modan* age. She was silent for a while, looking extremely lost, then said calmly: 'Father and I tried to think of her, rather than ourselves.' On 'ourselves' she drew with her arm a vague large circle.

Because both Tristram and I had so much to do before leaving for France, where we were to spend the summer with his parents, I went straight home from the consulate with my parents. Tristram stayed on at the Imperial. Five days later, accompanied by my family, I joined him at Haneda Airport.

'We are now Mr and Mrs Harder, non-consummate Mr and Mrs Harder,' Tristram hugged me in a possessive manner, as we walked on the tarmac toward the plane. With my family left behind the passport control barrier, it was the first staggering moment when I realised that I was a married woman.

2

I lost my nerve, I think, when Tristram, till then in my eyes a conspicuously ill-fitting *gaijin*, suddenly and with such ease fitted into the Westernness that proliferated at Orly Airport. Frantically looking round, I felt my eyes go blurred as if stung by a raw onion: everything but everything was written from left to right, everyone but everyone was a Westerner and I a brazen *gaijin!* I tugged at Tristram's blazer hem, for I was no longer sure if being merely his lawful wife could help me bridge the staggering chasm I felt gaping between myself and the surrounding Occident.

'*Puis-je faire un brin de toilette?*' I brought out the speciality expression of my university French. The lanky fair-haired Occidental turned and replied with some amused surprise at my ornate French: 'Yes, love, I'll be at the baggage claim, over there.'

Please remember, it is not every day that a frog from a well swims in the Atlantic, I mumbled aloud as I leant heavily against the toilet wall; and I could not help wincing as one would at a rancid bad memory when the mirrors above washbasins shouted back at me how incongruously and embarrassingly Japanese I looked.

Seeing was unsettling enough, but smelling was hideouser still and struck me with a fist of queasiness reaching down to my gut as I made my way to the baggage claim: the people who swarmed over the huge airport exuded odours of centuries-old fried animal fat and acidity from their super-active sweat glands: together, they made the entire airport smell of salad dressing.

Tristram's parents had sent the village taxi to fetch us.

23

The driver with a drooping paunch and a tartan tam-o'-shanter addressed Tristram as 'Monsieur Tristan' with a family retainer's deference, and at once I felt the behind-the-scenes presence of my parents-in-law and had to curl my toes inside my shoes, terrified: I wanted so much to be liked, approved, accepted by them.

'Why, darling, why worry your little head so? If they like you, it'll be an added pleasure; but if they don't, they won't be taking away anything from us, isn't that so?' argued Tristram, bless his noble sweet soul, but on that dusty warm afternoon in June, as we sped towards his parents' house, an added pleasure seemed to me more like an imperative necessity. If only I were a descendant of Napoleon or an Olympic champion swimmer, anything but Japanese and nondescript! I'll never forget how puny, insignificant and horribly alone I felt during that drive, which showed me little promise of the glory of *la belle* France to come. Rows and rows of dismally banal houses were distinguishable solely by the colours of their shutters as we passed by. And shutters there were aplenty, yet I noticed with mounting disquiet that very few of them were fully opened at four on the exquisite summer afternoon. Like bandaged eyes and sewn-up lips, they were either shut or kept mistrustingly ajar on their latches.

Leaving the suburban ribbon development, we came into the vast verdant countryside, but here too, farmhouses, spaced out kilometres apart, an unthinkable extravagance at home, had their sun-bleached shutters biting their lips mum. Can the French see in the dark like bats, I wondered and was not at all sure if I was going to like them, the French lurking behind their shutters.

My parents-in-law lived in a chateau, or at least it was entered as such in the telephone directory: no house number or street name, simply Chateau de Mortcerf in the village of Mortcerf.

'In order to be classified as a chateau, it ought to have more than four turrets. We have only two,' said Tristram, yawning, as the taxi driver went in through a small dark green door, overwhelmed by glossy flowering ivies, and

24

presently swung open the two huge wings of the wrought-iron gate.

My idea of a chateau was that of the Neueschwanstein of the Mad Ludwig's; my surprise and relief, therefore, were profound as the driver pushed his Citroën's droopy nose into the cobbled yard under an immense platan and caused a gaggle of ducks and chickens to scatter and to raise a rudest, most cacophonic protest. There were filthy pails of water and feed, a wooden ladder with two rungs missing leant against the stone-and-clay wall of the stable block which housed a Mercedes, a Renault, and some dilapidated garden implements. If this was a chateau, couldn't I cope with its chatelaine, I wondered as I stepped out of the car as cautiously as if into a scalding hot bath. Tristram came behind me and put his hand on my diffident shoulder and for that one touch, I almost wept, I'd remain loyal and grateful to him all my life.

He then led me towards a small two-storeyed house, smothered with climbing roses. 'Here reside our octagenarian cook and her niece,' said my husband, scholar, fluent in English, French and German. Not knowing the meaning of the word, I concluded that their servants were from Algeria or Nigeria or thereabout. We walked round a tall clipped hedge, presumably designed to shun the rude gaze of the Arab servants on their masters, and entered a shimmering open space of closely cut lawn, the size and the immaculate condition of which could only be found in national parks in Japan. But here no sign of keepers or warning notices, let alone a stream of Sunday promenaders lusting for ozone and chlorophyll. Just a few white chairs and a parasoled table, from which emerged two lone figures.

Mrs Harder skipped toward us, light as a feather, her husband following in her wake with a slow awkward gait. The setting sun was low in the sky behind our backs. Mrs Harder lifted her hand to shade her eyes and a half dozen ivory and gold bracelets clanked down her slim arm. In the distance she looked forty; closer to, a remarkably well-preserved forty-nine, but I knew her to be fifty-six. She was handsome, erect, and had a sort of antiseptic chic.

Her large green eyes pierced, appraised and challenged in one emerald sparkle which would have curdled my blood, had it not been for the fine network of charitable wrinkles around them and the mercurial charm of her smile. All in all, I wouldn't have liked to have her as my enemy, let alone as my mother-in-law.

'Darling Tristram, how lovely to see you!'

She threw her angular dark arms round her son's docilely offered neck. Even I could detect a foreign accent in her English, her thin shapely lips strenuously curling to produce a tone of harsh depth and undulating complexity.

'And this is your bride, what a pretty girl, a lovely monsoon complexion, sixteen and not a day older.'

As she spoke, she took hold of both my hands and flung me round as if we were dancing a square dance, till she positioned her back against the sun with me in the downstream of the inflamed light and the torrent of her guttural inquiries, which ended with her asking off-handedly: 'And what's her name?' A silence struck. Tristram was visibly taken aback. I knew he had written about me in a number of express letters from Japan. Not quite sure from whom Mrs Harder had demanded a reply, I opened my parched dry lips ready but still hesitated.

'Surely, Tristram, you know your wife's name?' Mrs Harder laughed.

'Asako,' Tristram replied, blushing.

'Ah, here we are, Frank,' Mrs Harder pulled me aside. 'Meet Sakki. You don't mind, do you? Eastern names don't sit easily on our clumsy tongues. Must cut down to two syllables. Frank, Sakki!'

Mr Harder, his pale long cheeks squirming in a shy smile, offered me his soft hand, and tears urgently rose in me. He was, after my mother-in-law, so gentle, flaccid and unthreatening. I could tell that he had once been a very handsome man. His nose and forehead were noble and with a receding but thick mane of white hair he looked a philosopher-poet, the image of Bertrand Russell. Against his wife's vitality and gleamy tan he in a long-sleeved shirt and a cashmere jacket seemed frail like a meandering tendril.

26

'One of my gout days. Had champagne in Paris last week. Fatal,' he said to Tristram, pointing at his right foot with a slender cane. His accent was again different from either his wife's or his son's: I could not place it.

'Listen, children,' said Mrs Harder and we all listened. 'We dine at eight. If you could unpack noiselessly, I'd be grateful. Frank must take an hour's rest before the evening.'

Her last sentence caused Mr Harder to shrug his shoulders with a self-mocking protest, which went unheeded, for she was already halfway down to the white stone house of the octagenarian cook. Mr Harder strolled off to recover his sunglasses and a pile of magazines from the parasoled table. Tristram proceeded to show me the house.

I had read Dickens's *Great Expectations* in Japanese translation and seen the film version of it in Kobe and I could still vividly recall the oppressing sensation, almost an acute heartburn, that Mrs Haversham's mammoth accumulation of objects and bric-a-brac had caused me. And now I was walking into my own experience of *Great Expectations*. In the library and and in the drawing room, underfoot, overhead, crawling on four walls or spread on every available flat surface, anything was on show everywhere; even a lock of hair or a menu immortalised in gilded frames; snuff boxes, painted eggs, shells, guns, armour and helmets all resignedly collecting dust and dead insects; paintings of all seasons and tastes cohabited hugger-mugger on the walls: an oil of a shot deer, for example, copiously bleeding on the white of snow next to a delicate gouache of young ladies inside a sun-streaked conservatory; beasts and birds, stuffed or embalmed, rampant or upright, heads or hides, all in order to eliminate offensive void.

I was beginning to feel my 'Mrs Haversham heartburn', when we walked into a small white room.

'Mother has decorated this room. All white. So *depouillé*, so stark. It's almost Japanese, don't you think?'

I choked. If he only knew what to *my* mother 'stark and uncluttered' meant! Before any guests arrived Mother would make a quick tour of the room, putting away liter-

27

ally everything in sight into a cupboard called *oshi-iré*, meaning 'shove in', excepting one seasonal scroll, one seasonal flower and one cushion per bottom. Here in Tristram's mother's white room, crammed with white sofas with rabbit-fur cushions and chairs and pouffes and whitish paintings, I spied white porcelain doves nesting round a white enamel-framed photograph and a white heart-shaped *bonbonnière* on a side table draped with white lace.

Upstairs, Tristram pointed at his father's and mother's bedrooms with the expression of an usher telling a late-arriving audience to be silent, then directing me into a room with a cascade of cotton curtain, called chintz, as greasy-textured as if manicured with egg yolk, he took my hand.

'All this may seem to you so strange and difficult to cope with, Sakki,' he began.

I blushed, for his sake: somehow Sakki was not his style. He must have realised it himself, he went on faster:

'But, you'll quickly get used to the way we live. This is a house of insomniacs. Earplugs, eye masks, Mogadon, Seconal we try them all, yet can't sleep. Since Father had his stroke a few years back, Mother, very highly strung at the best of times, sleeps even less, gets into a state over his health and puts everyone else on edge. Now, look here.' He went to the door and demonstrated to me how to open and shut it with the minimum of noise possible and made me practise twice in front of him. 'The house is of stone and echoes terribly. Your bedroom floor is not carpeted, just plain wood planks, and tends to squeak at every foot fall.'

'*I* have my *own* bedroom?'

'Of course, come, I'll show you.'

When a girl marries, I used to think, she sleeps in the same room with her husband, economy of space apart from anything else. But, this is indeed life in a chateau. I was thrilled.

My room, large and oblong, had two tall windows on either side of a fireplace with deep red damask curtains rolling down from the height of the ceiling. The walls, covered with the same red damask, were padded and bouncy to touch, rich to the point of being slightly vulgar like embroidered slippers made in China. Two beds lying side by side and the dressing table were also covered with the blood-red damask as was the padded *trompe l'oeil* door leading to my *own* bathroom, which, to my great relief, was spared the tyranny of red damask. It was simple and old-fashioned with the wall paper that endlessly depicted a shepherd and a shepherdess in love. A tall narrow window at the foot of the bathtub overlooked the park and trees beyond. So excited and pleased to have so much space to myself, I could not help squealing with the agony of joy: 'In Japan we'd put a family of four in this room. So kind of your mother. Shall I go down and thank?'

'Please don't. France is a big country.' With a short laugh, amused or irritated I could not tell which, Tristram left to unpack his suitcases in his own room.

'Every house has its cranky ways and style. You must adapt yourself to them like water to the contours of a pitcher,' Mother had warned me. 'And, don't wait to be told, use your eyes and quick thinking.' After unpacking, I put on a new silk dress and made a bun of my long hair at the nape. I went downstairs all eyes and quick thinking, exactly at ten to eight.

A warm, unstirred evening. I could almost feel a scatter of fireflies suspended motionless in mid air. At the bottom of the stairs I heard laughter and conviviality, Father, Mother and Son. I froze. I wanted to fly home. I held on to the balustrade, shifted my weight from left toe to right toe, then from left heel to right heel, remembering Big Brother's warning at the airport: 'you enter a big room, laughter erupts, but don't imagine that . . .' It was one of the most daunting moments of my life. If I survive this, I thought, I can survive the marriage, a dozen marriages, a dozen sets of in-laws.

I returned noiselessly upstairs and stood still on the landing for what seemed to me an eternity till it was two minutes to eight, then dashed down at a breakneck speed and emerged on the terrace into the arrows of blue and green eyes lifted from schnapps and Perrier water.

Mrs Harder was dressed in a white silk shirt and white linen trousers with a thin green belt, her bare feet in white ballerina slippess, her short blonde hair brushed into artful disorder like a Van Gogh haystack. She turned to Tristram.

'She looks lovely, but explain to your little wife in the country one dresses *à la campagne*, not as if going to dine at Tokyo Hilton. Is there a Hilton by the way in Japan? Oh, how clever of me. So there is one!' She finished her schnapps, put the glass on a tray and stood up.

'Let me, I will, if you like . . .' I hovered at once. Mother had said: 'Don't offer to help. Go and help.'

'Oh, if you insist. Just outside the breakfast room. The slaves will clear it away tomorrow morning.'

As I walked away with the tray, taking note that a so-called progressive artist would call an Algerian a slave, I heard behind me: 'Frank, isn't it nice to have young people round?'

At table my declining a glass of wine caused an impassioned interrogation from the elder Harders. Tristram, used to it by now, said: 'It's fine with me. A cheap wife to keep.'

'But, tell me, is it that she fears its effects? Or does she hate the taste or does she go absolutely berserk on a teaspoonful of alcohol, now, what is it?' asked Mrs Harder. Since 'she' referred exclusively to me, I ventured to reply.

'I just never began.'

'But, my dear girl, there's always the first time,' Mrs Harder persisted. A lengthy argument stirring much spit and froth ensued, talking on top of and in and out of each other, contradicting, agreeing 'in principle' and refuting 'in principle' and so on. What astonished me was that whilst the debate continued, not for a second did they neglect the act of surveying, aiming at, scooping, chopping, chewing, wiping the mouth and refusing or accepting food. As for me, having all my life coped with a single pair of wooden sticks, just to select and manoeuvre the correct cutlery left me little spare capacity for anything else, let alone for discussing my principles!

30

I consoled myself by recalling a French film I had seen in Kobe, in which Alain Delon was ticked off by his rich, well-brought-up friend for eating fish *with* a fish knife. I have not to this day discovered why the Western civilisation, having bothered to invent the fish knife, then requires one to eat fish without it. In any case, so profoundly humiliated was Delon that he proceeded to murder his friend and drop his corpse into the sea.

Mrs Harder changed the subject and went enthusiastically on to *The Brothers Karamazov*, which she said she reread annually in June 'ever since I could read English reasonably well.'

So, she's neither English nor American nor Canadian nor Australian, I began the process of elimination as direct questioning would be deemed gushy Americanism. Presumably not Russian either, why otherwise would she be reading Dostoevsky in English?

'I can see a slow questing train of thought going from here to there, Sakki!' Mrs Harder laughed and with her index finger traced a line from one side to the other of my forehead. I blushed till my earlobes tingled.

'Don't put your little brain to too hard a work. I'll tell you. I was born in Vienna, Austria. There, now, have more blanquette.'

I did not want more blanquette, but to avoid another spiteful discussion on the principle of an Oriental refusing to eat bovine baby flesh, etc., I served myself one tiniest morsel of veal, which, I could not understand why, provoked a groan of irritation from my mother-in-law, who herself as a matter of principle never took a second helping.

During the entire course of the meal not a word was uttered with regard to our marriage, my family, our journey, Japan, nor to what to me seemed the most fascinating subject of all, how we had happened to meet. Mrs Harder who professed her aversion to mean tittle-tattle at table ticked off the father and the son as they discussed the comparative prices of wine at restaurants in Paris and London.

31

'Sakki's silent mastication is music compared to the vulgar noise you two are making.'

After dinner we retired to the library, Mrs Harder and Tristram with glasses of unfinished wine. Mr Harder collapsed into a soft low sofa in his endearing gyrating manner. Despite his very distinguished looks he gave me a feeling of spinelessness, twistable in any direction. The only question that even remotely concerned my country on that first evening came from him:

'Tell me, Sukko, is it true the Japanese take their bath at a boiling temperature?'

'I hope you don't,' snapped at once my mother-in-law, looking beautiful and supple in the dim lamp light. 'You know what the French plumbing is like. Atrocious. When we came here the place had one douche. We redecorated the place to satisfy Frank's American idea of hygiene and comfort and put in four bathrooms.' (So, the Bertrand Russell was American! I looked down on my lap, lest Mrs Harder should detect another questing thought chugging across my forehead.) 'No sooner had the work been finished than Madame Malenfant, bless her, she was thirty-six years younger then, went inside the garden cloakroom and found a cesspool swirling round her legs. A nightmare. Anyhow, to cut a long and unsavoury story short, our system can't cope with more than two baths at a time. I gather, though, from Tristram, the Japanese take a bath at night, and we in the morning as a rule. So far, so good. But, tonight it so happens is my shampoo night. So go steady and not too hot, poppet. Now, on this desperately *hausfrau* note, shall we retire and hope we might sleep?'

We did; we had no choice. I bathed in tepid water barely rising to cover my navel, goose-fleshed all over. That was my first night in the bosom of my new family.

3

Frankly, I would have been just as happy and contented with tender long kisses, intermittently broken for air. But marriage was a more demanding business: it had to be consummated. The first night, Tristram was too exhausted and agitated by *déplacement* which he abhorred and by seeing his parents again, so he planted an indescribably lovely shower of kisses on my face as I lay in bed with my conjugation chart of French verbs and tiptoed out of my room. The second night, he looked at me with a lingering long glance throughout the dinner past a tangle of candles and Mrs Harder's arrangement of tiger lilies and cornflowers. His glances were new to me and made me feel unclean like greasy hands washed in cold water.

Being a Monday when shops were shut in the nearest town of St-Loup-en-Brie, we had *petit salé*, drank a large bowl of its bouillon and finished the meal with melting Brie and *fraise des bois* with cream. When we retired, after a short desultory game of Scrabble, Tristram took hold of my cold hand, in which, unlike in his, flowed no Nuit St Georges.

'Come, sleep in my room.'

I recalled at once my sister's cheeks, neck and earlobes flushed crimson as she had haltingly briefed me on the subject.

'Tonight?' I asked. If I could have a choice, I'd rather be put through it after a lighter meal.

'Yes, my love, tonight,' replied my husband and since he could not be accused of rape, I had to obey.

I ran the bath and while hot water fitfully spurted with loud wheezing I brushed my teeth, washed my face, plaited my hair and sat naked shivering on a closed toilet seat with my French verb chart. I looked at the wallpaper as one does when one is in a quandary, vacant but intense: a shepherdess on the swing, a shepherd with a flute, a sheep that looked more like a dog and a dog that looked liked a sheep. My husband walked in, bare feet in slippers, loosely wrapped in a blue paisley print silk dressing gown. I covered my nakedness with everything I possessed: hands, the plait, the French verb chart. His look of annoyance gave way to a smile of resignation: he turned off the hot water.

'This is enough to boil a lobster. It's amazing how Japanese manage to live the long years they do.' He threw my verb chart on to my bed through the half-open door, came very close to my tautened cold skin, untied his belt and, opening his gown, drew me inside and held me against his tepid white long nakedness. I can't recall how we managed to walk to his room without stepping on each other's feet.

When we were evacuated with Grandmother to the country during the war, village boys suggested to Kenji that, if he would let them have a look inside my knickers, they would let us both shake the persimmon tree which belonged to one of the boys' family and take all the persimmons that fell to the ground. Both Kenji and I were famished. He looked grimly at the tree before he knelt before me. He pulled down my pants and helped me pull them up again, then ran to the tree with a wild yell. Big Brother heard about this the next day at the village temple school and when he came home he beat and kicked us both with a savagery surprising for an undernourished nine-year-old. When Grandmother managed to separate us, noses were bleeding and Kenji's wrist sprained. Fumiko took me to the well to clean my bleeding nose and with the same cold blood-stained towel wiped my bottom, front and back, as if it were stained just because it had been exposed to the village boys' gaze.

Grandmother called it 'a soiled place' and used to bark at Fumiko and me: 'Girls, your soiled place must be aired and washed with soap and water every day!' A perfectly

34

normal young woman though I was, to think that of all available anatomical areas, to complete a marriage, the soiled place had to be involved! I must have been the most defensive and worried woman ever to be found between conjugal sheets as I kept recalling Fumiko's numerous advices; a towel at hand, for example, and I wracked my brain how to snatch the towel I had left on Tristram's bedside table when it would be over, for it should surely be over soon!

Mrs Harder's fine linen caressing my closed eyelids, one hand plastered over half of my face, the other flying everywhere in combat against the next unforeseen, I thought of my sister who had aggressively sworn that pain was soon to become pleasure. Pleasure? I don't know how I could have endured what seemed to me ridiculous brutality, had I not drawn as much joy from submitting to my husband's desire and *his* pleasure.

Only once during our first night did I open my eyes and see my husband's face. I had seen that face before. During the war in the country Kenji would take me to where the railway track came out of a tunnel. We would put rusty old nails on the rail and wait for a train to pass over them, leaving behind miraculously flattened iron jewels. Rigid with excitement, we would wait till the steam engine's face emerged from the black deep hole in the mountain, the face that showed the agony of having to drag its long writhing body out of the earth. That transfixed lone eye and that cavernous mouth had haunted me in my childhood and now I saw them again on my husband's face. Afterwards, I clung to him with tears of gratitude that he was finally out of the dark tunnel.

'In case I can impregnate you keep utterly still for three minutes,' whispered Tristram like a prayer over my head. I knew the adjective pregnant but the verb was unfamiliar; besides, forgetting, in a state of general shock, that all this in fact had much to do with procreation, I paid little attention to Tristram's words. Only some weeks later did he feel secure enough with me to explain that a specialist doctor had given him a most pessimistic, if not altogether hopeless, prediction as to his fathering a child. Something to do with producing very few live sperm. I found it odd that he should want a baby, for I had been with him when he had stalked out of a tearoom in Kobe because of a crying baby, his face wrung by pure horror and irritation.

For a land-hungry Japanese who had known little of country life, *la vie en chateau* in the huge seclusion of twenty-eight hectares, bursting with nature's summer splendours was pure bliss. I had difficulty in checking my wild curiosity and enthusiasm so as not to be reprimanded by Tristram: 'Darling, please! One thing I can't stomach, that's a nature gusher.'

Long before I was consciously awake, I was already impatient to get up, too jealous of every minute that might flit away without my appreciating it. In eastern France early morning was chilly even in July. I washed my face and brushed my teeth with a cold-weather stoop, each movement minutely worked out for utmost soundlessness. As soon as I had put on clothes and slung across my shoulder a Japan Airline bag, I picked up a pair of rubber-soled shoes at the door. I always drew a deep breath and shut my eyes as I turned the door knob exactly how Tristram had taught me and dared not breathe again till I safely landed on the non-squeaking marble floor downstairs, where I put on my shoes.

I loved my breakfast alone, leisurely and unintimidated, watching the streaks of heatless pale sun across the table, always so cheerful with blue-and-white English china and lace doilies. After several cups of tea, bread with honey and a variety of jams I had never known in Japan, I would tiptoe down to the garden cloakroom where I flushed out the used tea leaves and dried the silver tea pot to put it back on the side table. One final glance to see if I had left my plate and tea cup in not too unappetising a disorder, I walked over to see Madame Malenfant. It did not take me long to discover that neither she nor her niece was Algerian but thoroughly French. Aged eighty-four, Madame Malenfant had originally been engaged as a *poulaillère*, a chicken woman, 'then, Madame had a hell of a row with all the staff working for her then: the butler and his wife, the chambermaid and her husband who did the cooking, and the chauffeur and his wife who was laundress, and told all six of them to get out. You should have heard the din, I can still hear it, which stopped at a stroke when Madame promised them each two weeks' salary. They left the next day and I and my niece took over.'

Madame Malenfant insisted on cooking only on a wood-burning stove, refused to use the Westinghouse *frigo* and I watched with some anxiety butter sitting soft-edged and sweaty on the kitchen shelf through the summer months. I could have understood more of her simple hearty French, had she had more teeth left in her head. She was shrivelled small and wiry; her skin was waxy with criss-crossing black wrinkles which matched her peppered white hair, pulled back in a prune-sized bun. Dressed permanently in a faded blue frock, a blue apron, thick socks and lace-up leather boots, she smelt so strongly of the burnt wood upon which she forever hovered that even if Mr Harder were serious when he said Mme Malenfant had not bathed 'since the Armistice Day in '18' any unpleasant odour had been disinfected and cured in smoke.

While her unmarried niece, Josiane, was nondescriptly middle-aged, sullen and slow, her octagenarian aunt was as merry and quick as a pullet and, being a little deaf, yelled at the top of her lungs and burst into shrieking giggles at her own anecdotes, more often than not about chickens and ducks, thousands of which she had affection-ately addressed as '*tu*', fattened, plucked, and eaten. '*C'est sa nature*' was her favourite line. Everything in human and bestial world was explained away by '*C'est sa nature*'.

Waiting for the unsleepables to wake up, I then retreated farther afield to the walled vegetable garden, where I sat on a stone bench under a cherry tree, pondering when I should be welcome to be seen or heard at the house. Finally, at about half past ten I steeled myself to re-emerge at the sunny front of the house and with a brave, all-purpose smile went up to the breakfast room.

A few mornings after our arrival, as I hesitated at the doorway Mr and Mrs Harder went on slicing the baguette and asking for the honey to be passed. My smile lost its crisp upward edge and I wished I could evaporate.

'If you want to come in, Sokkie, come in, shut the door and stop the *courant d'air*, please.' Mrs Harder was *frileuse*. To illustrate the draught in question, she turned up the collar of her quilted dressing gown, her face raw and white like a fillet of sole.

'Tristram must have taken a third Seconal last night,' Mr Harder chuckled with a friendly malevolence. 'On top of dry martinis and wine and cognac, I wouldn't dare, myself. Valium twenty-five milligrammes maybe, but not three Seconals. Have you slept well, Sakkie?'

At this point I was still standing upright against the shut door.

'Oh, yes, very well, thank you, like a log.' I was pleased to use my newly acquired expression.

'Wonderful. I do envy you, Sakkie,' said my father-in-law who called me each day with a new variation of name vaguely related to Asako.

'What's so wonderful about her sleeping well?' Mrs Harder violently plunged the spoon into the marmalade. 'What difference does it make if you slept like a log? None. What matters is that Tristram can't sleep. Why should you, his wife, sleep so well while he can't? You are up early like a lark, but of what practical good use? None whatever. It's your husband's waking hours that count, for they are productive. You should have been rubbing his feet, comforting him, lullabying him to sleep. *You* slept like a log!'

I could not tell how she looked as she spoke: I did not raise my eyes.

'Letti, you are so illogical. The poor child can't sleep the sleep her husband can't!'

'*Allez*, go and see if your husband is alive.'

Had I understood every word, every lethal connotation of her tirade, I might have shoved the bread knife through

38

my stomach then and there; a cantankerous mother-in-law cowing her daughter-in-law into suicide was after all as common as a cat run over by a lorry in Japan. But, as it was, I took her Wagnerian outburst at its simplest meaning: when husband can't, wife doesn't and resolved to do my wifely best.

Tristram was alive and up, turning his room upside down and inside out. The bed was half dismantled; sausage bolster, pillows and sheets littered the floor; furniture all displaced, drawers of the desk and the chest were piled up on a sofa. He turned on me, his hair tousled and mouth in a self-pitying downward curve.

'My pen! You didn't borrow it, did you, by any chance? A Parker, nothing special, black body, chrome banded.'

'No, I didn't. You lose it?'

'Can't you see I've been looking for the damn thing for hours? Besides, *lost*, Not *lose*. If you must ask such a daft question, ask grammatically correctly: *have you lost it?*' He flung about his arms as if conducting busy traffic, then suddenly flumped straight down on the pile of pillows. 'Sorry, love, it's just that I must have it, must have it!'

I could hardly recognise him. Is this my Tristram? Have I married a Dr Jekyll and Mr Hyde?

'You drive to St-Loup, buy new pen,' I said sensibly.

'No, no! You don't understand!' He wailed and began rubbing his right thumb nail against his teeth. With the midday sun held back behind the closed shutters and all the lamps in the room lit, my tormented husband appeared more Dostoevskyan than an English eccentric. Why didn't I stay in Japan and read about these bizarre Westerners in translation instead of having to live with one?

'Mother gave it to me when I went to Winchester. I've written all my work with it. I know I mustn't be superstitious but I can't write without it. I know I can't.'

'Please, when you used it last time? Where? I'll look for it everywhere you went.'

'Good girl! I know I used it to jot down my traveller's cheque numbers before going to bed, there, at the desk. I may then have brought it to the bedside table to underline passages in *Civilisation*.'

First I went up to open the shutters, baked hot by the sun.

'Don't open it! Can't bear the light. For God's sake!' Tristram covered his eyes with both hands. For a split second I saw my brother Kenji's face, laughing, normal and sun-struck; I retreated from the window and began searching all the drawers, but no Parker pen.

'Get down on the floor and look under the bed, will you, you're closer to the ground than I am.'

I knelt down and swept the floor with my arm, bringing out a few dead spiders, dried leaves and two Perrier caps. I sat on the floor and examined inside the wastepaper basket, where, buried in the mass of Kleenex tissues and *Le Monde*, I found an old Parker, not even a fountain pen, but a refillable pencil type pen.

'Is this the pen?'

'It is! My God, it is! Aren't you wonderful, that's the pen!' He snatched the pen from me. I got up and briskly opened the shutters and the burst of sun and birds' chirping poured into the ravaged room. Tristram did not protest; he trampled on his pillows and eiderdown like a clown on a trampoline, spitting his ritual morning catarrh into a handkerchief.

'I hate losing things. Any old thing. It really upsets me. Can't bear it.'

Since I came to know him I had heard so often 'I can't bear it' spoken. I made a mental record to probe into the deeper menace and implication of that expression.

Whilst I put his room in reasonable order, Tristram combed his hair, put on his silk dressing gown, its matching cravat and slippers and went down for breakfast without either brushing his teeth or washing his face. 'Only the working class wash and brush up first thing in the morning,' he had explained to me. 'We civilised people do that all through the rest of the day.'

With the three Harders in the breakfast room behind the door that shut out draught and me, I crept my way up to the attic where Mrs Harder had assigned me a cubicle so that I would not be in anyone's way. I was thrilled with it, just in keeping with my size and height;

it had a desk and a chair underneath a square window called a *vasistas* in the sloping roof-ceiling. When Mrs Harder showed me the place I thanked her with grateful enthusiasm. She looked at me a little taken aback and suspicious, then, smiling, patted me once on my arm. 'It's not hard to please you, is it?' Encouraged by her sweet smile, I prayed afterwards till I felt faint in the back of my head, would she one day like me!

Shortly after noon the father and the son, washed and dressed, came out on the lawn; the father with a *Herald Tribune* and the book he was engaged to review, Tristram with Kenneth Clark's *Civilisation*, both equipped with sunglasses, straw hats, notebooks and pens.

At two Josiane bent and stretched her barrel of a body to ring the ship's bell hung on the kitchen house wall to announce lunch. The sole of my tennis shoes as pliant and eager as my appetite, I wound my way down the house from my attic. I loved walking through the large stone house in summer: one passes such distinctly varied strata of air; toasted hot by a window, chilly on landings, a moist warmth trapped in a long corridor, then finally into the exultant midday outdoor.

The table was set under the pergola between the kitchen house and the main house. Mrs Harder was late as she had to walk back from her *atelier*, a converted lodge by the old main gate beyond the wood a kilometre away. We stood round waiting and when her elongated white figure was perceived, I noticed we all stood less flabbily. Josiane brought out a huge plate of cold meat and *crudités* and cheese.

'In a household of working artists one eats little and drinks Evian at lunch,' said Mrs Harder.

Mr Harder in a drawling avuncular intonation talked about the book he was reviewing that week, the autobiography of a famous English newspaper proprietor.

'He's a fraud, Lord Samrock: not a mention of his parents, his birthplace, which, I reckon, was in a remote town in the Ukraine or a ghetto in Palestine. On the first page he's already a young Fleet Street tout. His style is gush and schmaltz laced with pathological name-dropping. So very Jewish.'

Between cheese and peaches I made a mental note: find out what schmaltz is and how the Jews became so ubiquitous and powerful. All that I knew in Japan of Jews was Shylock, Anne Franck, and Auschwitz. I had no idea that they had since so flourished as to be able to own a string of newspapers in England and be members of the House of Lords.

After lunch the elders retired for a siesta, and if Tristram had slept well the night before and had not lost or mislaid any of his precious possessions, he drew me into his cool, darkened bedroom and in his arms I thought of the bright green ivy which alone refused to wilt and sleep in the afternoon sun.

4

Soon came August and Sunday luncheon guests. Mr Harder invited them in his indiscriminately gregarious fashion. With wives, husbands and other appendages, the number of guests was normally about twenty but when the French telephone line functioned well, allowing him to get through to a larger and farther-located circle of acquaintances, the number could reach thirty or more. Mrs Harder loathed having them and Tristram and I lived in trepidation, trying not to step on her all too readily provocable nerve ends.

It did not take me long to discover that the gyrating and floppy-ankled Mr Harder of whom the world would say: 'Ah, there goes the poor henpecked husband of that fury, Letti!' was in fact an incorrigibly spoilt child who nearly always got his own way in the end. In order to justify his frequent visits to Paris he had taken on innumerable committee jobs and donated a fair amount of money each year to secure charity-cum-social positions. With a meek little smile on his Bertrand Russell face, he waded through the incessant barrage of his wife's reprimands like a fox through thorny bush, unscathed and indifferent. When Tristram told me: 'Father reviews books for a few American and English periodicals,' I raised a vivid Japanese groan and asked how such an esoteric and ill-defined profession could produce enough income to support a life in a chateau and those endless telephone calls, only to be punished by a curt reply: 'It's unattractive to ask questions about money.'

On Sunday mornings in August Mrs Harder dispatched Tristram and me to St-Loup with a long shopping list:

43

three or four *gigots* and a great number of *quiches lorraines, tartes aux pommes, aux myrtilles* or *aux framboises* and the local cheeses, Brie and Coulomier, not to speak of six large *brioches* for tea, 'in case the Yahoos are so damnably inconsiderate as to stay that late.' Madame Malenfant and Josiane cooked beans on the wood-burning stove and prepared a huge salad. It was the same menu every Sunday.

'But, Letti, the Kleins and the de Baschers were here only two Sundays ago. *Quiche, gigot, quiche, gigot*, it's cruelty to animals, can't you vary the food a bit?' Mr Harder whined.

'Cruelty to *which* animal, let's get that straight! Lamb or me? You aren't referring to the animals who come to eat the lambs, surely! If those Yahoos and spongers and degenerates must have a varied menu each Sunday, then, I pack up and go to the Mamunia this second!'

'It's a bit hot in Marrakech in August, I'd have thought.' Mr Harder said mildly with an innocent concern.

'Frank, you'll be the death of me! Yahoos eat *quiche* and *gigot* in my house and that's that.'

'Hospitality is one of the oldest human instincts . . .'

'So is incest, so is buggery!'

'Go, children, *quiche* and *gigot, allez-y!*' Mr Harder waved at us who had been standing at a discreet distance away. 'And, toilet paper for the garden cloakroom, don't forget. Not that horrid French brown stuff, but the double-ply white.'

'No, Tristram, I forbid you to buy double-ply toilet paper for the invading Yahoos. Enough is enough!'

I had to admit that there was a thrilling magnificence in her unrestrained anger. It was operatic and suited my mother-in-law's delicate but hard-edged face with its green eyes sparkling like poison drops.

'But, Letti, you never use that repellent brown paper yourself?'

'Allow me to point out that I am neither French nor a luncheon guest in my own house. *Allez, mes enfants*, what are you gaping for? *Dumkopfs!*'

44

'Hospitality . . .' Mr Harder mumbled sulkily and knocked his head in his boneless manner against the palm of his hand as if he had an errant stopple stuck in his ear.

As the Renault grumbled its nose out of the gate, pullets and cocks somersaulting in its exhaust fumes, Tristram put his free right hand on my lap. A limpid summer morning, when everything seemed newborn and diamond-edged in the cool sun and me in a car alone with my husband, his hand on my lap, I was choked; I was so happy.

'Don't be upset, I'll pay for the double-ply toilet paper and leave it in the garden cloakroom,' Tristram said, misinterpreting my silence of momentary married bliss. 'Mother wouldn't think twice about giving away thousands of dollars to political refugees or causes, yet when it comes to something as petty and commonplace as toilet paper, she turns pathologically mean. Not always, though; as with everything else with her, she is quite unpredictable.' Tristram paused, scanning with narrowed eyes the endless stretch of immobile corn, then to my surprise continued in a level dry voice.

'Mother left us when I was six. Didn't come back till thirteen years later. She is like that.' He sighed and patted my hand with his eyes set fast where the road was erased out of sight by the horizon. 'You've been very good, darling. I'm proud of you. Felicity tried to come between me and Mother and that was a disaster. You have a kind of reserve that would blunt a steel blade.'

I was so taken aback and flattered by this unusual sally of confidence that before I could check my gushiness a question dropped out of my mouth: 'Your father, he took her back? He was not angry with her?'

'No, seems not. The point is that as far as he was concerned, until her sudden departure, there had existed a perfectly agreeable marriage, no quarrels, no major discord. One morning he wakes up and finds her gone. So, when she turns up again after an absence of thirteen years and himself having had a string of mistresses, it was for him like getting to know and falling in love with

45

Mother all over again. She's still quite handsome; you can imagine how ravishingly lovely she was then.'

'You love your mother very much?' What a mouthful of inanity, I could have kicked myself, but Tristram bit his lips amply, giving the question a serious thought.

'Not as I loved Nanny Binn, no, but I loved Mother in a way as I imagine a Russian serf adored his cruel Tsar whom he had not even set eyes on. Myth and idolatry. In a similar way she was much more mother to me during those thirteen years. On my birthday, at Christmas and at Easter with her Teutonic punctuality arrived parcels of goodies from Harrods, or F.A.O. Schwarts, and at random intervals postcards from Tahiti, from Rio, from Panama and from Yucatan. Her letters were full of funny drawings and smelt of her palm that used to pat my head when she came into my room to say goodnight before going out with Father. The same *L'Heure Bleue*. I kept all her postcards and letters, spent hours staring at exotic stamps. She gave no address, I never replied.

'Father's successive mistresses tried to win my affection with lavish presents, but none knew how to. Mother had that special talent for choosing just the right gifts. Nanny Binn packed the presents from Father's mistresses and gave them to charities. I lived surrounded by Mother's. As I grew from child to adolescent, through her unbroken one-sided correspondence, she remained all the more fascinating and dominant, exercising much more power over me than Father, whom I could see any time I wanted.

'Then, one morning she sailed into the breakfast room, where Father was alone, tapped him on the shoulder with her gloves, took off her hat and kissed him on the head. "Darling, are you still drinking China tea with milk?" From that moment on, she resumed her former life with Father. The following week they arrived in Oxford together. I said I'd come up to their room at the Randolph. After thirteen years, I didn't count on her recognising me if we were to meet in the public room crowded with parents and undergraduates at lunch time.

'I'll never forget how my hand shook as I plucked up the courage to knock on their suite door. When the door

46

was opened I smelt *L'Heure Bleue* and knew it was Mother. She stared at me unsparingly as if I were a new dress being delivered to her. She was as lithe, blonde and elegant as I had vaguely remembered; only she had a repulsively pagan suntan and was dressed in a fuscia-pink silk dress. It was late in October. Oxford was damp and chilly and everyone wore a wintry pallor and woollies.

' "Tristram!" she hugged me finally. "Frank, this calls for schnapps, there's a bottle in my suitcase." No tears. No emotion. I drank schnapps for the first time and we talked like three over-jolly undergraduates and went down to lunch, where Mother said and I never got over this: "If you eat this sort of muck now, I can't imagine what you had to eat during the war!" '

'She didn't know the war?' I asked.

'She was in the South Sea Islands and Latin America most of the war years, painting, swimming, and fishing.'

'Alone?'

'Don't be silly, she was with H.R . . . with whom she'd eloped.'

'H.R . . . !' my exclamation hit the roof of the car and bounded back to my forehead with a spray of astonishment. H.R . . . whose retrospective exhibition in Tokyo marked one of the most important Franco-Japanese cultural exchanges after the war, long preceding the visits of Sartre and de Beauvoir, la Comedie Française or Mona Lisa!

'But, I thought he committed suicide.'

'He did. He threw himself into a volcanic crater in Hawaii a few months before Mother re-emerged at Mortcerf.'

'Did she push him?'

'Into the crater?'

'No, no, to suicide. By leaving him break heart?'

'*Broken-hearted*, darling. Who knows? He was getting on, sixty-nine or seventy, often drunk, repeating himself, almost thirty years older than Mother. He left all his paintings to the wife he had deserted for Mother thirteen years earlier. Mind you, all this I've learnt from newspapers. Mother never talks about her truant years. Not even indirectly. Not a word. She's nothing if not savagely disciplined. I do warn you, Asako, she is not easy.'

'Thank you,' I said with a small bow. Tristram laughed colourlessly.

'Don't look so frightened. She won't eat you alive. It's only that Mother doesn't forgive easily. I'll give you an example: during the war Mother's only sister, Katia, just divorced from a Swede, was staying in the *pavillon*, when German officers occupied the main house. Aunt Katia was, I'm told, beautiful and athletic. She was seen a few times riding with the German officers. Others said she had accepted food from the enemy. When Mother got to hear of this on her dramatic return to Mortcerf, she wrote to Katia by then living in New York, saying they were sisters no more. Yet Katia was the only surviving member of the family Mother was left with. Unless someone who had actually known Katia had told me this, I'd never have known I had an aunt.' After some thoughtful moments he continued.

'Perhaps I'd better tell you some basic facts about my parents so that you shan't put your innocent foot in it. Both Father and Mother are paid-up members of the French Communist Party. Mother out of ardent if misled belief in a socialist utopia, and Father under her influence and out of no belief in anything else. Father is American, Mother, you know, Austrian. Many of her ancestors were military grandees in the Austrian army who fought with distinction in Maria Theresa's wars and alongside Schwartzenberg against Napoleon. But, since the turn of the century their fortunes dwindled. To pay for her art classes Mother was working in a *konditorei* in Vienna where she happened to serve coffee and cake to Father, at that time a Harvard graduate, loafing in grand style in Europe. They got married almost immediately, he twenty-seven to her nineteen. The young married couple went on loafing round Europe till the date of my birth approached. Mother had the cute little idea' (Tristram's face wrung a very nasty grin on 'cute') 'of giving the child British nationality. Goodness knows why. Perhaps she believed that the next communist revolution would take place in

48

England or that the English public school system was ideal in securing her continued freedom to go on travelling. At any rate, she flew into London, rented a comfortable flat in Hampstead, hired Nurse Binnie, and brought me into the world with a British passport secured.

'Three years after Mother's reappearance I married Felicity. To my astonishment, Mother reacted with venom and hysteria. Every night she would ring me from New York where they were then living, ranting and raging without any logic and soon persuaded Father, who was as always completely indifferent either way, to cut all financial support to me. Enter Senator McCarthy. My parents were then in the main stream of New York's progressive arty-crafty set, due not so much to their own pen and brush as to their superb French cook who produced one of the best tables in the town. In due course they were put on McCarthy's black list and their decision to come and live in Europe helped expedite the break up of my marriage. Here we are, *gigot* and *quiche!*'

Tristram stepped on the brake in front of the *traiteur*.

That night, not surprisingly, I did not get to sleep till the early hours of the morning. Such premonitory sentences as 'Felicity tried to come between Mother and myself,' 'As an absentee mother she became all the more fascinating,' harrassed me like knives thrown at a girl tied to a board in a circus act. Between a wife and a mother-in-law I am sure there will always be a certain degree of tug of war; but how can a poor wife cope with a mother-in-law who remained an unseen goddess for all of thirteen impressionable years in her husband's life? I was up against a *dramatis personae* who had blustered through the scenes of her life with stamina, passion and screaming egotism the like of which I had never imagined possible. And what a staggering variety of character attributes there was in this family drama: no two persons seemed to be of the same race, nationality, domicile, hair or skin or eye colours. I felt quite faint as I compared my kaleidoscopic in-laws with my family and relations, confined to one race, one religion, one colour of skin and hair and eye, and glued to a scatter of islands in the far far east.

I rubbed my cold feet together under the heavy bedding, telling myself, more butter, more cheese and red meat, Sakkie, you must build up your strength against the high-protein aggression of your amazing in-laws.

Guests arrive, having just motored seventy kilometres in a sun-baked oven of a car. Hosts and guests make a dash forward like *sumo* wrestlers in the ring, arms stretched out, the maximum of teeth exposed, fingers impatiently groping for each other's elbows, arm, or bulge. And to think the misanthropic hostess has just been heard hissing under her breath, 'Here they come. Yahoos, degenerates and *pique-assiettes!*'

'Letti!'

'Darling!'

'How divine you look.'

'You are too sweet.'

Smack, wallop, bodies coagulate, heads narrowly missing a frontal collision; two red mouths in the lewdest movements wriggle forward then sideways toward each other's cheek like dolphins squirming out of water; abruptly bodies separate in order to continue the same process with the next arrivals. It was very loud, the good manners Western-style. 'A nail that shines gets hammered down' was the kind of Confucian maxim on social decorum I had been fed on. A well-brought-up girl was expected to withdraw and erase her glitter if she were so uncouth as to possess any. But, here, one was expected to flash and amplify one's delight and gratitude.

'You must make an effort, darling. Go out and mix,' Tristram encouraged me; but too proud to appear insincere and too squeamish to welcome tactile greetings on such a hot afternoon, like a sun-shy plant I remained most of the time alone, just watching. I watched my father-in-law so at ease, happily gyrating on the axis of his Perrier glass in his natural habitat, a company of people, lots of people. I saw my mother-in-law gripping her son by the wrist and dragging him everywhere rather like a ballerina with her relunctant choreographer at a curtain call. As she kissed a new pair of tendered cheeks, her clasp on her son's wrist remained firm and I could see him itching with embarrassment. I melted, I felt for him, I adored my anti-gush husband.

The diversity of guests was amazing: a typical Sunday would produce a glutinously knit group of Greek communist refugees and several excitable French leftwing intellectuals, instantly recognisable by their outrageous gestures and unctuous voice soaring at the end of each sentence. No less regularly present would be a small but conspicuous crowd of foreign artists resident in Paris, who were totally unknown in their own countries but somehow managed to get accepted in the French capital: an unpublished writer from Ireland passed as 'a Joyce of our time'; a mediocre photographer from New York would be introduced as 'a Capa from Greenwich Village' and so on. Painters, photographers, sculptors and cinematists and theatre directors were welcomed by Mr Harder because many brought with them decorative young girls.

The Sunday extra help from the village, Aristide, the Harders' gardener-handyman; Hortence, his wife and their daughter, Mireille, brought out all the food, china, cutlery and linen and put them on the long trestle table set up against the kitchen house wall, guests helped themselves, and sat down at the white cast-iron tables scattered round in the dark-green shade of the walnut tree. After the guests began tucking in, Mrs Harder surveyed the scene of hearty guzzling with an audible sigh and disappeared; few guests took notice of her absence till, sipping their coffee, they heard the irritable tapping on a typewriter through the upstairs window: Mrs Harder choosing just such a moment of postprandial hush to write letters of complaint to the *P.T.T.*, the *Electricité de France* or some tradesman or other.

Mr Harder smiled wanly and out of sheer habit knocked his ear against his palm in search of an errant earplug; Tristram, who of the three Harders spoke the best French, went on placidly talking, not allowing himself a lapse of a single preposition.

About five o'clock, *France Culture* would be turned on

with jarring loudness on the old radio upstairs. Here and there on the lawn the more sensitive guests took their cue and stood up. At this crucial stage, Mr Harder more often than not turned defiant and asserted his right to be the master of the house.

'Do stay for tea. What do you mean, overstayed? It's only five. Of course, you must stay for tea. Mireille! Hortence!'

By the time everyone had had tea and brioche, the sun was low and the lawn shimmered like a honey-coloured sea. Preceded by a sudden stop of the radio music, Mrs Harder would descend and announce that it was really time for Mr Harder to rest. She could not be more charming and cordial as her guests took their enthusiastic leave.

'I've always enjoyed giving these parties for the sheer delight of being able to discuss the departed guests afterwards *en famille*.' Mr Harder urged us to give him our impression of the personalities we had encountered during the long afternoon.

'Nothing could be more depressing; the faster we forget them, the better,' retorted Mrs Harder as she sipped her infusion of verbena for her nerves.

One evening in early August, an English couple came to stay overnight. The husband was a celebrated novelist and an advanced alcoholic, most of whose 150 pounds was collected round the middle of his short unwieldy body. His sallow-faced, upright wife turned out to be an eminent psychologist on urban childhood. The husband had such an unlikely shrill voice to which he and his wife obviously enjoyed listening and the dinner conversation quickly became a monologue, interspersed by occasional syco-phantic interjections from Mr Harder. Mrs Harder showed her boredom and drank much more than usual. As we were moving toward the library, she cried with a brilliant panic, 'Oh, beds! Sakki, come upstairs and help me turn down the beds.'

'Oh, please don't bother, Letti. We'll turn them down ourselves,' said Mrs Conway, alias Dr Heaton.

'No, you won't, Flavia. The one thing I enjoy in house-keeping is to turn down guests' beds. Come, Sekkie!' She eyed me sternly, led the way upstairs and walked straight into her bedroom, where, as on any other night, Josiane had turned her bed down and lit the lamps. Mrs Harder kicked off her shoes and threw herself on the bed.

'Oh, boredom of all boredoms of all times and memories! Pity me, God, I hate oldsters. They stain me with their old-age mildew. Sakkie, be an angel, give me a little massage, will you, on the back on my neck and shoulders.'

Without waiting for my response she unbuttoned and peeled off her silk shirt. Mother who had taught or rather bullied Fumiko and me to learn finger-pressure massage had always worn a cotton kimono and than a thin towel put between her skin and my fingers. Mrs Harder's bare skin under my fingers felt porous and suctorial.

'Oh, how good it is, yes, there, there, oh, lovely . . . lovely . . . if you knew how those geriatric blubberers depress me! I feel just as young as I did at eighteen, there are few things I can't now physically perform that I could forty years ago; then I catch myself in a mirror and I don't recognise the old hag I see in it. That must be me, I say, but it is not what I feel I am. Hateful. So unfair . . .'

Hot and bothered from the physical exertion, I felt embarrassed at my mother-in-law's abandon. I would rather have her as cantankerous, tyrannical and unassail-able as I had thought her to be rather than this piece of soft flesh writhing in regret.

'Sakkie, you are a tough little nut,' she went on, her head resting on its side and I saw her lipstick smear the starched linen pillowcase. 'You are blessed with an insatiable curiosity, you'll never be bored. You can cope with anything. Be kind to my son.'

She turned over and her pendulant breasts, much more copious than I would have imagined from her wiry body, followed suit with heavy reluctance.

'You know I am intolerant and very selfish. But, after

all Tristram is my only child. Frank hated the baby. Couldn't bear the inconvenience, the noise, the smell or anything else that came with it. He nagged and nagged till I was fraught to the point of screaming: oh, anything to stop this nagging! I had myself sterilised. I was twenty-seven. I can't say I've been a good mother. I've lived my own life. But, he's my son. You must be kind to him. Darling Tristram.'

I had an aunt who had turned dotty and rancid when her passage of blood stopped, but she resigned herself, got over it and was now a nice old aunt. She often said to my mother, 'What bliss, getting old. I want less and less.'

Mrs Harder, having had so much out of life, now at fifty-six, wanted more and more, much more. I felt sorry for her who fought so hard to stay young, desirable, and abreast of the young.

The weather broke early: on August 15th we had the first storm and thereafter each morning we discussed the prospect of good or bad weather, a thing we had not done since June.

In the middle of the month Mrs Harder invited an Italian sculptor well-known for his active support of the Italian Communist Party, together with his mistress, her son and the chauffeur. Needing all the beds in the house, Mrs Harder asked Tristram and me if we would not mind getting a room in St-Loup for the following weekend.

'Hotel Sauvages in town is all right for a simple meal, but not for sleeping. Apart from the noise, I find it trying having to go out of the room and down the stairs to the public lavatory in the courtyard.' Tristram scratched his forehead, then lifted his face with a bright smile. 'I have a better idea! I'd like to show Asako Fontainebleau. We could stay at Bas Bréau in Barbizon.'

'Of course, why not?' began Mrs Harder. '*Allez-y, allez-y!* Take her to the Ritz, the Carlton, the Majestic, anywhere she fancies. Buy her the Chateau de Fontainebleau, why not, you can afford it, heavens, what with the tiara and all the rest!'

There was in her tone something ripped apart and twanging, more than mere annoyance or jealousy of a daughter-in-law, something erupting from a well of long-lasting rancour.

I saw the fine wrinkles I loved at the corner of Tristram's eyes harden like a rake. On these occasions, due perhaps to his English upbringing, my husband had far better control of his temper than his parents. He contracted then stretched both his hands a few times as if to encourage circulation, and spoke:

'There's no need to be sarcastic, I don't think.'

'Oh, dear, oh, dear, must one wash dirty linen in public?' Mr Harder wrung his napkin. He had the annoying habit of always having to crumble his bread and torture napkins.

'Soukie is not a member of the public, she's our daughter-in-law. And, Tristram, whilst you're in the mood, why not an eternity ring from Cartier's eh? I have noticed your wife isn't exactly rich in rubies and diamonds.'

'But, Japanese women c-consider jewellery a g-gaudery. Gaudy n-n-not rich . . .' stuttered Tristram, no longer able to control his vexation. 'God, it's getting too s-s-sordid!'

'What did you say?' Mrs Harder leaned towards Tristram.

'The boy was quoting from Shakespeare, Letti. Rich not gaudy, *Hamlet*,' intervened Mr Harder. 'Tristram, what about this one? "Nous avons bien diné. Nous sommes une famille Anglaise" '

'*La Cantatrice Chauve*, Ionesco!' Tristram replied desperately.

'Right-o! And on this highly literary note, shall we, to bed?' With a charming little inclination of his head Mr Harder pushed his chair back. Tristram strode out of the room. Mrs Harder picked up the knife her son had knocked on the floor with agility, a rich reward for her arduous daily Yoga practice.

'He's sensitive, Tristram, a sensitive boy,' said Mr Harder as if he were talking about a young neighbour.

'A queer fish. Good thing that I didn't go on procreating more queer fishes like him.'

'Darling Letti, your grammar! One fish, ten fish; like one sheep, ten sheep.'

'Frank, you are sweet! You can go through the downpour of life's injustice and affronts as if you were born with invisible wellies and mackintosh.'

She planted a little kiss on her husband's temple as he patted her hand placed on his shoulder. To the uninitiated it could only have suggested conjugal harmony of many uninterrupted decades. I bowed and, murmuring good night, backed out of the room as they, heedless of my exit, went on talking:

'Barbizon isn't what it used to be, though.'

'With the group tourism, no place in the world is what it used to be, dear heart.'

'Oh, Frank, remember our honeymoon in Greece with no riff-raff about?'

Tristram was sucking his knuckle, prostrate on top of his bed. 'I'm not that rich,' he whined. 'It's a vicious slander. Mother never forgives, never forgets. Darling, I'm not that rich . . .'

'Of course, you are not rich, you are . . . well-to-do.' I chimed as soothingly as a lukewarm compress and to my joy it seemed to relieve him of his mental congestion and the flush of red subsided from his face.

'Well-to-do,' he smiled. 'Asako, your English is getting better. Maybe, darling, what would you say, if we stayed in a nice little quiet inn by the Seine? I'll take you to see Vaux le Vicomte as well as Fontainebleau and Barbizon.'

'Anywhere, I am happy!' Being a new girl in France, any town, any inn, any river held a dazzling fascination for me. I tried not to read too much into Letti's outburst and the even more mysterious mention of a tiara.

The last Sunday in August, Mr Harder surpassed himself and there were over thirty guests to lunch. After coffee

56

and liqueurs I saw Mrs Harder stroll away in the direction of her studio with a newcomer to Mortcerf, a swarthy bull-fighter of a man in his mid forties, so I took the opportunity to go upstairs to my room to wash and freshen up. I opened the bathroom door and stopped.

There in my bathtub a woman was lying with her sandalled feet resting on the taps. Her eyes and mouth were solemnly shut, her kinky reddish hair straggling over her small face. Her clothes looked expensive but were put together with higgledy-piggledy carelessness. At my entrance she neither opened her eyes nor tried to rise, but hastily put on a pair of ludicrously large dark glasses.

'Excuse me, are you not well?' I asked politely.

She remained immobile. At a closer look I noted she had a dry spongy fair skin with pale freckles. Her colourless lips had the texture of crumbly biscuit, and I was enchanted with her turned-up 'Susan Hayward' nose, the type all Japanese girls dreamt of. I guessed her to be a few years younger than I.

'Can you hear me? Something bad with you? Can I help? If you like you can rest in my bed. It's more soft . . .'

'Go on talking. I like the way you talk. Like your voice too. Go on,' she said. That was how I came to know Juliet Sugarheim, my first Western friend. She stayed in my bathtub for at least another half an hour.

'You look funny in the bathtub,' I could not help laughing.

'Whatever you tell me I am, I believe you. I'm just fine in here. So relax. I can't (when she said this I knew her to be American) connect with lots of people, especially people eating and drinking and trying to impress. Haven't you suffered deaths when, talking to those people, their eyes start wandering round the room over your shoulder? I drop like a rag doll. I have a rabbit, Tarquin, he's divine.'

'Where is he?' I looked round, expecting to find a rabbit hiding in the laundry basket or under my bed: with these weird people one never knew . . .

'If you listen, I'll tell you,' was her reply but with

neither snappishness nor the imperativeness the written words might suggest. The most striking thing about her speech was that she talked as if she were really talking to herself, sorting things out, settling accounts, back-checking, mostly spoken on inhaled breaths. 'He's at this minute in my bathroom at the Ritz, sitting in a blue plastic pail filled with shredded Kleenex.'

Rich and weird with a neurotic rabbit, I thought. Pet animals often end up assuming the worst characteristics of their owners.

'How many boxes of Kleenex a day does he eat?'

'He's not a goat, dummy, he doesn't eat it, he pees and shits on it. All I do is take out the dirty Kleenex shreds and add some more. Two boxes a day, about.'

Talking about the rabbit brought colour to her cheeks and she finally pushed her dark goggles above her fore-head, opened her eyes and deigned to look at me. The greyish pupils floated uncertainly on the egg-white wet eyes which, presumably due to the dense humidity, were capable of a disconcertingly long unblinking stare.

'You're the Oriental girl the young Harder married,' she said as if to put the record straight, then shaking her head, added: 'Frank Harder is my dad's old friend. A spooky couple.'

Spooky, I made a mental record to look it up later in the dictionary, but the sound pleased me and I laughed a little. Juliet looked at me with surprise.

'You're terrific,' she declared. 'I'm told I must learn to laugh and open up. I need positive people round me. If you agree to take off your shoes, 'cause I must keep the floor clean for Tarq, I'd love you to come and meet him. Wouldn't you like to come and see us at the Ritz?'

'Yes, next summer, maybe, I'd like to.'

Not quite right in the head, perhaps, but by her genuine goodwill I was touched. Next year sounded rather unfriendly, so I added: 'Tristram lives in London, you see, so we are going back in two days. I'll come next summer. I'll take a bus to Paris from St-Loup.'

'Yeah, that'll be terrific. Too bad you're going so soon.'

'I found an American girl called Juliet resting in my

bathroom,' I said as I played Scrabble with Mr Harder and Tristram that evening. Mrs Harder had skipped supper and gone to bed early with a bowl of fruit and a camomile infusion.

'What an unholy mess she's turned out, poor old Daniel Sugarheim,' said Mr Harder. 'It's a tragedy that the Sugarheim empire has no son and heir and not even a decent heiress.'

Tristram was more specific: 'She certainly has appalling taste in men. The dago painter she brought with her was a really nasty bit of work. Paris is full of professional gigolos, ants swarming over a sugar heap. Quite revolting.'

'Is Juliet's father famous?' I asked.

'Come, come, Asako, even in Japan you must have eaten or at least heard of Chips Patata or Patata crackers and Popkiss? It's like Schwepps and Tate and Lyle and Sainsbury all rolled into one,' said Tristram.

'But, Tristram, you are wrong about that South American painter, you know,' said Mr Harder, belatedly reacting to Tristram's earlier comment as he peered at the Scrabble board. 'I liked the man. He's rather *sympa*. Letti tells me he's immensely talented. She took him to look at her paintings, and how often does she do that? He must be quite a genius.'

'Oh, Father, Father . . .'

'Poor Daniel Sugarheim,' mumbled Mr Harder rather like a benign cow chewing the same old cud.

5

The afternoon we arrived in London, it was raining just the way it does in Japan in autumn: a friendly absorbent humidity creeping into every crack and cranny of the city's life and people's mood. My skin, my nostrils and my lungs felt comforted at once and I wrote to Mother, full of hope: 'In London I am alone with Tristram in our own house, being Mrs Harder, not a daughter-in-law.'

Tristram had a four-storey terraced house, facing south over a patch of green grass which was fenced in by glossy black iron railings and called a crescent. Four bedrooms, three bathrooms, a large sitting room, a small library-cum-study, a dining room, a kitchen in the semi-basement and lots of stairs. It was woolly everywhere: the blue-grey carpet covered all available space, even bathroom floors had holes cut out for basins and toilets and pipes to grow out of it. Only the kitchen floor was spared the wool and was covered with greedy-pored, oil-shiny cork. On sunny mornings as I walked on the carpet, my toes dipping into a sponge-cake of wool, I saw shimmering dust somersault, twirl, and reluctantly realight elsewhere.

Mrs Apps, the char, welcomed us on our arrival by slapping her hands together under her loose chin.

'Oh, gawd, you've gone exotic, Doctor!' *This* to her master and employer; then to me: 'What's your name, ehn? Where're you from? Miss your family? Bet you do. Tea, Doctor?'

After those narrow-eyed, watchful and untrusting French of the Seine-et-Marne, I thawed at once in Mrs Apps's bossy inquisitive warm-heartedness. She was short, tub-shaped with a pleasant smiling face, as wrinkled and

60

powder-pink as a Chinese lantern. She arrived at eight in the morning from across the River Thames worked unflaggingly till six in the evening on numerous cups of sweetened tea and little else. She questioned everything, gave opinions and unvariably prognostigated disasters, all unasked for, on a variety of topics, then at regular intervals exclaimed how hard she worked; but her arms in the act of cleaning seemed to me to be confined to easy-going circular movements, for I saw in every corner of the house an age-coagulated triangle of dirt. Before a week was up, I was seized by a compulsive desire to beat the woollen dust trap, scrape out the muck in the corners and move all the furniture to see what lay underneath. But, as I was no more than a bride invited into an already existing and functioning household, I had no choice but to take this elegantly over-stuffed and dirty house lying down and try not to take a deep breath as I moved about, inevitably disturbing a sediment of woolly dust.

At Mortcerf I had been initiated into the Occidental dislike of empty space; here I was confronted by the love of colour unity: once blue, blue it had to be all the way. Accordingly, in Tristram's bedroom, painted and wall-papered in sour blue, everything else was blue: in his bathroom I saw blue toilet paper, blue Kleenex, blue soap, blue laundry basket, blue toilet brush, blue nail brush, and blue tooth brush. Only Colgate was defiantly red and white.

What Mrs Apps called reception rooms I would have called an over-endowed museum. In order to get at narrow strips of space left between innumerable paintings, Mrs Apps was obliged to use a small feather duster. Five antique chess sets of carved ivory and of papier-mâché were said to be so valuable that she was not allowed to wield even her duster, she had to blow at the dust. The tail of the grand piano carried two enormous glass vases filled to explosion with dried dusty flowers as the piano was an early nineteenth-century gem for which, according to Tristram, water would be death and disaster.

The museum clutter extended under foot as well: colourful Bedouin rugs were strategically scattered about

61

the place, under a coffee table, beneath a Venetian suit of armour and over the traffic-worn patches of fitted carpet, all ashen-faced from decades of foot grime. Under the dining table was a long-haired blue-and-white Chinese carpet, inside which hibernated a wide variety of desiccated or rotting food. In these circumstances I was grateful that I was allowed to keep my outdoor shoes on everywhere inside the house.

Feeling myself a stray cat let in by the backdoor into the woolly comfort of my husband's museum house, I was inhibited from asking too many questions. I did not ask, for instance, why my husband was addressed as 'Doctor' by his char and in most of his correspondence. Only months later did one of his chess friends tell me: 'Ah, that's because he's a D.Litt. I'm a D. Litt., too but I don't tell my maid to call me Doctor. Tristram is like that. It's his style.' Nor did I question why the linen cupboard was filled to the ceiling with sheets, napkins, doilies and mats with D and B, but not H for Harder, monogrammed on them. Touching the spine of the monogram, stiff and proud like healing cuts, I ventured only this much: 'Why put your initials on things you use exclusively in your own house? Guests steal them, Mrs Apps?'

'No, no, it's just the style of things here; you see, Doctor's family's been rich for a long long time.'

Like a polite house guest, I asked no more, content that from all accounts I seemed to have married a highly stylish gentleman.

It was also his style to let Sido-Basta, a ten-year-old dachshund, live with us inside the woolly confinement. She was obese in the shape of a hot-water bottle with a tiny bat-like head and sad reproachful eyes. She smelt and snored and twitched in her sleep. Tristram was devoted to Sido.

'I like the picture of a dog in its basket by the fireplace, radiators gently coughing, butter melting on hot toast, a pipe, a good book and music, Telemann or Shütz or Scarlatti, nothing more modern, to me that is home. Now that I'm married again, I'd love to spend as many evenings as possible at home. I'm really a *casanier*.'

To complete his picture of domestic bliss, Tristram took my hand and made me caress Sido in her pungently stinking basket. Under so much attention Sido turned coquette, rolled on her back, opened out and wriggled her four ridiculous legs. I had owned dogs which were treated as such and contented as such. I had loved them dearly, but they knew their place and lived outdoors on their four legs and slept in a dog house and when they died were buried in our garden corner, where we put flowers and bowl of rice every August, the month in which the dead returned to pay us friendly visits. Here in England, because of an unsubstantiated belief that dogs preferred our way of life, the poor beasts had to live in the house just like us.

'Felicity had the idea rather like that of the Chinese communist leaders who, as soon as they conquered Peking, ordered annihilation of its canine population so that their food could be given to starving humans. I think she neither really liked dogs nor approved of them. I hope you do, darling.'

I replied, I love them.

Back in London Tristram was a working man, although not the way I understood the word work. His gallery in Conduit Street, Beaufort and Harder, was open ten to five Tuesday to Saturday, but he never got there before eleven, often not till after lunch, from where he moved on to various appointments. Having been used to a father who worked on his feet in a white dentist's uniform from eight to seven, I was charmed by his free-range life style, which, appeared nevertheless to earn enough to support himself, his wife and his dog in great comfort. The way he dressed to go to work struck me as being equally unconventional: tweedy suit or double-breasted blazer and grey flannel trousers, with a coloured or striped shirt, daringly topped off with a dotted or striped tie. With his pockets irregularly bulging with what his father termed as 'British impedimenta': a pipe, a pouch of tobacco, a gold toothpick, a Dunhill cigar cutter, a Smythson diary and so on, he looked at once well-to-do and Bohemian, casually distinguished.

The gallery was staffed by a young assistant and a secretary. To my 'Who is Beaufort, does he exist?' Tristram responded by inviting Colin Beaufort to dinner. He was short, plump and ugly with the unnerving habit of one eye opening much more slowly than the other: as the one eye remained recumbent like a sleeping lizard, the other flashed open, catching you unawares. An over-greasy fiftyish, had he not been so blatantly well-dressed and groomed, I'd have said he was a quick-witted and a joky head waiter. But, listening to him, no one was left in doubt that he had friends in high, very high places and knew the most intimate and confidential details of their lives.

'Maybe he is a tax inspector or a Russian spy, Tristram. He knows indecently too much!' I said after our guests had gone.

'Don't be silly. He is a multi-millionaire. Why should he spy or work from nine to five?'

'Multi-millionaire in gallery business?'

'Of course not. He's a commodity broker, speculating in sugar, coffee and that sort of things.'

'I had a feeling he'd not been rich for a long long time.' I took pleasure in imitating one of Mrs Apps's expressions.

'Your feeling is correct. He started from nothing and nearly starved.'

'But, he has a beautiful name, Beau-fort.'

'It's a comparatively recent acquisition. His real name was something like Shakim or Sakkarine.'

'Jewish?' I asked and was surprised that I had already learnt to imitate that slightly sibilant tone of my in-laws on the subject.

'*Naturlisch!*' said Tristram.

'How interesting, Mr Beaufort is the first Jewish person I have met.'

A piece of toast warped under a large blob of marmalade and, falling short of Tristram's waiting mouth, dribbled down the front of his silk dressing gown. I quickly handed him a knife with which he scraped off the offending smudge.

'Colin isn't as bad as some people say. A very astute

businessman and a very loyal friend,' said Tristram, removing the stickiness with a dampened napkin.

No longer just son of the family, but master of his own household, Tristram entertained frequently at home. Here again, like a rented pet, I tried not to get in the way of hired professionals who arrived at five in the afternoon and knew the kitchen and the dining room and the pantry far better than I did. In practice the only contribution I made to the evening was to light the candles at the right moment and to sit unobtrusively at one end of the table, adoring my husband at the opposite end who, with so many candles between us and his airborne caramel hair glowing like a halo, looked the image of a saint burning at the stake.

Eating is not one of the most attractive-looking human activities; so why do people combine this act of basic animal need with higher human aspirations such as social climbing or communication of charm and intelligence? Myself, I'd be so much happier to be asked to meet persons of quality without the onerous ritual of eating. I could not help wondering why a professed stay-at-home like Tristram was so obsessed with the interminable repetition of eating in other people's houses, then promptly inviting them to do the same in our own house.

Soon a day came when it was revealed to me how dead serious the feed-me-feed-you merry-go-round was in civilised society. Tristram showed me an old notebook, minutely filled with names of his friends and acquaintances round the world with the number of luncheons and dinners each had asked him to against the number of meals he had given each in return. Cocktails were marked in parentheses. 'They really don't count,' said he. 'A barbarous invention of American Yahoos and almost an insult. I suppose you could say I enjoy the idea of asking people more than actually having them; but I equally hate not being asked back. If someone, after having been to my house twice running, does not invite me back, I stop asking.'

I looked at him in disbelief, but he was not joking but undilutedly serious.

'Not counting cocktails and teas, fifty-seven per cent of those whom I had entertained returned the hospitality last year,' he said with a mathematical precision which betrayed his rancour.

'Only half of those people who come here?' I gasped.

'In a cosmopolitan city like London one cannot avoid a low percentage of returns,' said Tristram. 'A galaxy of what one might call illustrious spongers, celebrated artists, politicians in power, famed beauties, and so on feel they have made a handsome return by merely being there.'

He spoke with philosophical calm, but I could tell that the forty-three per cent of unreturned hospitality dug a deeper festering wound in his soul than I would have believed possible or seemly in someone as intelligent and sophisticated as Tristram, and who was besides not without a sense of humour! But then, in many ways he was still the boy abandoned by his mother who could shock me by casually remarking: 'When Felicity and I divorced I had a written undertaking from her to the effect that she would not see my friends. I gave her mine not to see hers.'

Yet, paranoid about being unwanted as he was, there was in him much of his misanthropic mother, and the ambivalence was intense: half an hour before leaving the house for an important social event, having downed at least two dry martinis, it was his wont to heave a long petulant sigh:

'Oh, how I hate going out, putting on a show, parading myself, I wish I could be eating poached eggs on toast at home! And we have such a nice cosy house. Asako, you really must try and spare me these ordeals!'

I refrained from comment, chewing the inside of my mouth, and I was right to do so, for only a short while later, I would be marvelling at my husband as he pranced into a brightly lit drawing room with a loose-limbed debonair charm, saying 'Hey-low!' to everyone. It was I who dawdled behind, intimidated by the laughter and stock-taking glances shooting at me out of the crowded room.

That first autumn in London, Tristram did not mislay

his Parker pen too frequently and seemed to enjoy life. I myself was excited, curious and thought myself one of the luckiest Japanese as I visited the historical monuments and museums. I was more than comfortably off on the six pounds ten shillings weekly pocket money my husband gave me; he paid butcher's, greengrocer's, Barkers's and Harrods's bills direct by cheques and for other household expenses I kept an account of the money he advanced me each Monday morning. Tristram also paid for my English classes and when he discovered that I had studied the piano for six years in Japan he engaged and paid for a Mr Goldberger to come every Thursday afternoon to give me lessons.

Mother with a touching repetitiousness urged me in her letters to be so very very grateful to my husband, 'for if he had married an English girl he wouldn't have had to spend money educating her for the Western style life. He is your master, your teacher, your fate. Without him you'd be nothing.'

I was inspired; I hand-washed Tristram's underwear in soap flakes as he was allergic to any washing detergent; I shampooed his hair and rinsed it with fresh lemon juice twice weekly as his pale fine hair became greasy quickly; I massaged him when he complained of tension in the back; shopped, wrapped and mailed medicine, teas, books and crystalised ginger requested by his parents to their winter address in rue de Grenelle in Paris. Having learnt to type at the YWCA in Kobe, I made myself useful at the gallery on Mrs McCay's days off and also at the openings of exhibitions. Soon I began actually chancing upon people who knew me by my first name in the street. I felt I belonged here and was on the whole very pleased with my life. At rare moments when I felt dejected and home-sick, all I had to do to take heart again was to think of ten million other Japanese who were cooped up in the Japnese archipelago, ignorant of all that I had seen and heard and learnt, however hard the initial pain of learning might have seemed at times.

In the new year my parent-in-law after a holiday in Marrakech arrived in London and took a service flat in

Curzon Street. Simultaneously, Tristram was plunged into a state of gloom and despondency.

'Nothing to do with them being here, it's like this every year,' he said. A statement like this reduced our age difference at a stroke and his intellectual superiority to nil. Just a spoilt little boy, I smiled, and did everything to cheer him up.

'No use, Asako, sweet of you to try, but I see a year of waste behind me and another ahead of me, all of 365 bloody long days. I know a man who every seventh year on January first arbitrarily changes his occupation. Not just a job or an employment, but the whole scope of his life. A brilliant, industrious, disciplined man. Be it designing speed boats, farming in Lincolnshire or cooking in the best kitchens of Europe, having achieved near perfection, come the seventh year, he chucks it all away and starts from scratch. Every new year's day I think of him and depression rises like damp in me . . .'

'Ooom, aam, uum!' How I wished to be his rock and inspiration and help; but words failed me and I was left with a samurai grunt. What could a novice wife and an apprentice European do for someone who, according to Colin, is 'probably one of the most brilliant brains of his generation.'

I did what I could: tell facts. 'You're an excellent scholar,' I began. 'You have written six books and you are not yet thirty-four. You have lots of friends. The telephone rings and rings. Everyone wants you. A fashionable gallery in Mayfair, a lovely house, Sido, Mrs Apps and me, all here to make you happy.'

To my great surprise, it worked. Tristram put his glass of whisky on the bedside table. 'What a really nice person you are. I feel I might sleep tonight. Help me, go on, tell me anything else that you can think of that I should be pleased with and grateful for.'

I sat on the floor with my back against his bed and tracing the scalloped lace that bordered the hem of my nightdress like a string of beads, re-enumerated in detail his good fortune. He soon fell asleep.

Colin of whom I had heard someone remark: 'Colin's

aiming to shove his way into the House of Lords by throwing lavish parties' organised a soirée for my parents-in-law at his Chester Square house. Thirty-four to dinner and at ten thirty fifty more had been asked to drop in for coffee, dance and breakfast.

'Oh, impossible, they'd be too proud to come *after* dinner,' I laughed.

'You'd be surprised,' retorted Tristram. 'The English upper class would sell their mothers, do anything to get free booze and eats. You wait and see.'

'But, wouldn't it be better to do it well with a small number of people and go to bed at a sensible hour?'

'Colin loves a crowd, he'd be lost and uncomfortable with six or eight. Besides, with a Labour Government in, he has so many Labour peers and MPs he's got to add to his list, yet he doesn't want to appear too much of an opportunist by turning a cold shoulder on his old Tory friends.'

Truly, I was amazed. I thought one had to do something far beyond the call of duty, like conquering a new continent or sinking Napoleon's fleet to get ennobled in gallant old England. But, just feeding influential stomachs! I remembered Mrs Harder's scathing comment on American civilisation: 'It's quite unabashedly *oral*. Don't forget, the majority of Americans are immigrants who have starved once.' I had not understood this last summer, but now I concluded that the British too are oral, if sumptuous meals could buy one's way into one of the world's most dignified institutions. And to think that during the war the British had known only a moderate sort of rationing, not the morally and physically atrophying near-starvation we had suffered . . .

Tristram insisted on my wearing a kimono.

'You look so lovely in it. Do wear it, darling, to please me. Mother'll be thrilled, too. She hasn't seen you in a kimono,' he crooned. I put on the best and most formal of all my kimonos.

When we arrived at Colin's, I found Mrs Harder in an unmistakably Parisian and *haute-couture* black dress, a simple straight bodice and thin straps, no fuss, no furbelows, just the essence, with some exquisite gold jewelry. She cast me a quick glance.

'Chôchô-san, how lovely to see you!' She threw her head grazing past my ear in a picturesque embrace of a mother-in-law. I told myself I was beginning to show some symptoms of persecution phobia, but for the rest of the evening, no matter how many kind or flattering remarks were lavished on me and my kimono, my father-in-law repeating: 'Enchanting, you look a real dull, a reall dull!' meaning 'doll', my morale stayed at the level of my *tabi* socks and all I wanted to do was to go home, jump out of my Madame Butterfly costume and cry.

Eight to a table, conversation meandering from a slimming clinic on Lake Garda to a suicide by cyanide of a lady called Nicco, of whom everyone except I knew the most private and appalling details, on to the inevitable Bay of Tong King, we waded through a lengthy meal on which one dyspeptic-looking gentleman commented: 'You couldn't call this warmed-up leftovers, could you? The Vietnam war must have given a tremendous boost to our host's fortune.' It started with rolled smoked salmon stuffed with caviar and cream, which, eaten together, tasted exactly like cod-liver oil; then a gelatinised soup with a blob of sour cream, went on to Beef Wellington and ended with baked Alaska, carried ceremoniously into the darkened room with sparklers.

As the desert plates were removed, the gentleman on my left, distinguished and upright, one of the few who managed not to look like a waiter in his evening suit, leant over to me and said, 'Japs blew it off in Burma,' and tapped at his knee. A wooden leg. I felt the down on my nape stand up in horror. As soon as it was politely possible to leave the table, I stole upstairs to the host's bathroom, putting my palm over my obi centre, an afflicted spot.

The door was not locked, I went in. The light was on. I saw a pair of gold sandals perched on the taps.

'Juliet?' I said very softly.

'The Japanese girl!' affirmed the voice from the bathtub. I locked the door.

'I'm so glad you are here!' I said and meant every word.

70

Juliet, brusque, timid, anaemic, neurotic and the mother of a tamed rabbit. With an unexpected hot lump in my throat I sat on the edge of the bidet.

'I'm not glad I'm here, though,' Juliet said petulantly as she pushed up her dark glasses. In Colin's orante bathroom, every square inch sullied by an interior decorator's eager touch and with several minor Pre-Raphaelites nailed on to the wall, she looked like Ophelia floating down the river. She had on a loose Arabic gown with bits of mirror and mother-of-pearl and plastic sequins splattered all over it. Her small face was so albinic that the pale bran-like freckles seemed to rise and float above her dry skin; her thin white lips were distinguishable from the rest of the face mainly because, when opened, they exposed the wet red of her mouth.

'You look pretty. I like that. Unusual, too.'

I thought it was the nicest, most straight comment I had heard that evening and was pleased I had bothered to put on a kimono.

'Where is Tarquin?'

'In Paris, at the Ritz. The head porter's son, Jean-Piérre, is baby-sitting. This quarantine business is *gyastly!* I sat next to a feller at the dinner – did you eat any of that pretentious garbage? I ate only spinach and potato. I'm vegetarian, you know? Am thinking of going whole-hog macrobiotic. Brown rice, sesame and no acidity. Anyway, this feller swears he'll smuggle my Tarquin. He wants a thousand pounds. A thousand! Daddy says no one respects anyone who overpays. So I said, if it's dollars, OK I'll pay. D'you know what the guy said? I don't bargain, lady, a thousand pounds or no rabbit. He's a cool customer all right, but precisely because of that, I have a feeling he might get Tarquin safely.'

'What is his name?'

'Don-no's the answer. The British never open their lips when they introduce you: "Yew knoh sew-and-sew?" All I could make out was that he's a farmer and a freaked-out keep-fit nut. Talked some sense about trees, pesticide and fauna. You know I majored in botany at college before I flunked out.'

71

'You've made the Ritz in Paris your home, why smuggle your rabbit into England?'

'I have no real home. Just now I feel like living in London. People don't stab you in the back as they do in Paris; besides, we talk the same langauge and that's a help when I go to shrinks.'

Look up *schrinck* or *cherinque*, I made a mental note and asked. 'Are you with the South American painter?'

'Nope. Not with him, no more. A long, hair-raising story. But Toma is here tonight. I've seen him.'

'I wish you could come and live here!'

'You do?' Juliet put one hand on the edge of the bathtub and pulled herself up.

'I would love it,' I said with vehemence.

'Sweetie, if *you* want me to live over here, I'll tell the guy, OK, a thousand pounds sterling.'

This sweetie was deeply touched by this important declaration of friendship. I gave her a hand out of the bath and helped her fold the towels and bath mats she had been lying on and followed her downstairs to look for the pet-smuggler.

The after-ten-thirty guests were arriving. The taped music had been put on at the loudest volume and a tightly packed crowd shimmied and wriggled in the drawing room denuded of most of the furniture. The scrimmage, the friction and the heat were appalling: I saw beads of sweat, like fat worms, crawl out of the hair, slide down the dancers' foreheads and drop to the floor. Those not indulging in the dance scrimmage were talking themselves hoarse, leaning against the walls of the corridors and landings, sitting down on stairs or drinking in the library.

'There he is,' Juliet cried on an inhaled breath as we managed to make our way into the library.

'That small feller with a GI hair cut, kinda gangster, see him?'

I spotted the man who looked both 'kinda gangster' and a choir boy. Not tall, five-feet-five or six and although slim I had a feeling he weighed more than he looked with muscles tightly packed round the bone. His short clipped hair covered his head like a thick coat of tar, with mossy sideburns reaching down to his jaw bones. He looked extremely young and boyish, possessing none of the spruce elegance of Colin's other guests whose trousers' pleats could have sliced cheese. His dinner jacket had the tired air of tinned vegetables and in lieu of a black tie, a velvet ribbon was tied in a dropping bow. He was not handsome like Tristram, no Gainsborough's young man in blue, but had a strong interesting face with a protuberant dimpled chin, thick brows drawn straight across like a beam over a set of large dark eyes. One striking feature about him was his carriage, upright and unforced, so unexpectedly gracious.

He said something to a group of smart young men standing round him and, throwing his head right back, suddenly burst out laughing. The impact of his laughter, with such attack and abandon, galvanised his listeners into equally wild laughter and made others turn. Ju flinched and waited for the laughter to subside, cleaning the large lenses of her dark glasses, then went straight up to him.

'Hey, can I speak to you?' Her voice was throttled.

'About your cat.'

'Rabbit.'

'Rabbit, of course, sorry, rabbit. Let me suggest we talk in quiet and peace,' he said. Rather pompous for a smuggler, I thought, and his accent was crisp, not cockney like Mrs Apps's.

'Where?' Juliet recoiled a fraction of an inch.

'Come.' The young man took Juliet by the elbow. She turned in my direction with the frightened look of an innocent suspect being taken to a police station.

'Shan't be long. A business talk.' The man smiled at me as a smooth conman would with a slight bow of his head.

I retreated behind the plexiglass shelves filled with Colin's art investments, priceless bronze and silver and porcelain antiques, which separated the library from a small den with a low circular sofa and matching pouffes, on one of which sat Colin, glued to a telephone, making his customary call to New York at this time of the night.

I turned round and watched the candle-lit room beyond

73

the plexiglass shelves, where I could survey a long table which served as a bar with two waiters with their backs to me. I saw a forest of bodies instantly recognisable as English with drinks in their hands, just as one can always detect French women by the way they choose melons and cheese.

My idle eyes were soon drawn to an inaudible little scene enacted amongst used glasses and full ashtrays at the far end of the drinks table. A man's hand, squat and dark, and a woman's stringy bare arm wearing a gold bracelet I recognised: my mother-in-law's from Cartier's. The man's hand lay inert and empty on the table while the woman's played with ice tongs. The man turned his hand over in what I interpreted as a placatory gesture, exposing his thick pink palm, into which the woman deliberately plunged the tongs. His fingers curled up and closed like a starfish round the steel. I could see the amount of force applied to the tongs from the way her arm strained and showed long sinuous ripples. After a little vicious twist into the palm, she let go of the tongs and her black slim body swiftly disappeared out of my view.

I edged closer to sneak a look at the man's face. Toma, the painter, stood there. To my consternation the man whom Tristram had called 'a nasty bit of work' at that precise moment lifted his eyes from his palm. Our eyes met. His insolent stare betrayed neither surprise nor embarrassment. It was just smouldering black. I quickly hid my face behind a massive Chinese bronze urn and stood there petrified. Oh, Buddha, spare me involvement, it is more than enough to cope with my own problems as it is! I envied Colin who was still screaming into the telephone, rattling off prices and quantities, oblivious of anything else but rubber and lentils and copper . . .

Toma stood right in front of me, grinning in a way that made me feel furious.

'I saw nothing!' I lied.

'You saw, but you won't talk,' he said unhurriedly.

'No, I will not.'

'I like Japanese, they are proud people, die for their

74

honour.' The way he stressed 'Ja' of Japanese made me
cringe with distaste. I heard myself react:

'I won't die for *your* honour. Juliet is my good friend.'

'Mine too. I adore her,' he smiled and his swarthy cheek
shone like spilt oil.

'My husband says you are a day-go. I don't know what
that means, but not a gentleman, must be. May I go?' I
took a step forward to his right. He swayed to the right,
blocking my path, and exposed a raw of square white
teeth. 'One day when you want to know what a pissed-
off ass your husband is, come to me. You'll find me in
the Paris directory. And, my name is not Dago. Dano.'
He stepped aside. I toddled away as fast as my Chôchô-
san skirt permitted.

6

I asked Tristram if I could accept an invitation from Ju to spend the following weekend in Folkestone.

'Folkestone? But, why Folkestone?'

'She's always wanted to see Folkestone. She tells me it's a romantic port town.' I lied as I felt meeting a pet smuggler would not go down very well with him. Tristram laughed and kissed me on the parting of my hair. 'You really are a funny thing. All right, then, I'll go alone to Lady Symmington's luncheon on Sunday.'

Ju hired a small automatic Ford and drove it herself. We stayed at the Clifton Hotel and waited as Ju had been instructed by the smuggler who had left for Paris a few days earlier armed with Ju's letter to Jean-Pièrre, the Ritz concierge's son, and a five hundred pound advance in cash.

It poured on Saturday and went on pouring on Sunday. The rain kicked and beat down on our casement windows, the humidity literally blurring our vision. As each hour passed, my confidence in Ju's smuggler lessened.

'We should not have trusted a man with a name like Pom. He's gone, Ju, and your five hundred pounds gone down in the pipe. Let's go back to London. It may be sunny there.' I whined.

'I have a hunch he'll make it with Tarq!' Ju said with her jaw set obstinately, sitting on the floor with her back against the radiator.

'What is a hunch?'

'I won't tell you, Nasty! Get the dic and dick the hunch yourself! And, while you're at it, it's down the drain, not in the pipe, OK? . . . Oh, Suki, Suki, he's got to do it,

76

he's got to bring Tarq!' Ju wailed, banging her thighs with her fists. She was only a year younger than I but she certainly did not behave her age when she was not having her own way.

On Sunday afternoon we were sitting down for tea in the lounge with neither thirst nor appetite, but for sheer want of anything better to do, spreading the suspiciously scarlet strawberry jam on a soggy mattress of buttered toast amongst the whispering and ageing English seaside tea eaters, when Pom, unshaven and clad in a plastic anorak, sauntered in with a bulky moss-green canvas bag slung from his shoulder. Ju and I gazed at the bag with an intensity that could have drilled four little holes. Reaching our table, Pom laid his bag on the floor as gently as if it were an egg.

'Tar-quin-nnne!' Ju gasped on a choked breath and turned on me with venomous triumph: 'Didn't I tell you he'd make it, didn't I? He's made it, you meany!'

Pom unstrapped the top of the bag, revealing a gourd-shaped wicker basket neatly embedded inside and we could see a luminous white ball of fur snugly nested in a mass of shredded Kleenex. Ju wrapped herself over the basket and went through her usual string of Tarq talk, not so much in voice but in a nasal caress.

'He's a dear, I must say. He's been very good,' said Pom and pulling a chair, wearily dropped on to it.

'Isn't he? Isn't he good? A dear boy! I can't wait to go to my room. Pom, eat all our toast and scones. The service in this hotel is gyhastly. If we order fresh tea, we'll be here till dinner time. Ours is still hot. Here's my yellow jam. Suki, give him your red jam. No, don't tell me how you did it. I don't want to know. It scares me. And, Pom, when you come upstairs for the rest of the money, please take off your shoes. OK? Fine!'

I had never seen Juliet so alert, so in command and sure of herself. She darted way ahead of us to her room to spread clean towels along the radiator before letting Tarquin loose on them.

When Ju handed him five hundred pounds due on successful completion, Pom said, 'Ta,' which was a pity, for even Mrs Apps refrained from using 'Ta' in conversation with me and certainly not with Doctor Harder, who considered 'Ta' too common to be suffered in his house. Pom did not count the money, shoved it inside his trouser pocket, then lay on his side on Ju's bed and watched her with one eye that was not quite buried under the crook of his elbow as she tried to cajole Tarquin into a new pink plastic pail, three-quarters filled with shredded Kleenex. I was struck by the gentleness of the one visible eye of this cockney youth. When Tarquin at last consented to hop inside the unfamiliar pail, I saw a vivid colour spread from his cheek to earlobe, but exhaustion quickly wiped the colour away. He shut his eyes and fell into a deep sleep.

Ju, so conditioned by her rabbit who, she claimed, started even at a clink between her two bracelets, put on the censorious look of a night nurse and shushed me if I as much as uncrossed my legs. In the algae-green dark of a rainy afternoon by the sea, we sat caressing Tarquin in turns and listening to Pom's rising and falling snortle with the hushed respect for a hero's hard-won repose.

Ju had only to mention that Tarquin would not like Claridge's with lifts clanking up and down, guests returning late at night, and ubiquitous toilets being flushed all hours of the day; Pom found her for no extra charge a newly decorated furnished flat off Grosvenor Square with two bedrooms with two bathrooms, a kitchen and a sitting room, and even went out of his way to interview and select a Swedish cook-housekeeper, Anita, on whose passion for cleanliness the Mayfair agency who recommended her used the adjectives: fiendish and atavistic.

Most weekday afternoons as soon as my English class in Oxford Street was over, I jogged down to Ju's flat, ran up the carpeted stairs at the double, hopped impatiently whilst Anita vetted me through a spy-hole in the door, and the moment it was opened, I kicked off my shoes and darted in to spend a penny.

'Bless Anita's rubber gloves and Ajax and Harpic!' I

groaned with relief. 'You can't imagine how horrid the school toilets are, Ju!'

'Public loos, yuck! You should have seen the ones in Paris. OK, after pee, it's tea. Anita, tea!'

Our opening conversation was nearly always lavatorial, which somehow helped put Ju at ease, for even with me after only a day or two's separation a strain of self-consciousness grew in her like bacteria in stagnant water. Once the tea tray was brought and left on the velvet-covered pouf, we settled down to Tarquin's level and she relaxed, finding in me an ideal listener, for I would listen with devout, lip-reading concentration to anyone who would be so good as to talk to me in English without charging a fee. I groaned soulfully to punctuate everything she had to say. As Ju had no spare aggression to criticise, judge or intimidate me, I felt my shoulders loosen after an hour with her.

Ju, whom her father, Daddy Sugarheim, had dispatched to Europe in order to distance her from shrinks and other undesirables, had not a modicum of initiative or condensed will-power to organise and shape her life. She therefore lurked most of the time in the flat lit by lamps even in the day time with Tarquin warming her feet, reading books on animals, trees and herbs or watching television hour after hour with the same uncanny stillness as the rabbit. But, the world at large always knew how to locate an heiress to a legendary fortune, especially with the extensive contacts in Europe of the Sugarheim Foundation for Arts and Science. An impressive number of invitations to dinners, balls and charity galas found their way to her flat. She attended them only if the hosts insisted on sending an escort to fetch her.

'I haven't been a Sugarheim all my life without some damage,' she said. Like Tarquin who cowered low with vivid suspicion and foretaste of disaster at an approaching stranger, Ju was convinced that nearly everyone sought her friendship with no intention other than to make use of her name and money.

'And there's this too . . .'

'What?'

'My nose. When I became eighteen Mammy booked a room in a clinic in New York and sent me to have my nose done.' When she came home her mother laughed, spilling dry martini on her poodle. 'Haven't they taken off a bit too much? Ah, well, better than your face looking a map of Israel.' Ever since, Ju obstinately hid as much as possible of her face behind a curtain of dangling hair and huge tinted glasses when she went out. "Cos, you see, I've been messed up.'

'But, Ju, your nose is adorable. A Susan Heyward. And even your old nose, the longer one, many Japanese girls, a hundred thousand of them, would risk a painful operation to have a nose shaped just like that, I swear.'

'It's not the shape, nor the size, Su-ki-i-i!' Ju groaned in a tone coming from somewhere deep and gaseous. 'It's the association, the judgement, the prejudice that needs a surgical knife.'

It was the shrinked Ju talking, so I repeated with loyal obstinacy: 'But, yours now is a Susan Heyward, no question, I swear.'

'OK, OK!' For the first time since we met, Ju was over the top, as she herself would put it. 'But, damn it, what would a Susan Heyward nose be doing here on a body and soul of Israel?'

'But, after operation many Garbo-shaped noses sit happy and proud on map-of-Japan faces.'

'Gosh, you're dense today. Japs are no Jews!'

'Japs no Jews? Y-yes, q-quite . . . but, listen, Ju, I hear we have synagogues and excellent delicatessens in Japan as there are so many Jewish Japanese. You see how uncomplex we are?' After a gulp of undaunted breath I ventured my final sally: 'Maybe, who knows, Susan Heyward was Jewish?'

'Ough, she wasn't, she wasn't!' Ju flung herself, narrowly avoiding Tarquin, on to a giant cushion, her furious face hitting the silk cover with a dull thud.

Oh, God, I thought, what's so special about these people. So exclusive, so touchy, such intolerant racists! Prima donnas! I was glad that the Tokugawa Shoguns had for three centuries banned the equally touchy and

80

intolerant Catholic missionaries from our islands and that today Japan is a nation of sanguine religious promiscuity and indifference.

At any odd hour of the day or night Pom apparently dropped in to see how Juliet and Tarquin were getting on in their new cocoon. He was invariably worn out and unwashed, with a half eaten jar of honey in his anorak pocket.

'I'm sure he thinks I'm running a twenty-four-hour gas station here,' said Ju contentedly. 'He comes in with that *crai-ee-zy* laugh shaking our window panes, gets refuelled, then out he goes again.'

'Where to? I thought he was a farmer.'

'You can't farm in London, silly! He works, he does. Not everyone can work in a nine-to-five sort of way. He works damn hard for a better world.'

'For a better world? How?'

'Stop laughing, or I'll kill you. The feller's a little strange, I admit that, but he works, for a better world, you've heard me! It's called World Elsewhere and there are two centres. One in Drury Lane where he teaches meditation and yoga and so on; spiritual salvation, you know, for ten pence, a pound or whatever people can afford. The other, in Notting Hill Gate, it's for immigrants, drug addicts, the homeless, the junky people. I can tell when he's spent the day or night in Notting Hill Gate. He comes in, cross-eyed exhausted, lips white and cracked, depressed. But he never forgets to take off his filthy shoes, goes on his knees to say hello to Tarq, and you won't believe this: Anita, "a fiendish and atavistic cleanliness nut," remember? well, she adores him. There's nothing she won't do for him. This morning she washed the stinking gym clothes he'd left behind.'

'Eee-ma-gine!' I expressed my surprise in a manner I had recently copied from an elegant London hostess whom Tristram had described as 'the best listener, thereby her immense popularity.'

'Yeah, imagine, and wait for this, as if two Worlds Elsewhere weren't enough, he goes to body-building and *calatee*' (I guessed she meant karate) 'classes every day he

81

spends in London. Obsessively disciplined about it. Sweat, agony and bliss, he says. Suki, you know what a *latismusdorisi*, no wait, a *latismusodrisi* is? A kind of muscle somewhere in your back. He says he can now let them rise or go flat at his will. He hasn't a teaspoonful of flab or untrained muscle on him. Anita and I saw him take off his dirty shirt. His chest looks like the shell-armour of a crab. He goes on the binge, eating tons of blood-dripping steaks and grilled liver for his latismuso-what-not, then, feeling terribly guilty, lives for weeks on nuts or yoghurt and bean-curd. He's like that. Crai-ee-zy!'

'But, Ju, how can he afford karate lessons and red steaks? A farmer-smuggler. Besides, how did he get invited to Colin's party?'

'He owns a small farm, which must bring in something. I asked him how come he knew Colin. Apparently, Colin helped to sell furniture and pictures left to him by his mother, which, to everyone's surprise, fetched a lot of money. He bought a second-hand Volkswagen and went to India and Japan.'

'Japan? You can't drive all the way to Japan in a second-hand Volkswagen! We're islands and very very far.'

'Who said *in* a Volkswagen *to* Japan? Bought a car, full stop. Went to India and Japan, full stop. Two separate things, dummy!'

Juliet's tetchiness made me smile under my navel; and the following Monday when I arrived at Ju's flat to find her and Pom seated on the floor with their legs stretched out, leaning against the wall side by side like two criminals waiting to be shot, eating scones with morello jam, I smiled again under my navel. He had just come up from the country, having collected on the way a fresh supply of Tarquin's organic hay pellets for which Ju paid, adding an extra five pounds for petrol and time.

I could not delay one moment to ask him: 'What did you do in Japan? When was it?'

'You know a place called Itto En near Kyoto?'

'In Yamashina? That Buddhist-communist camp? You mean you went all the way to Japan to join that crazy camp?'

82

'It's not a camp, Suki, it's a living temple, a commune run on Buddhist principles. I lived there for three months.'

'Did you give up all your personal possessions to the commune? Beg for alms from door to door?'

'Oh, yes, I did all that before I was allowed to work on the commune farm, driving tractors, pruning, digging canals, and cleaning the floor. I was particularly useful to them in milking and looking after cows, which for some reasons your compatriots all hated doing.'

'Why did you leave Itto En after only three months?'

'Simple. I was told to go. One morning, cold and blowy in early March, I was summoned to see the chief priest. He had a bad cold and was lying between two eiderdowns and a thin battered sleeping mat, a bamboo pillow under his neck. The sliding doors were fully opened, and it felt like being in a birdcage, winds driving past and peach-blossom scuttling in and out. From where I sat I could see only the top of his bald head. His voice was hardly audible. His interpreter was a middle-aged donnish man who had spent a few years working in a kibbutz on the Dead Sea. "Master say you too raw, too eager to push charity, try too hard to prove something, but what it is this something you don't know. This agitates you, agitates us. A nice boy and sincere but come back later, many years later, after shaking off dust and desires and strong bad dreams of this world. That's what Master say." '

'I remember every word he said and how cold it was as I packed my rucksack. The children walked with me to the station and the interpreter bought me a bag of *mikan* oranges for my journey.'

'You gave up Buddhism after that?' I pursued him.

'No, not one bit.' He smiled a smile which lit up his whole face with such mirth and total candour that I could not help smiling in its wake, a pure contagion. 'I then went to India and stayed in an ashram in the Sahia Mountains near Poonah for four months. I can't boast I found *atma* nor could I go so far up the scale of yoga as to attain the state of *smadhi*, you know, a kind of death, but I did have moments when I was conscious of getting near to it.'

His eyes went hazy as if falling asleep as he continued. 'I don't regret for a second my pilgrimage to the East. In India I found my body, in Japan I discovered an attitude to death very much to my liking.' He shut his eyes, the wings of his nostrils fluttering.

'The way of warrior is to die. Never hesitate, choose death. Nothing complicated. Morning and night, prepare yourself for death. To fear death is not to live.'

'But, Pom, *that . . . that* is from *Hagakure!*' I was flabbergasted: of all persons, Pom knew this eighteenth-century code of samurai ethics by heart! I did not even know it had been translated into a foreign language. *Hagakure* had been banned from the school textbooks by General McArthur, condemned as anachronistic right-wing literature, but I knew it thanks to my reactionary brother Kenji who read and reread it with tears rolling down his cheeks.

'But, surely, Pom, you didn't learn that at Itto En?'

'Don't forget, after Itto En I stayed two more months in Japan and studied the way of sword.' Pom laughed with the soft percussion noise of a xylophone as he was always careful not to laugh in his normal explosive manner in Tarquin's presence.

'Spooky,' said Ju with distaste. 'Morbid.'

'Not a bit,' said Pom. 'Morbid are the slow late deaths with oxygen pumps, pinned to kidney machines or getting fat and creaky-jointed before a TV set. My father held on till eighty-eight, mentally blank, physically a mess, then an unlamented death. I never thought I'd live beyond twenty-one, but twenty-one came and passed. Came twenty-two and passed. And, here I am.'

He grabbed the bread knife from the tray and held the point of its blade ceremoniously on the left end of his abdomen. His eyes screwed shut and his face wrung in a hideous grimace, he inhaled a sonorous long breath, then began drawing the knife horizontally across his belly at an excruciatingly slow speed. When the blade finally reached the right end of his abdomen, he fell forward, his back rigidly straight, gurgling a plausible death rattle. The moment his forehead touched Ju's antiseptic white carpet, he sprang up with a lusty guffaw.

'That's how I'd like to go.'

'You've seen too many samurai films,' I said, unimpressed, for I had seen Kenji enact disembowelment countless times with much gorier details and more acrobatic death jerks; but Ju let out a long shrill hiss, with tears in her eyes.

'Don't ever do that again! You scared me, you scared me!'

'Darling little silly, just play-acting.' Pom crawled forward on his knees and kissed her on both pale freckled cheeks, minding not to crush Tarquin who cowered between them.

Tristram just then was engrossed in an investigatory research into a Burne-Jones that the leading auctioneers had recently sold to B Gallery. In the whole polite art world my husband alone believed this to be a copy by one of Burne-Jones's diligent disciples. Once he dug his teeth into the flesh of a case like this, he did not let go. He slogged at it with intense concentration, read through endless piles of books, scurried round the country looking for hitherto unknown documents or other copies by Burne-Jones's disciples. What with this and the gallery he had little time for concerning himself too much with my daily activities. As long as I was at the piano practising scales as he left the house and found me working on my English homework when he came home, he was blithely indifferent to how I filled the time in between.

One Friday afternoon, however, I returned to find him already home. He asked me what I had done that day. When I said I had been to see Juliet Sugarheim at her new flat in Mayfair after my English class, he was surprised.

'She's still here? Does this mean her rabbit is finally dead?'

'No, Tarquin is here.'

'But, how?'

'Please don't tell anyone: he could be sent to jail.

Someone she'd met at Colin's party, a man called Pom, smuggled it in for a thousand pounds.'

'You couldn't mean the famous Admiral Pom?'

'Oh, no, he's not an admiral. We call him Pom but I think his family name is Pommard or Poomeries. He's very good to Ju and Tarquin. Ju adores him. He drove her to buy new herb and bran pellets somewhere in Sussex yesterday. What is he like? Not tall, a sort of Japanese height, not fat, not skinny, black short hair, lots of forehead and eyes. Laughs like a cannon.'

'Of course, it's the Earl of Hersingdon's young brother! The de la Pomme-rois go back to William the Conqueror, it's a very old family indeed which produced many naval heroes in our history. The father of this Pom of yours had won many important sea battles in the war, the First World War; but then, years later, oh many years, the old boy, by then a widower, fell helplessly in love with his Irish maid, married her and in no time a son was born, your friend, Pom. His profligate lordship was nearly seventy and the new countess not yet thirty. But, I think this was the last brave sally the old admiral could muster. According to Colin, long years of his illness literally ate up the family fortune even with the blessing of all the fine gravel he sat on in Hampshire, and towards the end of his life he had to sell his French and Italian minor masterpieces. Colin himself managed the sale of some fine tapestries and furniture still in the Hersingdon family possession when your Pom's mother died of cirrhosis of the liver. I seem to remember Colin telling me that the present Earl, presumably your friend's half-brother, was trying to auction Falaise Hall, the family home, with about a thousand acres of land still left round it. Tell Juliet that the boy is well-nigh penniless and not the stuff to make a good Sugarheim executive. I think he left King's College, Cambridge, under a bit of a cloud, exactly what it was I can't remember.'

That Pom had no university degree seemed a shocking disadvantage to me, coming as I did from the country where to enter or not the right university was of monumental importance to a man's life.

'But, tell me,' pursued Tristram, 'what about his lordship?'

'*Who*?'

'Pom.'

'He's a lord, Pom?'

'Afraid so. Does he adore her too or is he simply after the Sugarheim money?'

'Well, Lord Pom is very fond of her.'

'Darling, please!' Tristram sizzled, an egg dropped in hot oil. 'Never, but never call him Lord Pom. You're not his over-familiar barber.'

'I'm sorry, I'll be careful!' New to the game of titles, overt or covert, played by those who either had them or had not, I knew I had a poor instinct for getting the subtleties right. With things I knew little about, I followed my mother's advice implicitly: apologize at once, and save time and ill-tasting breath.

Ju, too, being American and a Sugarheim, could not fathom what the barony added or did to her adored handyman-lackey, or for that matter to herself. When I finished telling all that I had learnt from Tristram, she took a long whistling breath, rolled over to the velvet pouffe next to which Tarquin had subsided like a landing hovercraft and stroked him for a long while.

'Daddy might like it. Lord and lady. He's not that orthodox.'

I was startled. Lord and lady? Man and wife? Is this how young well-bred people should get engaged, without first letting marriage detectives loose? I wondered, conveniently putting my own outrageous marriage on a mental shelf of oblivion. 'You mean . . . Ju, you marry him, just like that?'

Ju buried her lips in the cool of the rabbit's fur into which she whispered. 'But, I lah-ve himmmm!'

'Does *he*, though?' I was a rock of common sense, feet firmly on the ground. Ju winced a little and burying her face further, said carefully as if Tarquin were an oversensitive microphone. 'I'll ask him.'

I could see that Pom genuinely cared for Ju as he did Tarquin. He felt, I am sure, responsible for the two of them, having been instrumental in their settling down in England and being a man of strong protective instinct. He might well wish to protect them on a permanent and more lucrative basis. A man without a university diploma, what could he lose anyway?

'And your stepmother?' Ju's mother had died of cancer of the throat a few years back.

'Lillian? She'd love it. His lordship and all that. She's famous for the big parties she throws. But, Suki, why worry what they think, what about me, think of me, think how happy *I* would be!'

'I do think!' I replied solemnly. She was my only real friend and it was very important to me, her happiness.

On Friday, Pom drove Ju and Tarquin and Anita to Falaise Hall for the weekend and when I rushed to her flat after my class the following Tuesday, Ju opened the door and yanked me into her arms.

'I'm so happy I can't stand it!' cried Ju. True to my waterlogged national trait, I wept with joy into her flaxen hair. Anita brought the tea tray and standing arms akimbo over us, complained of the inadequate sanitation of Falaise Hall: 'Three toilets that work for a house with forty rooms, Mrs Harder! An idiot girl from the village to clean, if that could be called cleaning and an old old cook who is deaf and almost blind and can't smell either. And as to the Earl! He's a filthy old wreck, coughing and spitting and cursing into the same old handkerchief. He wears woollies, sweaters and a tweed jacket and is still shivering as he won't have the fires lit. Inside the house it is colder than Stockholm in January.'

As soon as Anita left, Ju declared:

'I slept with him and I know he loves me.'

I was so shocked that for no reason at all I grabbed hold of the toast rack and put it on my plate. The first cogent thought I could bring out was: 'You must marry him quick then!'

'I will!' Ju bit off almost half of the buttered toast and chewed it lustily. 'I sent Daddy a telegram this morning. He'll probably call me any minute now.'

'What did Anita think of it all?' I was slowly recovering

from the shock. Only after this inane question did I realise how silly it was of me to make a song and dance about her night with Pom, as she had slept with others, including Toma the Dago, with no disastrous consequences.

'Anita? She's Swedish, she's thrilled. Besides, Suki, look, I'm safe.' She picked up an ornate calendar with every day of its months filled with a pill. 'When I left New York my shrink gave me this. Terrific stuff. Why don't I get you one, eh?'

Out of my cardinal loyalty to my husband I had not told Ju that with Tristram I had little need for the pill. I did not look her in the face as I mumbled, 'I'm all right, thank you.'

I could not help telling Tristram that Ju had spent a weekend at Falaise Hall with Pom and that they had slept together.

'There's a lot in common between the English upper class and Jews,' said Tristram. 'Especially their heavy-handed sexuality. Both a randy lot.'

Whatever it was that they had in common, Ju, in her wary, gauche rabbit-like way, was up to the hilt in love and positively glowed and blossomed in it. So much so that when her father did ring I heard her declare:

'Daddy, with Pom I shan't go near another shrink, I swear!'

The first Sunday in June Juliet Sugarheim married Lord William Arthur Valerian Pommeroy. Ju was twenty-two and Pom twenty-three. Daddy Sugarheim and Lillian arrived with a troop of over-dressed, over-excited relatives and hangers-on who filled two floors at Claridge's and gave Ju away with exceeding pomp and opulence.

The Earl of Hersingdon, a gaunt, tall, desiccated Rear Admiral who called Pom 'my dear William' talked to Daddy Sugarheim ad nauseam about the sadly neglected state of Falaise Hall. When he began listing what was urgently needed at Falaise Hall from up-to-date dairy machinery to a completely new roof and electric wiring, Daddy Sugarheim, with the seasoned agility of a millionaire before a begging bowl, pirouetted away into the crowd.

The newly-weds with Tarquin in Pom's old fishing bag and Anita with a feathered hat left with the Sugarheims for Southampton the following noon to board the Queen Mary for New York. Lillian Sugarheim, who made Pom guffaw by asking, 'Don't you think it's more impressive if we called Ju Baroness rather than just Lady?' had planned a second equally huge and expensive reception in New York exactly nine days later.

'After that, I'll show Pom a bit of America before coming back here to settle,' said Ju after she had changed into a travelling ensemble by Givenchy. 'Daddy's London office has already been told to look for a nice quiet house with a small back garden for Tarq. I asked them to find it not far from you, Suki. Oh, even for a short while, I'll miss you, miss you, miss you!'

I suspected I would miss her and Tarquin much more than she or he would miss me, as I was the one to stay put, whilst they were off to a whirlpool of new experiences with Pom. I nodded, as my lips were locked in a huge effort not to cry.

Tristram and I came home at five o'clock, feeling heavy with after-the-fête languor, dislocated and out of rhythm with the day. An odd time to come home so dressed up: Tristram looking like an Ashley Wilkes in the MGM film *Gone With The Wind* and me like 'a real cute geisha gal' as one of the Sugarheim contingent had put it; yet, the sun was still lingering in pale apricot on the red tiles of the houses beyond the crescent. I untied my obi, sat at the piano, but too listless actually to play, mentally picked out a tune by merely looking at the relevant keys. A Bach sonata in B flat. Tristram mixed himself a drink and sank into an armchair like wet cement.

'Remember I mentioned to you the *histoire* behind Pom's having had to go down from Cambridge? Colin told me the full story at the reception.'

Tristram who taught me the word, *Schadenfreude*, had a jealous nature, which for most of the time his intelligence and sense of style kept in rigorous check. As a matter of

principle he conditioned himself punctually to congratulate or praise the success of others; but jealousy was there
nonetheless like a tenacious odour of smoked fish.
Detecting a smirk of *Schadenfreude* in his tone, I knew
the *histoire* would not be flattering to Pom, 'a penniless
second son who's bagged an American heiress'.

One evening in his second year at Cambridge, Pom
turned up at his mother's Chelsea flat and, kissing her as
charmingly and affectionately as only he could, looked
into her already alcohol-blurred eyes: 'Mummy, come to
my wedding tomorrow. Kensington Registry Office at
four. Will you?' He wanted to save a beautiful Mexican
girl from deportation: she had overstayed her welcome in
the United Kingdom on a tourist visa, working undeclared
in a healthfood shop in Islington. The Dowager Countess
staggered to her feet and telephoned her solicitor, but
Pom had just turned twenty-one and there was nothing
the law could do to stop him from marrying the stranger.
The marriage with two salesgirls from the healthfood shop
as witnesses proceeded, but the following day the girl was
arrested by the police on allegation by Interpol that she
was a leading member in an international drug-smuggling
ring. She vociferously protested that she was being
persecuted for her leftwing political convictions and that
the drug charge was a frame up. Naturally the matter
attracted extensive press coverage. Pom refused to believe
the allegation or to listen to his mother's wail of reason,
till it was found that his wife was in fact already married
to an Algerian student awaiting trial on drug charges. The
marriage was annulled. End of story.

'That was the background to Pom's departure from
Cambridge.' Tristram shook his glass to rotate the ice
cubes, downed the rest of his drink, and gasped.

'Oh, God, what a ghastly reception! Poor old
Hersingdon, how he managed to keep his phlegm with
all those rent-a-celebrity crowd, flash bulbs, and gossip
columnists. Typically Jewish, all that orchestrated PR
racket.'

'That was anti-semitic.'

After a short pause Tristram lifted his glass to salute

91

me. 'When we next play Scrabble I won't give you a twenty-point handicap. Your English is now clearly good enough without.'

'I really don't understand,' I muttered. 'Is it because the Jews killed Jesus Christ? But, Jesus was a Jew. What does it mean to be Jewish?'

'A lot of things when you happen to be one, I guess,' said Tristram, shutting his eyes and sliding down on the armchair till his legs stretched almost parallel with the floor. I watched him a full minute before I thought of Chagall's 'Sleeping Poet' that I had seen at the Tate Gallery. A young elongated body of a poet with his small head resting on a rucksack lay at the bottom of a dark green garden with a white horse looming in the background.

I had never lived with anyone else to the same degree of physical proximity as I did with Tristram and here he was, a supine parcel of a man, my husband in name and law. What is he? Why is he? Do I know him any better than, say, Chagall's 'Sleeping Poet'? Why is he so white, so long, so remote? I know how many Seconals he'll have to take tonight; what size pyjamas he'll slip into; what little comforting items of praise will lull him to sleep . . . but, beyond these, what was there that I knew of essence about him? Even when we were locked in each other, our skins in a damp coagulation, even then, even thus, I never stopped feeling quite alone and uninvaded. But, so new in marriage, doing my determined best to stay being married, I abstained from questioning the quality of our marriage. Didn't Confucius advise: better not take the lid off, if there's something rotting inside?

That was *enryo*, the supreme of tact. *Enryo*, literally meaning 'far-reaching consideration' was as irrevocably a part of my Japaneseness as my nose, legs or skin. *Enryo* is indispensable to the smooth running of such an over-populated country: that is why it has been considered one of the highest virtues, but it is a negative, frightened little virtue, so considerate and self-effacing as to be nonconstructive and almost silly. A penniless man invites a starving man to lunch; the latter declines, because with his *enryo* he sees that his friend has invited him trusting in his *enryo* to decline it.

From the start of our marriage I had a huge *enryo* dustbin into which I threw everything that appeared disconcerting or even remotely threatening to our marriage; then, having banged the lid over it, faced Tristram and the world with a fresh, all-purpose smile. I would have said Tristram was a rare Occidental who instinctively understood *enryo* and had much that remarkably resembled 'far-reaching consideration' in his make-up, but he had neither my firm dustbin lid nor my mental sloppiness which greatly aided my adaptability and survival. In him all his couped-up far-reaching consideration fermented and corroded the walls of his soul. Probably, this huge flatulence of unforgotten and unresolved *enryo* accounted for his insomnia.

'Darling, you're so full of inhibitions. You can't forever play Little Red Riding Hood,' was how he would admonish me whenever he felt our marriage was falling short of expectation, domestically, socially, intellectually, and sexually. What prompted him to utter this remark was varied and plentiful: the fact that I could not bring myself to undress in front of him; that I could not tolerate Sido Basta's presence in the room when I slept in Tristram's bed; that I could not call Mrs Apps by her Christian name; that I had an insoluble difficulty in swimming the disturbed sea of social invitations, counter-invitations and collided invitations; that I could not manage a bath towel as huge as a tennis court to dry myself when we were invited for weekends in the country – I had been brought up to use a small hand towel to both scrub and dry myself in the humid country where a thick western towel would have needed a week to dry – there was no end, according to Tristram, to my inhibitions. I am the kind of person who, without being guilty, if someone screams he has been robbed of his purse, turns red in the face. So, naturally, I bowed my head in shame and asked him to forgive me and he, being a gentleman, would lift my hang-dog face and find someone else to put the blame on, anyone handy from Confucius and General McArthur to my mother and ancestors; then, trusting that all was well again and sorted out, we lived, at least for the time being, in renewed hope.

7

My father-in-law was a different man this summer: he
had been made honorary president of Americans In Paris
Against The War In Vietnam, APWAV for short.

'It's a much more meaningful and forward-looking role
for an expatriate to play than, say, an honorary consul,
don't you think, Tristram?' he asked, glowing in his new
meaningfulness. He made decisions right, left and centre
in telephone conversations which no longer dragged on
and on but ended crisply once the point had been made;
obeyed more willingly his wife's and Dr Leboeuf's orders;
took a nap; kept off champagne and strawberries and had
been free of an attack of gout for the longest period in
recent years; and dictated on the telephone his presidential
contributions to APWAV pamphlets to his secretary, Mrs
Harp, an energetic widow aged seventy-five, who also ran
a home for stray dogs and cats in Neuilly.

'He's like a man supercharged on hallucinatory drugs,
Mother. It'll kill him, Such *frénésie!*' Tristram who had
learnt French and English simultaneously as a child had
a charming way of superimposing a French pronunciation
on a similar English word whenever he became emphatic.

'But, my dear boy, can't you see how he loves it and
thrives on it? He must be allowed to have some fun in
life. Besides, unless you were totally devoid of political
conscience and compassion,' Mrs Harder put her arm on
her son's shoulder, her ivory bracelets, fluorescently white
against her deep tan, jangling down the length of her
slim forearm, 'you would surely agree that those bloody
Americans must be kicked out of South East Asia and
quick! Till then, no shilly-shallying, we must act relent-

lessly.' Then, with a burst of domestic charm, she smiled at us. 'Lovely to have you both here again!'

Since last summer, I suspect my mother-in-law has resigned herself to try and get 'used to the muck as you go along'. 'Come and meet our son's new wife,' 'Have you met our Japanese daughter-in-law?' or *'C'est ma belle-fille japonaise;'* although in whichever way she introduces me there is invariably an adjectival phrase qualifying me, she seems to have accepted with her characteristic chic that I am her son's lawful wife, a *fait-accompli* that cannot be undone.

Her resolution has prompted her on my second visit to Mortcerf to make a conscious effort to call me by one constant name: Soukie, instead of, as in the first summer, Sikki orSaké or Seiko, and to take me on her late afternoon walks.

One afternoon we are seated on a stone bench in the vegetable garden.

'Soukie, you understand me, don't you?' Mrs Harder suddenly grips my hand. 'I can't live without beauty. The love of beauty pervades my entire world, what I do, what I don't do, whom I like or hate, how I stand politically as well. That is why I love it here, *en pleine campagne*. In Japan (with an emphasis on 'Ja' of Japan) I think you have an inherent feeling for nature and appreciation of nature's humblest little miracles. Have I shown you my Sesshu? It's my treasure. It's a beetle climbing on a cucumber leaf: the way the shaggy frail cucumber tendrils twine round a bamboo stalk, exquisite! You could almost feel the poor little beetle out of breath as it . . . *look out!*'

Mrs Harder lets out a catastrophic screech and begins violently hitting her left shoulder with her gardening gloves. I was told by Tristram that his mother was an exaggerated herpetophobe. Turning quite cold myself, I hurry to her left, holding up the basket as a shield. A grasshopper drops to the ground and Mrs Harder bangs her white espadrille on it with enough ferocity to stir a cloud of white earth.

'There!' She grinds her foot in a semicircle to make sure the insolent beastie is crushed.

'There,' I join in lamely. I have seen an enchanting Sesshu of grasshoppers dancing and playing music. It was about then, I think, that I began questioning if my mother-in-law's political commitment weren't as bogus as her professed love of nature and its little miracles.

This being my second summer in Europe, I understood better what people were saying either in English or in French and began to detect a stench of sham and pretence as I sat amongst my parents-in-law's guests.

'Napalm and automatic rifles on one side and the barefoot Vietcongs brandishing sliced bamboo spears on the other . . .'

'Shake-speare, *en effet, n'est-ce pas?*'

'What? Oh, ah, *oui, oui!* Oh, that's a good one.'

'After thirty years of hell with Marie-Hélène he's now perfectly happy being alone with a Doberman bitch.'

'Who's she?'

'A Doberman-Pinscher, darling, a dog.'

'My worldwide capital and income are locked up in a Lichtenstein company, what they call an *etablissement*, which is in turn owned and managed by a Panamanian company, and as I'm not resident in any one particular country for over ninety days in any one year, no country in the world could possibly tax me.'

'Letti will kill me for saying this, but . . .'

'Who is Letti?'

'Sh! Our hostess, Madame Harder.'

'She's extraordinarily well-preserved for her age. A figure of an eighteen-year old.'

'She paints, you know. Works at it like a maniac; yet, like most dilettantes she's had exhibitions only in smart cultural backwaters like Lausanne, Antibes or Baden-Baden.'

'What are they like, her paintings?'

'Abstract, of course. Intense, jarring, self-opinionated, the kind you couldn't possibly live with.'

'I bet you, there'll be half a million or more American soldiers on Vietnamese soil by this day next year. A hundred francs? I'd go to a thousand francs. *D'accord*, as they say here, five hundred!'

'How much further can we go in our permissive society? I tell you, right to *luste morte*, ecstacy killing., My dear, we're coming to that!'

After being exposed to such conversation all afternoon in turgid summer heat, I would stagger into my bed with a headache and a sense of indignant disappointment. Not bored, no, they were neither boring nor lacking in malicious wit, but often I could not help wishing I hadn't understood so much of what had been said. Tristram maintained that there was no greater sin in life than to be dull and boring. My parents taught me that one of the greatest sins was to be inconsiderate. Father was proud of a proverb he knew in English and taught it to us as something of extraordinary virtue. He would look heavenwards and bark, 'Do to as-as as you would have as-as do to you.' He added that it meant what Mother always told us, the very same thing, be considerate. We children were duly impressed and whenever an opportunity arose reprimanded each other:

'Oh, that was not as-as-as!'

Having lived in Europe for a year, I began to wonder if it was in fact such a virtue, this, to be as-as-as, or even a good policy, for everyone round me had a fierce streak of inconsiderateness which was probably their strength and basis for success. Ju, having been a Sugarheim, could demonstrate the inconsiderateness of the extremely rich; my mother-in-law, that of the proud aristocracy; Tristram, that of the weak and sensitive. Ju, for instance, despite her sweet and charitable nature, would not think twice about ringing up her hostess, five minutes before she was due, to announce she was not coming simply because she was feeling 'lousy'. She would plunge at least a dozen people into a frenzy of activity and trouble to find a pair of the best seats on an over-booked aeroplane or at a sold-out opera house, then for no justifiable reason would cancel the seats without so much as 'I'm sorry'.

In the case of my rivetingly undull and unboring mother-in-law, her lack of as-as-as struck me as being all the more inexcusable, because she was an artist and a communist. With her professed love of humanity she ought to have known better than to shatter the self-respect of others who diffidently came into her orbit, her own daughter-in-law, for example.

In the heady atmosphere of APWAV, it was natural that Mrs Harder should begin working on what she considered the inexcusable political and social apathy in Tristram and myself.

'You two, much as I love you, disappoint me, exasperate me, even. Don't you have any feeling for the suffering of the millions of oppressed and deprived? Ehn?'

Tristram would raise an evasive chuckle, gyrate a little like his father, clutching at his unlit pipe, stutter and cough and begin talking about Vermeer or the blocked drain in his bathroom. So, Mrs Harder tackled me next time we went out snipping the dead heads in the rose garden.

'Soukie, darling, you really must work on your husband. He is too young and intelligent to be so selfish and smug. He calls himself a liberal, an agnostic, a pacifist, sends money to Lepra, Save the Children Fund, the Wild Life what-not and Amnesty International, but what does this really amount to? Nothing! Just suds and bubbles. The world is full of well-meaning supporters of those non-starter organisations. Nice to have them to supper, to go to the opera with, maybe, but that doesn't contribute one iota to actually changing and reshaping the world. When the revolution comes, theirs will be the first heads to tumble. You'll see!'

When Tristram and I went shopping in St-Loup that afternoon I duly warned him about his well-meaning head tumbling.

'Sweet,' he said and kissed me on the temple as we stood waiting for our bill to be added up at the Codec. Public kissing. Something he would never have done in a London shop, France must have that peculiar effect on men, I thought, blushing and far from being displeased.

'No doubt you have noticed that I try hard not to discuss politics with my parents,' said Tristram wearily. 'I find their political shenanigans embarrassingly naive and predictable, worse, how can I put it . . . ?'

'Phoney?' I said helpfully, using one of Ju's favourite adjectives.

'Ye-e-ess,' Tristram twisting his whole body and facial muscles as if one single word, yes, were having a difficult delivery; he was a scholar and writer of high style and used his every word discriminatingly. As we drove home he continued, 'Not exactly phoney, because they are sincere in their own callous, selfish way, but I'm afraid, despite all their frenetic involvements, this selfishness in the last analysis condemns them to an unrelated, dilettante, marginal existence. Rather sad.'

He pronounced 'rather' with a long 'ah' as in 'lather' which I always found irresistibly charming. I snortled a little giggle of delight.

'What's wrong?' asked Tristram sharply.

'Nothing wrong. Something nice,' I replied and suddenly yearned for my brother Kenji. Tristram, so leaden intense about himself, would have never understood why I had felt like giggling at his 'ah'. That little mental itch was unexplainable to a soul that could not laugh at itself.

A *manifestation* of the APWAV was held on a Sunday in Paris and as the success of the demonstration would be judged by the number of participants, both Tristram and I were pressed into joining. Tristram who dreaded the inevitable over-chumminess amongst those who stood united against the foe was reluctant to the point of being resentful. On Saturday night he drank heavily at dinner and took two Seconals. 'I confess I'd rather be dead than trekking hand in hand with fat Americans and skin-and-bone Vietnamese. Oh, and, let's not dress up. You've heard Mother go on and on about the poor Vietnamese refugees.'

The following morning, however, when we assembled for the drive into Paris, Mrs Harder was impeccable in radical chic: her feet in sleek white Ferragamo pumps, white trousers well pressed and an exquisite blue-on-white tunic shirt, a St Laurent. Mr Harder, as he came downstairs fussing with the clasp of his bulging Hermès briefcase, was dressed in beige summer suit, looking like an expensive lawyer on his way to court.

'Oh, dear, you both look exceedingly smart,' said Tristram slouching morosely in his old rubber-soled buckskin shoes and the oldest of his Kilgour and French blazers. He then cast an unhappy glance at my discoloured gym shoes and dungarees with rounded knees.

'Thank you, darling,' replied Mrs Harder cheerfully and continued without turning a hair. 'There's nothing I dislike more than upper-class socialists dressed like assistant cameramen and spouting the foul language of the gutters. I know for a fact the proletarians resent such a charade. They see through it and despise you.'

No one seemed to have remembered, but it was going to be the very first time I visited Paris. In the life of every imaginative Japanese there were times when he thought he knew more about Paris than Nagoya or Kanazawa. Paris, without which Montaigne said he would be 'less of a French'; Paris for which Madame de Stael died longing in exile; Paris of Victor Hugo, René Clair, Foujita . . . The excitement that throbbed in me as we sped towards the capital of France was not of discovering the unknown but of recognizing what had become so real in my imagination.

I ducked my head low behind Mrs Harder's bright Dior scarf, hating to miss the moment when the tip of the Tour Eiffel would heave into sight, first as a speck above the low spread of the city, then growing higher and grander, till I would stand conquered at the foot of the symbol of Paris.

The reality, however, was tragically undignified. The approach to the city was an endless line of horse-meat butchers, car salvage dumps, hovels, grimy cheap hotels and kilometre after kilometre of huge advertisement for Marlboro and Volkswagen and *Vache-qui-rit* cheese . . . My eyes frantically looking for signs of *my Paris*, I whispered to Tristram who had a rare capacity to read close-printed newspaper without feeling sick in a moving vehicle.

'Are we in Paris yet?'

Before he had time to lift his eyes from a day-old *Herald Tribune*, Mrs Harder's L'Heure Bleue flew towards me.

'Of course, Soukie, I have forgotten, this is the first time you've been to Paris! My dear girl, what wouldn't I have given to be able to see Paris for the first time again. It's a wonder. It's a dream. For the first time! Frank, it's a warm day, let's take Soukie to Closerie de Lilas tonight.'

'But, Letti, I've told you, I've already asked Muriel de Bergerac-Foucaud, Rosebud Schwartz and two others to Prunier's.'

'Oh, how depressing.'

'You know Muriel. She's such a hypochondriac that if she eats anywhere else she thinks she'll catch hepatitis.'

'But, Prunier's! Why? So staid and dull for Soukie.'

'Oh, please, I'd love to go to the real Prunier's.'

'What do you mean by the real Prunier's?'

'I have been to Prunier's in Tokyo.'

'I give up! Those *Ja*-panese!' Mrs Harder turned round furiously and faced the road ahead. 'Frank, did you hear that? They have an imitation Prunier's in *Ja*pan. What's next? Crazy Horse Saloon, Deux Magots, the Seine, the Eiffel Tower, bet they have them all by now. Those *Ja*panese!' Her contempt exploded on every Ja of Japanese.

'I believe there are at least sixteen cafés called Deux Magots in the Tokyo region alone,' said Tristram to Mrs Harder's disgusted groan and to Mr Harder's chuckle.

After a heavy silence that suffocated me with shame for my copycat compatriots, Mrs Harder said in a tone of voice from which I knew she was addressing herself to Tristram and not to me.

'Notre Dame looks hideous, washed white by Malraux's order. Wait till you see it. Looks like a wedding cake.'

'So I hear,' replied Tristram, turning the page of the *Herald Tribune*.

I felt like bashing their heads together: Notre Dame looks hideous. So I hear. Yawn-yawn! What criminal indifference, what smart-ass blasphemy! But, just then I had no time for their blasé heads: I had to look and look, for now at last there was no question we were in Paris.

'*Con-Cô-do!*' I gasped. '*Chan-ze-ri-sey!* And that's *Tew-il-ee!*'

'Tuilleries, yes, how well you know, Soukie,' Mr Harder said mildly as he changed gears.

After Japan and London, neither lovers of symmetry, the meticulous Parisian symmetry and the bold, almost reckless, extension of wide, straight avenues dumbfounded me. What my learnt-in-Japan Paris had not prepared me for was the sweeping stretch of houses and windows and shutters. Those perfectly proportioned houses of five or six storeys with grey roof tiles and voile-curtained windows, corseted by white thin-boned shutters, to me, were as graceful and beautiful as a long procession of grey-haired slim ladies in white lace robes. I flattened my nose hard against the car window, and quickly the vapour of my excitement blurred my vision. Erasing the mist on the glass, my eyes caught a garrulous belt of water gushing along the stone curb, making pigeons waddle aside; I could almost hear Charles Trenet, accompanied by the inevitable accordion. Had Mr Harder not braked hard then and there, throwing us violently forward at the sight of an empty parking space, I'd have melted in a slosh of tears.

'Oh, Christ, just look at them!' Tristram gnashed his pipe between his teeth, as we entered the Luxembourg Gardens. I knew what he meant. Our fellow demonstrators 'against the War in Vietnam' were for the most part a moth-eaten lot, middle-aged to prematurely senile Americans and English-speaking expatriates. By just observing the women's smudgy blouses and big-thighed trousers I could smell the complex odours that many years' wear had given them since the last dry leaning. Not a single Vietnamese in sight: I was the only Asiatic to be seen.

The march down boulevard St Michel and along the Seine and over the bridge into place de la Concorde and ending outside the United States Embassy was a godsend for me. I could not have had a better way to get to know the city. The Sunday crowd along the sunny banks of the Seine, mostly tourists, were indifferent, being too preoccupied with calculating French francs into their own currencies, but were respectful of our purpose which was spelt out in red ink on two split double sheets:

STOP THE WAR IN VIETNAM!
NOUS SOMMES AMERICANS CONTRE LA GUERRE EN VIETNAM

At the gate of the United States Embassy Mr Harder made a speech. His irresolute, oscillating manner, which could be charming in an upholstered drawing room, was disastrously ineffective in a public place, especially against the roar of traffic from the place de la Concorde. Tristram studied the toes of his shoes, while Mrs Harder looked grim and frozen. Finally my father-in-law's drawling speech on which he had worked for weeks came to an end and the petition was perfunctorily received by an Embassy duty officer.

Another fifteen minutes of trudging brought a selected bunch of us to a sprucely kept white town house in a quiet leafy street. Forty-six pairs of hot dusty feet filed inside, trampling on acres of Chinese carpets, and here for the first time we encountered Vietnamese, cool and immaculately dressed young men in rubber sandals. They darted about the house with noiseless jungle-trained steps, serving drinks and trays of fried bits of food. Every time they came near me they shot a quick searching glance at me, unsure which part of turbulent Asia I came from. Mr Harder introduced Tristram and me to a corpulent, short man. 'Meet our host, Monsieur Pong Pee Too'. It sounded like that but could have easily been Pin Pong Tar.

'*Enchanté, enchanté,*' he grinned till his cold observant eyes disappeared behind folds of sallow flesh. When the APWAV demonstrators had finished consuming all that was offered on the circulating trays and our clothes had absorbed an exotic cooking odour, we shook the boneless warm hand of Monsieur Pen Pen Ten or whatever and filed out.

'If I hazarded a guess,' Tristram began as the four of us sat in a taxi to go to Prunier's.

104

'Don't,' snapped Mrs Harder.

'What?'

'I say, don't hazard a guess.'

'Oh, it's really like that, is it?' Tristram's tone implied: 'I guessed as much.'

'Not at all like that. Letti's dramatising it,' said Mr Harder, sitting in the front seat next to the taxi driver. 'What he really is, no one knows. No question the war is vastly profitable to him, but he's very helpful and generous to us.'

When the taxi stopped Mrs Harder said threateningly, squinting her eyes at the meter, 'Frank, at least ten, all right? I'd go to twenty myself.'

'Letti thinks that is how a fair distribution of the world's wealth can be accomplished: tipping taxi drivers with a ludicrously large sum.' Mr Harder tipped five francs which was enthusiastically acknowledged by the driver.

The real Prunier's, I had to admit, was a bitter disappointment: charmless, institutional and wooden. We did not sit long before the four guests arrived. I shot to my feet out of sheer dismay. The dago the painter was walking toward us with three other people who turned out to be a wizened tall American married to the Comte de Bergerac, Rosebud Schwartz, a dark sullen South African dress designer, resident in Paris and her friend, a Dutch sculptor, whose nose and high cheekbones were big ripe strawberries.

'Isn't she cute! Honey, you don't have to get up to greet ladies, however ancient they may seem to you, as no doubt I do,' said the Comtesse as she patted my offered hand. I shook Rosebud's hand, then the sculptor's, and as I stood undecided as to what to do next with the dago, his stubby fingers gripped me by the arm.

'Hey, don't you remember me? We met in London.'

He gave me such an ingenuous friendly smile, showing his big square teeth, that I began laughing from relief and nervousness. 'Of course, how are you, Mr . . .'

'Watch it, not Dago, Dano.'

'Yes, Mr Dano,' I dropped to my chair and saw Tristram extend his hand over his left shoulder to shake

Toma's hand without quite looking at him, who reverently kissed Mrs Harder's hand and sat next to her.

As soon as the new arrivals were seated, the Comtesse began gratefully sipping Vichy Celestin which Mr Harder, always an attentive host, had ordered in readiness for his hypochondriacal guest.

'Much as I adore Ping Pong Toh, his so-called cocktail eats are gyhastly. Simply gyhastly! That's why, Frank, I could not bring myself to join your trek. A civilisation that could stomach such muck may justly deserve napalm.'

Mrs Harder tut-tutted at this irrelevancy but the old American girl did not hear her: she was already addressing me in her painfully husky voice as if she had no saliva to lubricate her vocal cords. 'You people eat sparrows' nests and suck the soft brain of baby monkeys, don't you?'

'She's not Chinese, she's Japanese, Muriel,' said Mr Harder.

'Great people, the Chinese.' The Comtesse went on unruffled. 'Have been there four times. Chou En Lai's a great pal of mine. So's Mao. A great man, a giant. Japan had better listen to her great neighbour.'

Overcome by the grandeur of the society she kept, I nodded and grunted, yes, yes, oh, yes!

No one paid any attention to the great friend of Mao's but went on calmly studying the menu. When the Comtesse chose artichoke and poached turbot, I followed her example. Rosebud, who smoked throughout the meal in order to stifle her appetite, referred to her red faced sculptor as 'this drunken son-of-a-bitch' or 'the bastard' and gibed cruelly at his financial dependence on her; but to my relief and joy, the sculptor minded not one bit of this and ate and drank in the best of humour. If over a year ago someone in Japan had said: 'Asako, one day you'll be in Paris and eating at the real Prunier's with a countess and a fashion designer and a sculptor and a painter and believe it or not, you'll wish you were back in Mikage,' I'd have laughed and said it was unthinkable. But now I had to admit that it was actually happening. They were so predictable and rigid and intolerant in their

dogmas and self-assigned images, those progressive intellectuals, and to my chagrin, they were rude to waiters.

After the meal, with her lipstick eaten away Mrs Harder
looked tired and pale, but kinder. I could not help looking
fixedly at her as she kissed the dago good night outside
the restaurant.

'Come and stay with us in the country, Toma. Soon,'
she said. 'I'd love you to see my new work.'

'Oh, do,' joined Mr Harder. 'I'll let you try my Vosne
Romane '57 just to prove the point I was making to you
earlier about the tannin . . .'

'Come on, Father, you can't keep everyone standing on
the pavement; besides, we have an hour and a half's drive
in front of us.' Tristram impatiently waved his arm in a
vague direction of Mortcerf. Stars were less visible in Paris
than at Mortcerf but as I looked up I saw one star falling.
During the long silent drive home, Mrs Harder suddenly
said: 'Tristram, don't you think it's about time Soukie
stopped calling us Mr and Mrs Harder?'

Tristram who took the wheel on our way back said
gently.

'Yes, Asako, call Father and Mother Frank and Letti.
It's not as rude and saucy as you think.'

'Y-yes, I will, if I m-may . . .' I stammered as I bobbed
my head in a sort of thankful bow.

'Sweet of Mother, I've been rather uncomfortable about
your calling her Mrs Harder. I think she's getting to like
you.' said Tristram when he came into my bedroom to
say good night.

'Oh, thank you!' I said, sitting up correctly in my bed.

'If I didn't know you, I'd think you were making fun
of us all.' He shrugged his shoulders and shut the door.

Over two months since Ju had sailed for America, yet not
a word from her, not even a postcard; so, when Tristram
lifted an airmail letter out of a bundle that Josiane had
brought to the breakfast room, saying: 'Here's, I think,
the longed-for missive from your friend,' I yelped a wordless scream of joy.

'Honolulu, Hawaii!' Tristram grimaced as he examined the postmark. 'I couldn't think of anywhere less inspiring. What on earth are they doing there?'

'They are in Hawaii? Ee-ma-giinne!' I opened the letter.

My darling Suki, hi! Pom and I, we are A–1. Terrific. Has been on macrobiotic diet for a month and as a result with five minutes in the sun we get the world's best sun tan, no acidity in our body, see? Mine doesn't last. Pom's does. Not fair. Macrobiotic eating, by the way, isn't the only thing that bothers my very American parents. Pom must get a job, says Daddy. Must show interest in corporate management and market research and economic analysis, blah-blah. Lillian then joins in: we'd rather you didn't swim starkers on Centre Island beach; and, must you go marching in Central Park in that unbelievable get-up, dear? Please ask Pom, will you, not to pester our dinner guests – senators, congressmen, mayors and newspaper proprietors – about the war and his anti-nuclear bug; tell me why you must sleep in sleeping bags in the garden when you have a perfectly adorable bedroom?; Sweetie, your rabbit gives me hay fever and please tell your Swedish maid not to bully our black servants, so on, ad nauseam!

Don't misunderstand, Suki. Daddy adores Pom, loves him like a schmaltzy Jewish mamma. Yet, he can't keep away from a CIA-type background investigation on anyone he cares for. It's not natural for a man to prefer honey to good steak, said he one day, then within a week confronted us with the findings of his inquiry agency: Pom had experimented with hard drugs back in '64 which probably damaged some of his brain cells, that's why he now craves for such an immense amount of primary sugar.

'So, I've married a Sugar,' Pom laughed like a firework, you know how he laughs, not at all repentant, but Daddy, mean and square, went on: 'If you think you've married Juliet as a free meal-ticket . . .'

'Mr Sugarheim,' said Pom, sitting on the floor with Tarq on his crotch with that beautiful straight yoga back of his. 'You've researched on me enough to know I am not a materialist. I detest possessions. Your Cadillacs and jet planes and Renoirs bore me. I appreciate the joint account you opened for us at Morgan Guaranty Bank, but if you didn't, I'd have loved your daughter just as much and made a living, not in

108

the Sugarheim style, but in our own way. With my war loan and a cottage at Falaise Hall I'm not exactly a pauper in need of alms. As long as starvation exists in the world, I cannot bring myself to work for a multi-national food business. If I did, I'd give everything away free and you wouldn't like that, would you? Yes, I tried drugs. I was curious, but my brain is as clear as anyone's and if I like honey as some like Bourbon, if I marry a rich girl as some marry blondes, it is all in the law of cause and effect, which we cannot control. Ju, I think I've said enough. Let us leave tomorrow.'

We left in fact a week later. Anita stayed with Tarq in Dad's New York flat. They'll join us later on our return to Europe, in Paris. Pom will smuggle him in. Remember Folkestone? I'm sure you're wondering why the hell we're in Hawaii. We're on our way to Nepal and Cambodia and then to Vietnam. Why such outlandish places? A long story.

America is full of well-meaning radical-chic idiots at the moment. Students and kids under fourteen fill up parks and streets. 'They're marching against the Vietnam War to fill their own vacuum', says Pom. 'There's no real charity or love from 59th street to Harlem.' I can't tell you how superficial and phoney the anti-Vietnam War movement here is and Pom is sickened. For him, the only solution to this appalling mess is true understanding of the people in Indo-China. Pom is dead against communism as you know, on that Daddy and he agree one hundred per cent. Pom cannot forgive communism for their fanatic intolerance of alternative ideologies and religions. He thinks communism is powered by hatred and fear and elitist greed. He can't understand why so-called enlightened Americans are virtually forcing the Government to invite the Chinese and Russian communists to take over in Vietnam. Sitting in an air-conditioned New York penthouse wouldn't lead us to any enlightenment on the problem. So, Pom wanted to get to the horse's mouth. See what I mean?

Daddy saw us off at East Side Air Terminal where we boarded an airport bus. At the last minute he put all the quarters and dimes he had in his pockets into the automatic life insurance machine for us. Rather touching, says Pom. Typical Daddy, say I.

Here we swim in the Pacific, your ocean. We're staying in a cheap hotel, half eaten away by white ants. Can't stand the hotel WC so I pee behind palm trees on the beach. Bliss! This is the longest letter I've ever written since I wrote one to

109

myself after mummy died. Now you know how much I love you. Yours ever, lavatorially, Ju.

I went inside my bathroom, sat on the toilet cover and stared at one white floor tile for at least five minutes, and only one thought on every pulse rang in my head: *les jours s'en vont, je demeure* . . .

I had always admired those who can go to the extreme, precisely because it was not in my character to do so. I had too much far-reaching consideration and self-discipline and self-deceit for that. That my friend Ju whom I had first discovered drowned in paranoia in my Mortcerf bathtub and her rabbit-smuggling husband were now embarking on a kind of pilgrimage to the festering wounds of the world thrilled me, made me feel proud, yet somehow embarrassed me.

When I gave a resumé of the long letter, Tristram said: 'Sounds more like a voyage in search of heroin. According to someone I knew at Oxford who's recently come back from Katmandu, seventy-five per cent of his work as cultural attaché at the British Embassy there was to pick up unconscious young bodies from the ditch and ship them back to their often rich and mighty parents.'

About a month after our return to London I had a telephone call from Geneva. It was Anita.

'Tarquin is dead,' began Anita who warned me in advance that she would have to ring off abruptly if and when her current employer, a very rich, very old and very mean English lady, returned. 'Yes, Lady Juliet knows. I got on perfectly well with him, as you know, but I wasn't Lady Juliet. He ate and drank water as normal, his droppings were dry, but after a week he began losing weight and one morning I found him, I don't know how he got up there, lying on top of an air-conditioning outlet. He was dead. Knowing my lady well, I kept his body in the freezer till Mr Sugarheim tracked her down, don't ask me how, through the last cheque she had cashed or something. Of all the dirty places, Mrs Harder, she was in Bombay! She asked me to air-freight Tarquin in a special refrigerated compartment to India. Air India won't do it.

110

In the end Pan Am agreed to do it. She wanted to cremate Tarquin in a holy place called Benares. Lady Juliet said that an Indian fortune teller had told her she'd have another death before . . .'

Her employer must have returned. Anita hung up, saying dryly: 'Wrong number, Madame, no trouble at all.'

I visualised the ashes of the fastidiously clean rabbit being sprinkled into the water of the Ganges, teeming with animal excrement and burnt human bodies. It seemed to me that Tarquin had died because Ju no longer needed him. She was a different and stronger girl now. She had Pom.

Before I slept that night I prayed for the soul of Tarquin, the Buddhist rabbit:

Nam myo ho ren ge kyo,
Nam myo ho ren ge kyo!

8

A Monday in February. I was sitting, in the frame of mind of discarded underwear, on the closed toilet seat in my bathroom, the only place in Tristram's house where I could feel at peace with its small proportions and uncluttered simplicity. I was humming the third act overture from *Carmen* and Mrs Apps in the passage was heartily singing above the boom of the Hoover: 'Dublin fair city, where the girls are so pretty . . .'

No doubt February was made the shortest month to show pity on those destined to live in the British Isles: the month in which even in the heated drawing room the core of an upholstered sofa felt clammy and damp as my cheerless bottom sank into it and a mushroom of despair seemed to grow under every unaired carpet and rug. Must we get through wet March and showery April before the first glimpse of spring?

Every Monday after breakfast, I give Tristram my household accounts, take Sido out for a walk, and when I return Tristram having checked the book, gives me my weekly allowance and some cash to top up my household float. On this particular Monday in February he opened the front door as we returned and asked me to come into his study.

'Darling, what is this Clinique Swiss Performance Extract here?' He pointed at one entry ticked in red pencil. 'Ah, that . . .' I blushed. Yes, I had to admit it was not exactly a household item. 'It's the face cream someone said I ought to use in winter. Very very nourishing. It was so expensive, more than my whole week's allowance, that I thought I'd ask you to buy it for me, but I forgot

112

to. I should have asked you before. I'm sorry. But, Tristram, I have only one face!'

My father would have been undone by this argument: he'd have roared with laughter and that would be the end of the matter. But, Tristram went on, grim as sulphuric acid. 'All right, leave the Swiss Extract as it is, I'll pay. There's another item to which I'd like to draw your attention. Toothpaste. You seem to get through an inordinate quantity of Colgate family size. One large tube lasts me several months. The amount you're buying is a fantasy.'

What did he think I had done with the toothpaste: sold it on black market in order to send money to my starving family in Asia, or secretly kept an alligator in my laundry basket and polished its teeth with Colgate night and day? I bristled with indignation. 'But, Mother told me to brush my teeth morning and night and after every meal so that I can be buried with my own teeth.'

'Whatever use could you make of good teeth *then*?' retorted Tristram. I had to raise one of my Japanese groans, for I did see some macabre logic in his argument. 'And, darling,' he continued. 'I don't think you're practising the piano often enough. According to my calculation Mr Goldberger's lesson costs eight pence a minute. Do you realise that?' asked my husband who would fight to pick up the bill if we went out to a restaurant with friends; who would himself telephone Alan's the butcher in Carlos Place for the best and dearest cut of meat when we had important guests to dinner; who insisted on sending the linen to the most expensive laundry in town; who had only a few weeks earlier insisted on buying me at Harvey Nichols a twelve-hundred-pound mink coat, which I did not want.

'I don't really think it's my style, Tristram, I look like a furball.' But did he listen to me and save himself twelve hundred pounds? No!

'Nancy Mitford says a good fur coat hides all ills in winter,' he insisted. So, thanks to Miss Mitford, whoever she might be, I was forced to look like a tea cosy bristling with hair. A tea cosy at twelve hundred pounds was no extravagance to him, but toothpaste was. I did not know whether to laugh or to weep. Just now, my brilliant husband ought to be feeling on top of the world and inclined to pamper his little wife: his article on the fake Burne-Jones had just been published and caused a stir far in excess of the average art-world scandal. Confronted with his irrefutably documented and lucid argument, the auctioneers and the B Gallery had been obliged to drop the libel action brought against Tristram and to acknowledge their error in print. Tristram's article also brought to public notice the more serious matter of the role and conscience of the fast-growing industry of auctioneering, the taxation of art heritage, and the veritable draining of nation's art capital abroad and so on. As a consequence, he had been offered an attractive contract by one of the leading publishers to write a book on the twilight world of disciples who copied their masters' work with a disturbing perfection and both the Ashmolean Museum and the Courtauld Institute invited him to lecture later in the spring.

Yet, the young scholar with a Gainsborough profile with impeccable manners in public, having mailed off to his bank a cheque in the sum of £2,000 as advance on his Master-Disciple book, would turn and nag his wife about a tube of toothpaste! I blushed and grew hot with distaste at something so totally incomprehensible to me. Then, a scene that occurred at Mortcerf in the summer came back to me with a startling new meaning. It was during dinner:

'How are you enjoying your London life, Soukie?' My father-in-law asked me. Whenever there was a pocket of silence amongst us, he chewed the inside of his mouth like a benign goat and came up with an innocuous question such as this.

'I like it very much. Only, I get skin rashes round the neck from nervousness when we go out too often and give too many dinners at home.'

'Tut-tut-tut!' Mrs Harder lightly tapped on the table. 'No belly-aching, my dear. So long as you're eating from Tristram's table, you don't gripe about a rash on your neck. Economic independence is the only language of feminine independence I care to listen to. I did modelling and worked in a coffee-house in Vienna to pay for my art classes. I don't pretend I earn much as a painter, but the commitment is there and I do work hard.'

As I recalled this conversation I felt a centipede crawling up my spine. Mother had never earned a penny in her life: she spent, frequently overspent, what Father earned.

'If your mother hadn't been so extravagant, I wouldn't have had the impetus to go as far as I have,' Father often admitted, not without gratitude.

Coming from a country where women produced the greatest literature of the nation as early as the eleventh century, thanks to the fact that they were totally dependent on men and kept out of politics and business and other foul affairs, I felt I was past the juvenile shrieks of independent new womanhood. But, it takes both men and women to make up the world and since I was in a world where a well-to-do male can be so emasculated as to question the other half's right to brush her teeth five times a day at the former's expense, I had no choice but to seek for myself this sordid, muddle-headed nonsense, economic independence of women.

'Could I be paid for my odd Saturday receptionist work at the gallery when Mrs McCay is off?' I asked.

'N-no, not ree-ally,' said Tristram with an elegant gyration. 'A bit embarrassing . . .'

'Why?'

'You're my wife.'

'Aha-a-a!' I made a mental snake-coil of myself to cogitate on this esoteric reply. If wives who work for money are considered embarrassing by men who monopolise the means of production, then, when and how will a wife ever achieve economic independence? Out of my snake-coil I surveyed the world around me: how difficult, very difficult it was to earn half a sixpence as opposed to spending it. And yet here was I, the titular mistress of the house, where marmalade and honey were transferred out of their commercial jars into crystal or porcelain jars at the average loss of, say, ten grammes every morning, because, according to Mrs Apps, 'Doctor wouldn't hear of just plonking an Oxford Vintage marmalade jar on his tray. It's common, says he, see?'

Besides, in my husband's household each time a fuse was blown or drain pipes were blocked or a TV set or an iron was bought without a plug or a bulb inside an overhead lighting fixture died, Mr Simms, the caretaker, was called in to attend to the problem.

'Mother taught me how to mend things. I can do them all. Would you pay me if I did the work instead of calling Mr Simms in? It'll be mended so much more quickly?'

'Certainly not. These are not the sort of work you should be doing. Mr Simms can't make ends meet unless his income is supplemented by these odd jobs paid for in tax-free cash.'

'But, what about *my* ends meeting?'

'Don't squeak, little one, it's unattractive. I'll raise your allowance to nine pounds ten.'

I made neither progress toward my economic independence nor peace with my dependence on Tristram. In me flowed samurai blood, and even a two-millimetre worm has half a millimetre of pride! What annoyed me till I felt itchy behind my ears was that I was such a cheap wife to keep: My parents supplied practically all my wardrobe through my dressmaker, Mrs Ikushima in Kobe. She had my measurements; I sent her drawings of what I wanted, copying and adapting what I found in the latest fashion magazines. Father paid for them and Mother airmailed them to me. Ju had often said I was much better and more originally dressed than she was who paid staggering sums to well-known English and French couturiers. And for formal occasions I could rely on my kimonos and I don't think Tristram had the faintest idea how hideously expensive kimonos and obis were. The first time he coerced me to ask for a kimono suitable for a charity ball: 'Something quite regal, darling. I see it as black with only burst of colours here and there,' I felt guilty asking Mother for it, but she wrote back at once: 'Don't worry, your father says; "since we did nothing that is normally expected of the bride's parents, the least we can do is to

116

send Asako kimonos and dresses her husband will not be ashamed of." '

Whenever a new parcel arrived from home I sat on the carpeted floor and bowed three times eastwards. Fortunately, Japan seemed to be flourishing: Father's private practice was bringing in a lot of money, whilst his university hospital work secured him prestige and agreeable benefits. The richer the nation grew, the more psychosomatic and hormonally disturbed people became and Big Brother, too, could now afford a second car for his wife whom he had married about a year after I left Japan. Fumike was now in Singapore, as her husband with the Mitsui Trading Corporation had been posted there. She could afford a luxurious air-conditioned apartment and two local servants and belonged to the best golf club. Kenji had dutifully fathered a son and to everyone's astonishment turned out to be a doting father; so much so that he decided to have a position he could proudly print on his visiting cards.

'When my son grows up and is asked what his father does, I don't want him to blush and answer, he doesn't do anything.'

He did not wish to work for or under anyone. He made his wife agree to sell their house in the choice area of Tokyo which had been given to them by her indulgent parents and with the proceeds set up a company dealing in timber and plywood and moved to Matsumoto, a highland town in the foothills of the Japan Alps, where his wife's family owned a huge forest land. In less than eighteen months he doubled his working capital, thanks to a building boom in Japan. He wrote to me: 'Being the president of New Life Forestry leaves me little time nowadays for judo and karate practice. If you ever decide to chuck your *gaijin* and return home, count on me, I'll build you a house with the best *hinoki* timber as fragrant as incense.'

'Born Tokyoite? That's good enough. Be my guest, eat my sushi!' is the cliché that comic-raconteurs have mouthed for centuries to depict what we consider as the most attractive male characteristics: compulsively

117

generous, open, quick-tempered and straight like a bamboo split clean down its length.

'I'd rather be dead than save today's money for tomorrow' was the vein in which a dandy in a kabuki play would speak. The Japanese associate manliness with generosity. Kenji, though not a Tokyoite, was so generous and 'split bamboo' that when a friend emphatically admired his bicycle or binoculars he suffered agonies of remorse afterwards: 'Was I mean and dastardly not to have given them to him?' He once saved a puppy from drowing in the Mikage river, gave its owner his shirt to dry and wrap the miserable animal and came home sneezing.

'A dog has fur. You don't.' Mother slapped him on the head.

I had a sneaking suspicion that my husband would not only not risk getting wet to save me out of the polluted Thames water but if I were arrested at Harrods for suspected shop-lifting he might walk away pretending not to know me. I may be maligning him without proof: but I must confess I'd be very reluctant to put him to the test. Of course, there would be many marriages that could not withstand such tests, but after three years of married life, I believe that in the final analysis it was the ungenerosity of Tristram's soul that put me on my guard and prevented me from giving myself totally, emotionally and physically, to him.

When I first came to London my husband gave me a weekly allowance of six pounds ten shillings, which was now raised to nine pounds ten shillings. Why always this ten shillings, I had often wondered. Now I knew. It was a small but potent psychological reminder that in his house every penny, let alone a shilling, was carefully watched.

I would have asked my brother without the slightest compunction to build me a palace with the best *hinoki* timber, but I preferred not to ask for anything except for the barest essentials from my own husband who dared question my brushing my teeth more often than was customary amongst the foul-mouthed breakfast-in-bed-eaters! Half-a-millimetre though it may have been, it was fierce, my pride. Even with an affluent father and brothers, the Japanese government's exchange control being as strict as it was, I, alone and unaided in a foreign city, needed to be all the more proud in order to withstand the humiliation and loneliness: I began brushing my teeth with salt except in the morning and at night.

9

Tristram planned our summer in France with his usual meticulousness, juggling dates to fit in with the gallery's summer closure, Colin's holiday and his Courtauld lecture. Then, sticking to his lifelong rule of never attending to correspondence except on Saturdays, he asked me to write my mother-in-law of our arrival date.

'And, don't forget, not "Dear Mrs Harder" this summer; it'll have to be "Dear Letti".' I wrote on a Wednesday in mid June.

'Not a word from Mother,' grumbled Tristram over a week later. 'I wouldn't be a bit surprised if they're galli-vanting somewhere between Leningrad and Goa.'

Nor would I. The way my parents-in-law thrived on frenetic displacement was scarcely believable. After a month's visit to Mexico in December and a trip to Prague and Budapest in early spring they had managed a holiday in Majorca and another at La Napoule between two quick visits to London and New York to see some heart special-ists. Finally, in the first week of July Letti rang. I answ-ered the phone.

'We're off to Weimar. I'm designing a backdrop for an anti-American-aggression opera performed at the Schiller-spielhaus there. The music is by the famous Augenhirsch, a Buchenwald survivor. The premiere is on August 3rd. I'll send a telegram to let you know when we'll get back to Mortcerf, precious, and will tell you all about the town of Goethe and Schiller and Cranach when we meet.'

Whilst losing things was on the top of Tristram's list of hates, a sudden change of plans came second. He so dreaded having one of his guests ring up to say he could not come at the last minute that he made me answer the telephone when it rang after teatime on the day of a dinner party. He himself defied fever, toothache, electricity cuts, taxi strikes, storms and other obstacles and seldom, if ever, broke an engagement.

'Typical of them to bugger off like this,' he said vengefully, biting his thumbnail as a therapeutic gesture, his teeth merely sliding up and down the nail's surface with a grating noise but without actually damaging it. 'So inconsiderate. I wouldn't put it past her to ring me up in a few days' time, saying: "Hello, darlings, Weimar is off. Come right away. Bring two sides of Fortnum's smoked salmon and half a dozen smoked trout, will you? Be an angel, pick up some medicine at *Dr Buchenwald's*. And that potent stuff your quack prescribes for sleeping. *A bientôt!*" '

I could not help laughing, for his imitation of his mother was viciously accurate.

'Ah, well, let's stay put, what else can we do?'

We stayed put and soon a Berlin Hilton postcard arrived from Frank. 'Enjoyed our last capitalist meal, quite superb. I want to visit the zoo, but Letti won't. Afraid of catching ticks from animals in summer. We're told a government hospitality Zum car, complete with a driver with a bouquet of red carnations, will be waiting for us on the other side of Check Point Charlie. Love, F and L.'

'So, they did bugger off! London's empty. I'll go mad if I just sit here waiting for Mother to ring.' Tristram threw the card on the table and stroked his hair wildly. 'We'll go to Italy! Colin has a villa outside Florence. I'll ask the East German Embassy here to contact Mother at the Schillerspielhaus with a message that we'll await her summons at Colin's.'

We packed what we needed for both Italy and Mortcerf and flew to Rome, where Tristram rented a small Fiat. Under the gigantic shadow of crumbling and decomposing ancient stone piles, people gesticulated and their voices fluctuated up and down as if they were perpetually and urgently bargaining. No one, walking at a brisk speed, took notice of anything: neither the murderously whizzing

121

little cars, the oncoming herd of similarly vociferous passers-by, cats, prams, beggars, nor the police, but concentrated solely on the rising fumes of their own arguments, and this frenzy of talkativeness in the ancient capital did not abate even at nightfall. 'They don't sleep here! They love noise, clatter, chaos, those wretched Italians.' Tristram whimpered nightly as he surrendered to a larger dose of Seconals.

We Japanese pride ourselves on possessing the world's oldest building, the Isé Shrine, the dynastic shrine of one hundred and twenty-one emperors. The shrine was rebuilt every twenty years with wood and paper in exact imitation of what had been there before and the latest one looks just as old or new as the very first one must have done two thousand years ago. In Italy God dwells in stone and tinted glass and iron; His durability seems very much a part of His holiness and I have never seen so unrestrained a glorification of bricks-and-mortar as at St Peter's. I read a lot when I was a pretentious university student and one of my favourite poems was Rainer Maria Rilke's Pieta, which had never failed to touch me with its stoic calm. But as I stood beneath a gilded arch, jostled by summer tourists, my eyes watering from the white fumes of candles which cost the pious many hundred lire, even Michelangelo's Pietà could not move me, for the surroundings suggested nothing more sacred than a huge multi-national corporation headquarters, a bustling industry, boasting a stupendous accumulation of wealth and power, so utterly devoid of a sense of being inside the house of God.

I was disappointed, but said nothing, only ah-ah-ed and oo-oo-ed to please Tristram who had been so good as to take me to the Isé Shrine of the Catholics. Tristram, a professed agnostic, looked at everything from a scholastic height, yawning frequently after a badly slept Italian night, but later at Gucci's in Via Condotti he showed some liveliness: he had been much impressed by dapper Italians carrying handbags and keeping their trouser pockets empty and flat.

'It might also help me not to lose things.'

He bought himself a smart handbag, the size of a hardcover biography and a small soft pouch for me to put my pearls in.

We arrived at Assisi at five o'clock. The hotel was at the end of a cul-de-sac street. No sooner had we entered the room, guaranteed by the manager to be the quietest, than Tristram walked straight up to the window and opened it so imperiously, that the manager and I stood behind like awed courtiers attending on a bad-tempered king. He turned, triumphantly tragic:

'No good, just as I feared, look at *that!* A bus terminal, an Italian bus terminal!'

'Oh, Signor, they stop running at eight, and won't start till six in the morning.' The manager wrung his hands.

I saw way down below a large flat patch of earth with dusty grass here and there with four empty buses standing. I turned red in the face from hard efforts to control myself: here we are in Assisi of St Francis and my husband is going to spoil it all. Between eight and six there are ten long hours to sleep and sleep! I'd have spanked and given no dinner to a boy who behaved like this!

Tristram, drawing himself to the dignified height of a martyr, repeated icily that he would not sleep a wink over a bus terminal. Just then loud radio music of *Dimmi Quando Tu Berai* blared up from somewhere down in the bus square. Tristram stalked out of the room, then the hotel. The porter, stunted under the weight of our large suitcases, filled with Tristram's reference books, pills and heavy Lobb's shoes, followed us up the stone steps.

'Don't tip him yet, or he won't follow us,' hissed Tristram looking colonial and handsome in his white linen shirt and trousers as he headed for another hotel, taking the stone steps two at a time. At the next hotel we were shown the two last rooms available with private bathrooms. The first, Tristram flatly turned down by merely sticking his head inside the door and hearing guests fluttering their newspapers behind the door communicating with the next room. The second room was at the end of the corridor, windows on two sides, a light, cheerful, lovely room. He paced the room, all ears. I stood

123

as rigid as in prayer as did the young and keen receptionist. Once you stop making counter-offensive noise yourself, an Italian city begins reverberating like an orchestra tuning up all round you. We heard insane motorbicycles tearing about the narrow echoing streets, grandmothers screaming at children, conversations exchanged between windows, church bells going berserk . . .

The keen and eager receptionist made it worse by saying that we would hear little if we slept with the bedroom windows shut.

'What an idea! I need fresh air,' said Tristram, the draught-loving Englishman.

'Ah-ha!' The young Italian darted to the bathroom. 'You open *jees* one. *Ecco!*'

The small window gave on to a narrow stone street and each Italian sandal that fell on it hit our ears like a well-aimed pistol shot. *Ecco*, that was the end or rather non-starter of Assisi for me. As we left the town it was already past six and I never did get to see a single Giotto. I never even set my foot inside Basilica di San Francesco. Later in Florence I bought a coloured guide book on Assisi to learn what I had missed.

We arrived at Colin's villa hours after midnight, more dead than alive. Colin and his friend, Edmond, had gone to dinner in Florence but the couple who looked after Colin were kind and willingly accomodated the guests who had arrived two days too early. We went to bed with bowls of apricots, figs, and grapes which we ate in the hard-won silence of the Tuscan hills.

Staying with Colin was like being at a small cosmopolitan hotel: people of varied nationalities, domiciles and races arrived at mealtimes from behind the hills or simply out of an unsuspected door in the guest wing.

They were mostly civilised professional people whom Ju's stepmother, Lillian, would have loved to ask to her dinners, describing them as '*interesting*, doing-things people': a syndicated columnist, a balletomane and author of many keep-fit books, a lawyer who wrote tax avoidance best-sellers, a drama critic and an agent for some of the world's most celebrated opera and ballet artists. They were neither creative nor innovative themselves, they were solely on the periphery of others' creation, risked little, but remained alertly and closely in touch with the vanguard of creative talent and led an enviably good life, often better and more stable than the objects of their attention.

Tristram appreciated the company, the good food and wine and the *dolce-far-niente* without the responsibility of having to run a household, till on our third day there arrived a new house guest, a twenty-seven-year-old novelist called Richard Pearce, whose latest and third novel had just been sold for £150,000 to an American film company based in Rome. That evening after dinner, the music critic of a London paper here to cover the Spoleto Festival commented that Arthur Rubenstein often said that he felt guilty about making a fortune for himself by merely playing the works of genius composers who had died in tragic penury: Mozart, Schubert, Schumann to name but a few. A long discussion ensued whether it was more desirable to be a posthumously acknowledged genius or a mediocre talent rewarded with fame and fortune in his lifetime.

'Well, look at our young Richard here, he's having his cake and eating it,' said a restaurant owner who annually sponsored one of London's most coveted literary awards. 'He's a Book of the Month Club writer at twenty-seven and, beyond dispute, a gigantic talent that'll defy the wear and tear of time.'

That night Tristram drank recklessly and fell asleep on the sitting room sofa. I covered him with my raincoat and a rug from our car and went to bed alone. He woke up at four in the morning and could not get back to sleep; hence began a bad cycle, what he termed 'a disturbed circadian rhythm'. He became despondent and finicky about food. I was familiar with the symptoms.

The Tristram of *Schadenfreude* was jealous without aggression or baseness: his jealousy damaged no one but himself, not that he thought himself inferior or a failure. He knew he had done as well as he could have hoped. But, I think, there was always within him a vague dissatisfaction and regret: 'had I been Richard Pearce, how much prouder of me Mother would have been!' Every time he uttered his mouthful: 'Grrreat people of this world!' I felt sick with distaste and pity for him, attributing his insecurity and complexes to his thirteen years of mother-lessness. As his wife, I so wanted to fold him to my bosom, meagre as it was, and salve his punctured ego with motherly unction. But, alas, I didn't have it in me, this tactile amplified gesture of mammal sympathy. It smacked of artificiality, too obvious, too slapstick for my taste; besides, I feared he might repulse me, snorting I was being gushy and American. As I pondered how else I could help him, time passed and he was sinking deeper into a morass of gloom, when, August 8th, a postcard arrived postmarked Berlin Airport.

'Tristram, they've buggered back!' Jubilant, I ran upstairs to bring him good news.

'Asako, your language! Where did you pick that up?'

'What?'

'Bugger.'

'From you, Tristram.'

'Not possible. Never mind. Don't use it again.' He looked at the card.

Hotel Elephante. Cranach and J. S. Bach lived here. The Goethe House was too grand with guards in posh uniforms and a manicured garden. Schiller's apartment, stark simple, spiritual and moving. Workers and children pick wild straw-berries in the woods near the Franz Liszt Conservatoire. The opera opened to a rapturous reception. A mountain of caviar and excellent Polish schnapps flowing. Back at Mortcerf August 8th. Join us at once. longing to see you. Love and hugs, Letti.

Mama's longing to see him; Mama's a creative artist, tall and slender and desirable: suddenly, there was fresh sap bubbling up his spine. Tristram sat up straight, bright-eyed.

'Can't wait to see her!' The ardour in his voice made me take a step backward.

'Sounds fascinating, her trip to Weimar,' I said, wondering why I had not said 'their trip'.

'She is a fascinating person,' said Tristram, then indicating downstairs in general, he lowered his voice. 'Why I find them so irritating is that whilst they have reasonably good taste, some education and charm, they're so completely lacking in real *élan vital*. They haven't lived!'

No, not everyone would have lived the way his mother had, I reflected; but I was grateful for the astonishing moral uplift her postcard had produced in her son. He began packing at once in order to leave right after lunch.

Colin did not dislike me, found me less intrusive in his relationship with Tristram than other women in his past and once in a while cast himself in the role of a kindly aunt with provocative advice. Before we left his villa, while Tristram went to the kitchen to 'do the right thing' with Colin's domestics he put his arm through mine and we walked amongst his roses.

'Mama says, "darling, we're home" and the son jumps, "coming, Mama, coming!" No, love, I'm not upset you're leaving so suddenly. I know him well enough. For anyone with a depressive nature the sky seems bluer elsewhere and his neighbour's cutlet always somewhat less fatty than his.'

As Tristram would not dare risk spending another night in an Italian hotel, he bent over his steering wheel and drove from Turin for the Col du Mont Cenis at a frantic speed; as a consequence, the experience I had longed for, to cross a land frontier, turned out a shattering disappointment: worn out, hungry, feeling unwashed and frazzled, the entire drama of leaving Italy and entering France was enacted in the dark through a lowered car window, less of a drama than leaving a supermarket. Ten kilometres after the frontier, Tristram stopped at the first hotel we could find, but the horse-hair mattress with a depression in the centre proved for him an even greater obstacle than Italian street noise and he finished sitting up in an armchair, falling asleep out of sheer fatigue in the early morning.

Tristram not breakfasting till after ten o'clock, we left

the hotel too late to avoid the dense August traffic on cross-country roads. When we finally arrived at Mortcerf, only a few barking dogs greeted us, not a soul in the street, not a single light did we find in the village. As I tumbled out of the Fiat we had rented at Rome airport and pushed open the green iron gate, the complex moist scent of a northern climate stung my nostrils: farm manure, dewy lawn, honeysuckle and flowering linden somewhere in the dark; and I realised we had travelled a long distance from the Tuscan hills of dust-white olive groves. Not our own home, but it was a home-coming of a sort, and I was touched almost to tears when both Frank and Letti, wrapped up in warm dressing gowns, came down the entrance stairs to welcome us.

'The poor boy is dead,' said Letti and made Tristram sit on a cushion on the top of the stone stairs next to her and brought him a glass of schnapps. 'Soukie, you really must learn to drive so that you can take over a part of the driving.'

'I know, I'm sorry, I'll learn to drive as soon as we get back to London,' I said and sat on the stone balustrade next to Frank.

The moon, slightly chipped but huge, suddenly appeared from behind the elm tree. Having grown up in Japan, one thing I know well is the moon. 'Ah, it is the seventeenth moon tonight, the stand-and-wait moon!'

'What is she talking about?' asked Letti to no one in particular.

'Sorry, I'll explain,' I said. 'After the full moon on the fifteenth night, the moon rises later and later, so the sixteenth night moon, we call it the wandering moon; the seventeenth, the stand-and-wait moon; the eighteenth, the sit-and-wait moon; the nineteenth, the sleep-and-wait moon.'

'Charming, Soukie. Now, Frank, give us your "*ich wittre Leben*"!'

'On, no, Letti, I do it so badly.' Frank in the seventeenth moonlight could be observed squirming with embarrassment, crouched low over his dangling legs.

'Oh, come on, do, Father. I love your *Walpurgisnacht*.'

128

Frank had majored in German literature at Harvard and attended Heidelberg University. With a little more coaxing and some more squirms, he began reciting in German. As I sat there in the mild breeze, the bright moon above, Frank's gentle sibilation rising and falling, a hundred moon-thoughts and moon-memories flowed back to me. I thought of my family at this precise moment, eight hours ahead of me, 135 degrees east in longitude, waking up, the sun already warm on their black roof tiles . . .

'*Es leuchetet beleuchtet borperlichen Ball. Ich wittre Leben* . . . The only proof of my one year slogging at Heidelberg University,' said Frank, looking apologetically in Tristram's direction, who had fallen asleep with his head hanging low.

'Soukie, you're the youngest, be an angel, go and fetch Tristram's sponge bag and pyjamas from the car. Now, beddie-byes for everyone!'

By the time I returned from the car, Tristram was lying on his bed in his underwear, Letti sitting at his feet, leaning against the bedpost. Letti took the pyjamas from me and helped him put them on. I watched and when he was snugly tucked in, I somehow felt inhibited from crossing the whole distance of the room and kissing my husband good night; so I said awkwardly, 'Sleep well' and with Letti and Tristram wishing me the same, left the room, went down again to the car to take out my toilet bag and nightdress. When I came into the house, I saw Frank standing by the entrance door, watching the moon. The sweetest, most vacant expression shone on his high forehead. Yes, he would take back his wife who had one morning disappeared and reappeared thirteen years later. . . .

'How are you doing?' he asked, still gazing at the moon.

'Not too well,' I replied, then realising Frank's question was meant only as a friendly noise, I added quickly, 'I wish I understood the poem you recited for us.'

'Oh, that, Goethe . . . it's a long time since I spoke German well. I thought what you told us about the moon was charming, the stand-and-wait moon.'

I had to go away, and quick: I just managed to say good night, choked by hot tears as I was. Frank had that effect on me.

On Sunday arrived the usual crowd to consume *quiche, gigot* and *tartes*. This summer it was chic to discuss China and the cultural revolution and Letti, like a cock shaking its ruby-red comb, was flaunting her most radical and rabid Chinese communist views. There was also much talk about the setting up of a tribunal to judge Vietnam war criminals in absentia which was to have its deliberation in Stockholm.

'We've got to find a few internationally known names to add some credibility and weight to the jury,' said an English Trotskyite.

'Jean Paul and Simone might be persuaded to come,' said a French lycée teacher who never failed to seize an opportunity to advertise his supposed intimacy with Sartre and de Beauvoir.

'Pity, Bertrand Russell is so ga-ga that one ends up being at the mercy of his young nurse-cum-secretary.'

Drinking Pernod under the dense shade of the spreading walnut tree, they discussed the composition and the diplomatic niceties involved in selecting the jury members in the manner of society hostesses making up dinner party lists: 'Oh, don't, that'll be a fiasco! Schwartzenberg hates the guts of Onna di Somala.' 'Xenia broke up Yollande's marriage: you couldn't ask them together.' 'Dick and Didier? Fatal. No one'll be able to put a word in edgeways,' and so on.

'The whole thing is a bullshit charade!' Tristram groaned with coarse disgust unusual in him after one such discussion. 'How could Mother play ringleader to these farcical carryings-on? It's pure embarrassment!' Nonetheless, this summer, his relationship with Letti seemed better. When Letti covered her mouth in horror, looking at his Gucci bag: 'Don't tell me it's yours, Tristram! My hairdresser has one. In fact every pansy in Paris has one just like that,' Tristram meekly emptied its contents and

130

put it away in his suitcase. They took long slow strolls, arm in arm, in the wood, stopping now and again to pull ivy off the tree trunks. 'My dear boy, as long as we keep off politics, and God knows we try hard to, I don't think I know any other mother and son who get along better than we do,' Letti would say and Tristram would blush and hold her hand in his as long as his style of understatement could tolerate it.

This left me with more time than in previous summers to spend alone with Frank. We listened to the records of Lily Ponce, Maurice Chevalier, and Harry Belafonte in the library; I played Scrabble with him; pasted his book reviews into his scrapbook; when his fingers were stiff with gout I typed his letters in connection with APWAV and the Stockholm Tribunal; and on his good days I would accompany him to view his aspens.

'It's a law in France since Napoleon,' Frank explained, uttering the Corsican's name with respectful emphasis, 'that a landowner possessing more than a certain acreage must maintain his woodlands in accordance with certain criteria.'

He took an excited, childlike interest in the growth of the aspens he had planted along the border of his property at regular intervals; but whenever he talked about his aspens Letti would protest, 'Oh, Frank, you try the patience of an oyster, or was it ostrich?'

'Oyster.'

'Oyster or ostrich, they are *not* aspens, Frank. They are just common-or-garden poplars!'

'Prussians are like that, you know, Soukie,' Frank would say to me the following day on our way to his aspens. 'They have to be right always. The so-called trembling poplars *are* aspens. My father had a huge estate on Long Island and there we had aspens and yellow poplars which at home we called tulip trees.'

'Tulip trees? Pretty.' I lifted the barbed wire for Frank to scramble underneath; then, arm in arm we would inspect the long line of aspens, gangling like young boys with not enough flesh to keep up with the sudden growth in height.

131

'Every ten years I plant them. Look, there, Soukie, those by the stream, you'd think they were there since the Congress of Vienna, eh? I only planted them when I returned after the war.'

'Do you plant them for Tristram?' I asked.

'N-n-no, not ree-ally,' Frank gazed at the gratefully bowing trees as if to find out for the first time for whom he had in fact planted them. 'These aspens . . . well, n-n-no, they're not for Tristram, not exactly. You see, Soukie, my mother left Tristram a substantial fortune in trust and as Mortcerf was a wedding gift for Letti and myself from my mother, as it were, I want Letti to have it. She adores nature and calm as you know. When it's her turn to go, well, I doubt if she'll leave Mortcerf to Tristram, who, as she rightly points out, a) doesn't need it and b) isn't really a country person. I think Letti has it in mind to give the whole place over to the persecuted and the deprived.'

I am out of my depth when rich Occidentals talk about death in the family. Such a chilling conversation between a son and his aged mother as: 'Mama, are you leaving that Hepplewhite table and chairs to Anthony or to Jessica?' would be unthinkable in Japan. Out of sympathy for those whose death is central to the matter, I can hardly lift my eyes till the conversation passes on to another subject. So, when at dinner toward the end of our stay 'the future of Mortcerf' was discussed, I bent low over my plate.

'As a matter of fact,' Letti said in an abrasively cheerful and loud voice which reminded me of a military band, 'I went to see Rosenthal when I was last in Paris and he assured me that there are ways and means whereby I could leave Mortcerf to a charitable organisation free from any gift or inheritance taxes.'

Tristram, not one to get involved in an unseemly squabble at the dinner table, began pouring water into his and Frank's glasses.

'Are you still thinking of an artists' utopia here?' Frank asked blandly. Although the place was entirely his till his death, whenever the conversation cropped up, he talked as if he no longer possessed any proprietary right to it.

132

He neither felt strongly enough for or against Letti's utopian plans nor possessed enough fatherly love for Tristram to fight to secure the property for him.

'International Artists' Asylum is what I'd like to call the commune here,' Letti continued, being dreadfully merry. 'Tristram would be the first to agree with me that in this age of greater social justice and fairer distribution of wealth, a bit of land like Mort . . .'

'A bit? Come, come, Letti, it's nearly thirty hectares of flat rich agricultural land we're talking about here,' Frank protested mildly.

'All right, Frank, but still, twenty-eight hectares of land shouldn't be selfishly enjoyed by one family, generation after generation. That's dynastic and decadent. It should be liberated and put to active use for as large a number of people as possible, people who need calm, peace and freedom to create.'

'But, Mother, if I may be so bold, why restrict the beneficiaries to artists alone, if your idea is to liberate the place to a greater wider world?'

'My dear boy, twenty-eight hectares do not a world make; it's logical and sensible to limit the beneficiaries, if you don't want the place to look like one of those disgusting camping sites near St Tropez. I want our beloved Mortcerf to be a haven for the politically and racially persecuted artists.'

Tristram then turned to his father and asked very gently, almost meltingly. 'Before Mother and the cunning old Rosenthal can liberate Mortcerf, how do you circumvent the Napoleonic law of equally divided inheritance?'

Frank writhed and sank low in his chair, his long wan cheeks looking longer with a non-committal smile, while Letti at this overt provocation lifted her chin higher.

'Tristram, more than a quarter of the old houses in France are uninhabitable because of the *héritiers* feuding and disagreeing on how to share or dispose of them. I'm sure you are above such squalid behaviour.'

Tristram raised a hollow laugh and changed the subject by asking Frank what he thought of the young Richard Pearce's latest novel.

Not until we were on board the BEA aeroplane bound for London did I feel sufficient security of distance to ask Tristram about the inheritance problem, and then only very obliquely:

'Do you love Mortcerf very much?'

'I do rather. In fact, more and more. You could say that it is the only real continuity I know.'

A jealous person who hates losing things, he began clinging to things with undue attachment when he knew he was to lose them or after having lost them. Now, he was becoming aggressively possessive and attached to Mortcerf. I thought of my mother who went into a sober mood every August, the month of the returning dead: 'We shall soon be a handful of ashes; then, fame, possession or vengeance, all will be of no importance. How nice!' I went on to think of Pom and Ju, by now perhaps otherworldly saints, levitating a few feet above the ground to which we ordinary mortals are bound.

And, talk of the devil, shortly after our return to London I was doing my Saturday stint at the gallery, when Colin strode in.

'Come to lunch, Asako. I have lots to tell you about your chums. I've just got back from New York.'

As we sat down in his immaculate dining room, Colin, looking sallow and bloated, sighed, 'My dear, after a long weekend chez Sugarheims I'm afraid you'll have to share this unhealthy protein diet, an absolute fad in New York.'

Over smoked salmon, steak and cheese, washed down with Evian water, he told me the latest news about Pom and Ju.

'Would you believe it, Suki, at this very moment your friends are somewhere not far from Saigon in a jungle infested with Vietcong and napalm bombs, running a thing called Saigon Sanctuary with some oddballs of the same bent as them, all Vanderbilts and Whitneys, of course. Saigon Sanctuary: S.S. Hear the sinister echo from the past, eh? According to Daniel (Colin called Mr Sugarheim by his Christian name with evident relish and pride) it's a sort of free-for-all dosshouse-cum-temple, and you know what a hawk and staunch Republican he is, well, Daniel swears that the whole thing's perfectly above board and Pom doesn't go out of his way to provoke the military police by hiding conscientious objectors or deserters. If you believe that you can believe anything, ehn? He mostly takes in young kids who've been shell-shocked, so says Daniel, and treates them with analysis, prayer, yoga and Zen meditation and feeds them with brown rice, rather like an RSPCA camp for strays with Oriental religious and macrobiotic overtones, see? All I can tell you, Suki, is that I met a number of Upper Eastside New York *chic-nicks* against the war in Vietnam who thought Pom's doing a terrific job and sent fat cheques to his so-called S.S.

'With half the American press camping out in Vietnam, as it were, my dear, they've become quite notorious. One Sunday magazine had photographed them in sari and loin-cloth chanting hare krishna, sitting cross-legged on straw mats laid on the hard earth, looking rather sexy, I must say. I cut out the article for you but I'm afraid the bull-dog-faced negro maid who obviously disapproves of Miss Ju's carryings-on threw it away.'

When I reported to Tristram what Colin had told me, he said, 'Men of action!' in the same vein as his 'Grrreat people of this world!' and went back to his tea and the Guardian, leaving me feeling short-changed.

10

Frank died of a massive heart attack, his third, at Stockholm airport on May Day. On May 3rd Tristram and I arrived at the Orly Airport to meet Letti and Frank's body returning on an Air France flight from Stockholm and found the dago already waiting there.

Lette was dressed in a bright fuscia-mauve Chanel suit in which she had probably started her outward journey. She bit her lower lip and crumpled her face as if to sneeze as she embraced Tristram and me. To Toma she offered neither cheek nor hand but said in a flat hoarse voice:

'Very kind, Toma. I need your help.'

And, the dago turned out to be extremely helpful in dealing with the customs, police and health control; he cleared the non-French corpse as if it were a box of exotic fruit. Tristram who abhorred anything to do with official procedures must have felt so relieved to have this aggressive and patient man to do all the dirty work, running from one end of the airport building to the other and back, that when we finally sat in a big black limousine following the hearse to the crematorium, he thanked Toma with a sincerity which I knew was more than just good manners.

Frank, being agnostic, had demanded that there should be no funeral rites and that his body be cremated and his ashes scattered on the soil of Mortcerf amongst his aspens. When we came out of the crematorium it was already getting late. Letti wanted to go home to Mortcerf; Tristram wanted to stay at a hotel in Paris, have dinner and go to bed; the limousine driver said he had been on duty since early in the morning and could not drive all the way to Mortcerf.

'Let's cut the cackle. I'll drive you to Mortcerf,' said Toma simply; gave only a fifteen franc tip to the sullen limousine chauffeur, ignoring a sharp hiss of disapproval from Letti; quickly transferred our luggage into his station wagon's boot and with no further ado told us where to sit.

I was surprised that I no longer found Toma detestable. In his crude, bossy, complacent way he was decent and straight. Ju had in fact told me: 'He's OK, Toma. You know where you are with him.' He was not a clinging sycophantic gigolo; moreover, his grief over Frank's death struck me as genuine.

'What beats me,' he said, 'is that Frank wasn't even an official guest of this so-called Bertrand Russell Tribunal, the biggest non-starter of the year, and why he thought he could do any good by going there just as an eager-beaver hanger-on, I can't imagine. To think he also paid for the journey and hotel rooms for the geriatric secretary and some useless APWAV members! Aside from everything else, he was clearly far from being well. Christ, it was only two days before he left for Stockholm that I urged him to stay quietly in bed and forget the whole bloody nonsense!' With the thick-lipped accent of his mother tongue, Spanish or Portugese or Aztek, whatever he said carried a ring of childlike blunt truthfulness which did not offend.

'You don't know Frank as well as I do,' said Letti severely, 'Like with dinner parties and luncheons, once arranged, he'd rather die than let others down.'

'Well, he did exactly that. It was just so stupid, plain stuu-pid!' Toma slapped at the dashboard and with an excess of fury flung his back against the car seat. 'And to think that without the May Day demonstrators the ambulance could probably have got him to the hospital in time. He was a real sucker all right!'

'What does a real sucker mean?' I asked Tristram later that night, having tucked him in and seated myself against the leg of his bed, the position I always took up when he was miserable. He had mixed a lot of vodka and wine and only with some difficulty could I persuade him not to follow them with Seconals.

'Father,' he replied.

'Yes, but what does a sucker mean?'

'Father!'

I looked up and saw his eyes staring out of his skull, tears rolling down fast into his hair and pillow.

Frank and Tristram had not been close; they were affable to each other like friendly neighbours and took a harmlessly malicious delight in exposing each other's idosyncrasies. I had often detected a tinge of rancour seeping into Tristram's comment whenever an opportunity enabled him to allude to Frank's lack of paternal instinct. Also, Tristram, the man of steely discipline who believed one half of genius was hard work, found his father's way of life wasteful. He privately declared to me that he could not accept occasional book reviewing as a serious literary profession and could scarcely conceal his embarrassment at his father's spoken French which, for someone who had lived in France nearly half a century, was fluent only in a broken, haphazard manner with a strong American accent.

And now that the futility of Frank's life was graphically brought home by the tragi-comic circumstances in which he had brought death upon himself, Tristram, man of style and analytical intellect, was revolted, whilst Tristram the son who feared any form of loss was seized by savage remorse, remorse too late and too near. Listening to the urgent vibration in the plumbing system of the hot water rushing toward Toma's bathroom, I remained mute.

The following morning when I tiptoed downstairs, I noticed dregs of coffee in one of the four cups laid on the breakfast table. Josiane, who was redistributing dust from here to there with a worn thin broom in the name of sweeping, told me that Monsieur Toma had just left. I was relieved that at least one element of tension had eliminated itself with exemplary tact.

Letti came down at nine, extraordinarily early for her and stranger still, already dressed; not just dressed for a

138

far niente day in the country nor for shopping grocery in St-Loup, but as smartly as if she were lunching at the Ritz. Tristram stood up, still in pyjamas and dressing gown, kissed her amiably, taking full note of her sartorial chic, but said nothing. Underneath the studied normality of a breakfast conversation, comparing the sleepability of the night, there was a kind of alert, watchful reticence between the two living Harders. At ten we were still in the breakfast room reading through the telegrams of condolence, when there rose a cacophony of chickens and ducks at the gate. Letti shot to her feet.

'Expecting someone, Mother?'

'Rosenthal,' said Letti and it was not only the name of the Parisian lawyer for the famous and the rich but a raw challenge that she delivered.

'Ah, *le maître* Rosenthal!' Tristram wiped his mouth in rough circles with his crumpled napkin, stood up and left the room. I was still undecided as to when and how I should make myself scarce, when a short, agreeably corpulent man with a hat and a briefcase was led up the front steps by Josiane. Letti greeted him graciously and, taking one nimble step backward to bring me into the picture, she said:

'Tristram's wife, Maître. Maître Rosenthal. Would you now leave us, Soukie?'

Leave I did. My fault, of course. Untrained in the art of timely entrance and exit in society, I asked for the request to get the hell out. I stole away to Frank's aspens whose thousand small new leaves fluttered and twirled as if they were cheering me: take heart, Soukie, we're glad to see you! The sun was cool and crisp; I could stay hatless in it for at least an hour, seated on a hardened mud rut, thinking of death, not the financial and legal aspect of it, but the irrevocable loss of a friend.

Maître Rosenthal was still with Letti behind the closed door when at two Josiane rang the bell for lunch. When I came into the breakfast room where the table had been laid for three, Tristram was there already, fiddling with knives and glasses, his entire attention focused on the muffled voices coming from the hall. As the maître and

Letti slowly descended the front steps and walked past the breakfast room windows he said: 'Goodness, he's put on weight!' He did not stop nervously clinking a knife against a plate till we heard the noise of the Parisian lawyer's car departing. Letti came back on quick airborne steps and as she entered the room she handed Tristram the *Herald Tribune*.

'Page seven. Frank's obituary. Muriel de Bergerac wrote it. Not long, but very nice.' Letti sat down and took a large portion of *omelette au lard* which Josiane had left on the side table. I never got to read the orbituary. No one thought of letting me see it. Taking into account my relatively short and occasional acquaintance with Frank, out of *enryo* I did not like to ask to read it. I watched Tristram read it and return the paper to Letti, who put it between the small of her back and the back of her chair. Without commenting on what he had read Tristram served himself some omelette. Josiane always mixed chicken with duck eggs for omelette and as a consequence the omelette at Mortcerf had a violent orange hue. The grease from the bacon and butter encircled the screaming orange mound and I always tried to absorb it by strategically placing pieces of bread.

'I am famished. Catastrophe always whets my appetite.' Letti took a break from serious eating and pulled a napkin from her napkin ring, her lips and the tip of her chin gleaming with grease.

Tristram was meticulously separating the white fat from the red flesh of the thick-cut French bacon, Tristram, who lost appetite in the face of a crisis, let out a noise half admiration, half horror at her statement. At the end of the meal Letti looked at us both.

'Shall we have coffee?'

Frank had been forbidden coffee by his doctors; when the four of us ate at home it had been the rule that we should also forego coffee. Caught unawares, Tristram and I remained silent. Letti swiftly answered the question herself: 'Why not? Soukie, you're young, go and tell Josiane we'll have coffee today.'

As I waited for Josiane to percolate the coffee I obstinately thought of the golden little hands of Frank's aspen beckoning and cheering in the sun. When I emerged in the hall with the coffee tray, Letti and Tristram were installed in the white room where Frank had been banned as, Letti had quite justifiably pointed out, he never looked where he was going and his shoes were seldom free of mud or worse, chicken or duck mess. I poured out coffee for them both, drank half a cup myself and took the tray back to the kitchen, where Madame Malenfant, seated, and Josiane and Aristide standing over her, were engaged in a heated debate. At my appearance their mobile mouths turned mute as if struck dumb by magic and watched me, distrustful and closed.

'*Merci, c'était bon, le café,*' I put down the tray.

'*Et, voilà, Madame Tristan, le courrier d'aujourd'hui.*' Josiane presented me a bundle of letters in exchange.

'*Ehm, Madame Tristan,*' Aristide stepped forward, forestalling my immediate departure and having consulted the looks in the eyes of the two women, went on, turning his *garde champêtre* cap round and round in his dirty hands. '*Le testament que Monsieur aurait dû laissé . . . nous nous demandons si Monsieur avait la gentillesse de . . . de . . .*'

The women at this juncture took the trouble to slap on their hearts in unison with their red hands.

'Ah, yes, the will,' I sighed and backed my way out of the kitchen, saying, '*Je demanderai à Madame Arder!*'

Letti and Tristram were no longer in the white room; they were walking to and fro at the far end of the lawn, heads angularly dropped, eyes fixed on the ground. The picture signalled warning enough. I stood still, prominently holding out the day's mail. Letti noticed me first and held out her hand. I ran up to her.

'Good girl, thank you, dear. Now, will you leave us?' Leave I did. I was getting used to being told to leave. I went up to my garret of peace and congeniality and slept at my desk with my head resting on my arms.

When I came down at six to take a walk alone in the wood Letti was in the library with some visitors. At dinner, looking worn out, she told us that the village schoolmaster had come to inquire if Madame was going

141

to continue the late Monsieur's annual charity of sending the village children by bus to the Chateau de Versailles. The chief of *sapeur-pompiers* of St-Loup had been to 'inform himself' if the *Veuve Arder* was going to give them a champagne reception on the forthcoming July 14th as in every year, and also the mayor had turned up to 'wonder' if Letti would go on donating five hundred francs a month for the children of unmarried mothers who were fostered with families in the village.

'And tomorrow a whole gang of people from Paris, APWAV and what have you, are coming. I'm beginning to wonder if I'll have anything left to live on after paying for all those lunatic charities Frank was committed to.'

Tristram, wiser and warier than to contradict Letti at this moment, smiled wanly and changed the subject to the explosive situation in the Middle East where Syria and Egypt seemed set to provoke Israel into war. Letti with an icy intolerance interrupted him:

'Ridiculous to feel sorry for Israel, Tristram. She's not a poor little state menaced on all sides to extinction. Far from it. She's as aggressive and cocky as a terrier that knows there's his master, Uncle Sam, at the end of his leash. It's the Palestinians one ought to sympathise with. You've got it all wrong, dear boy.'

Tristram nimbly changed the topic again, this time, to asparagus, Letti's favourite vegetable.

'I'll go to St-Loup tomorrow to see if I can find some fresh asparagus, Mother.'

'Sweet of you. Before I go to bed I'll make a list of things I need and leave it on the breakfast table.'

The following morning Letti was not yet up when Tristram and I left the house with her shopping list.

'Must ring Colin and Hawkins,' Tristram rubbed his thumb nail against his front teeth. Hawkins was his solicitor. The combination of Maître Rosenthal's visit and Tristram calling his own lawyer made me cautious, so I quickly said, 'I'll do the shopping whilst you telephone from the post office.'

'A great help. *Su-pa!*'

Tristram seemed to have had much to talk about with

them. He did not join me till I reached the *primeur* grocer to select asparagus.

At home, asparagus grows only in the volcanic soil of Hokkaido Island and by the time it reached us it was tinned and we ate it with chopsticks. Here, before my astonished eye, hot asparagus was held in the fingers, dipped into melted butter then lifted straight up, butter dripping at random on to plate and place mat, only to be lowered into the waiting cavern of a mouth. Letti's bracelets jangled up and down her forearm and a mixture of butter and asparagus juice trickled down her wrist. The outer fibre being straw-like, the effort to chew the flesh out of its hard sheath was again not a polite sight. I resolutely picked up my knife and fork. Just as Letti drew breath to comment on my use of a knife and fork, the telephone started ringing.

'Oh, bother, botheration!' Tristram stood up at once and hurried out of the room. It had always been Frank who jumped up to take telephone calls; there was nothing untoward that now Tristram should undertake the task. Letti neatly dabbed her mouth and fingers with her napkin and halted both conversation and eating, waiting to hear if the call was for her, but obviously it was for Tristram; he did not return to the table till several minutes later.

'It was Colin. He has to be in New York for a very important meeting on the 7th and wants me back, as he put it, yesterday. Our new show is scheduled to open on the 7th. I feel I really must go back tomorrow . . .'

'Oh, must you?' Letti said.

'Yes, Mother, I'm afraid I must. This new exhibition, a collection of costume and scenery designs for Diaghilev, many of which not previously exhibited, is a new departure for the gallery. I ought to be there at the final and most crucial stage.' Tristram put on a whining urgent tone, which I recognised as that which he used whenever he wanted to get his own way against the odds.

'Sounds very interesting,' Letti shot a mercurial smile at her son. The ways he said 'interesting' somehow deflated his original steam. Into a pocket of silence she injected calmly, 'I forgot to tell you. Just before you came

143

back from the town your lawyer rang to ask if you couldn't alter your appointment with him from four to five tomorrow in Threadneedle Street.'

Staring at his right hand resting on a crumpled napkin, Tristram, his duplicity exposed, replied in a vacuous over-jovial voice: 'Oh, good, good, I could do with the extra hour with Colin!'

I took a deliberately long time changing into pyjamas before I went to say good night to Tristram. As I had expected he was prostrate, hating himself. He clutched at my hand and pressed it to his red and wine-sweaty face.

'I'm not a liar,' he pleaded. 'Darling, you know me, I'm not a liar. Nannie Binn told us to be truthful. It's grossly unfair: I wanted to stay on and be of comfort to Mother for as long as I could, but there really is so much to do in London. That idiot Hawkins ringing up and leaving that message of all persons with Mother has botched everything up! I'm not a liar!'

'Of course not. But, Tristram, you did ring Mr Hawkins and Colin from St-Loup, *that* you did!' I said.

'I'm not saying I didn't ring. Hell, you simply don't understand what's at stake!'

The tiara in the past and the twenty-eight hectares today, I felt like retorting, but the thought of Frank's aspens being involved in a sordid legal wrangle between mother and son appalled me. I retrieved my hand from below his face, saying, 'I'll get you some hot milk. Then, I'll start packing.' As I warmed the milk on a low gas fire I recalled with a fond sense of relief that my maternal grandmother had lost everything during the war and had at her death left my mother only a wooden comb whose teeth, after many years of daily use, had worn to fit the exact shape of her skull. My mother used it now.

The two lawyers exchanged threatening letters but the mother and the son who employed them were highly soph-isticated people and their sense of style dictated a kind of behaviour which seemed to me just downright two-facedness: they wrote and talked on the telephone with a breezy friendliness; Tristram sent a book from Hatchards practically every week to help Letti through her long sleepless nights and followed it with Gentleman's Relish, Stilton cheese and candied ginger for which she fulsomely thanked him, saying that they stimulated her appetite dulled by grief and loneliness. Yet, I overheard Tristram on the phone to his solicitor: 'Oh no, there's no doubt in my mind that she hopes to marry the dago, or at least cohabit with him. You must realise, Mr Hawkins, that he being not much older than myself, sooner or later I'll just have to sit and watch all her assets drop into his hands.'

Under these circumstances I was not surprised to begin noticing signs of strain in him. His morbid possessiveness over his Parker pen now extended to his Gucci bag and Frank's slim dark mahogany cane whose round head was inlaid with mother-of-pearl and steel wire in an intricate Indian design, which he had taken from the umbrella stand at Mortcerf on our last visit there.

'For God's sake, Asako, take that frightful bag and that cane from your husband!' Colin urged me at the cocktail party the publisher gave at the Savoy to launch Tristram's *Disciples behind Masters*. 'He looks ridiculous, shaking hands with the cane and the bag squeezed under his armpit.'

Tristram, however, barred me with his squared stiff arms. 'No, thank you, darling. I'm managing perfectly well; besides, once I put them down I'll be bound to lose them.'

There was much truth in that. In spite of his almost pathological attachment to his pen and bag and cane, perhaps perversely because of it, he somehow managed to leave them behind or mislay them with an alarming frequency which was not only time-wasting but harmful to his nerves and to our peace of mind, that is, mine and Mrs App's. Too frequently seven o'clock would arrive with one or more of his precious items missing, and Mrs Apps, putting on her coat, whispered to me with a condoling look: 'At least I can go home and think no more about Doctor's pen, but you, poor Mrs Harder . . .'

Another eccentricity that had become more pronounced in him was his attachment to our house, *his* house.

'It's got to be cosy, beautiful and comfortable. We ought to be so pleased to come home and stay in it. It's so horrid outside . . .'

He spent hours selecting new materials to cover the walls and sofas; spent a fortune double-glazing the street-facing windows; bought three more antique chess sets, then tables to put them on. Simultaneously, his exclusive love of seventeeth and eighteenth-century music became an infatuation, and his dislike of anything later than that period, a veritable phobia. 'Mozart to me is a borderline case. Some of his later works are already too romantic and gushy.'

He stuck obstinately with Schütz, Telemann, Rameau, Bach, Scarlatti and so on; and morning or night when he was not actually asleep, his presence at home was deafeningly proclaimed by record after record of baroque music played on the stereophonic player in his study and diffused by two large speakers in the sitting room. Mrs Apps confessed that when she got home and took a hot bath to relax, she could still feel the thumping and banging rhythm of 'Doctor's music' in her body like someone who, having got off a boat after a stormy voyage, goes on experiencing the rolling of the ship.

Tristram's obdurate attachment to the baroque past, to the cosseting security of his own home were to a great extent an expression of his horror of and malaise with his time, with himself in it and with what was happening in the Middle East, in South East Asia and pretty well everywhere else. With his multiple negativism, if Nasser decided to close the Suez Canal, the pound sterling weakened, and his Victorian walking stick happened to be missing as well, to him, the end of the world was assured. And the way *Disciples behind Masters* was being received did not help alleviate his gloom. An enervating calm after such high hopes and promises. Reviews came out stragglingly, ranging from excellent to lukewarm to indifferent. The sales department reported: 'Things are not going too badly; we ought to sell out the first impression by the

146

autumn.' It was a respectable success, acknowledged and durable. But, Tristram had hoped for second and third impressions before the summer was out; he had expected a firework, a fanfare, a twenty-one gun salute . . . He had always enjoyed high esteem in the hushed world of academics, that was nothing new. This time, he had hoped for recognition from the wider public with its immediately enjoyable, vulgar and profitable appendage. Anyone else would have been more than satisfied to have already sold nearly five thousand copies and to have American and German editions to follow, but not my Tristram. He moped and sulked as if he had been betrayed by an illiterate public, mean critics, and uninspired and lazy publisher, bad publication timing, a national economic slump, the Middle East crisis, the oil embargo; in another word the whole universe had conspired against him.

It was just then that Colin, a confirmed balletomane, 'I adore the perversity of making girls hop about on a bleeding toe,' who assiduously worked for two sub-committees at the Royal Opera House, took two boxes for a gala given in aid of the Royal Ballet Benevolent Fund at Covent Garden and invited us.

Reaching our designated box, we found Colin in his element, like a windmill in a mild storm, passing glasses of vintage champagne to everyone who trotted into his orbit, not only his guests but to his friends and acquaintances who simply wormed their way there, having sighted champagne flowing.

'How was New York?' I asked him.

'New York?' He smoothed his stiffly lacquered hair, picked out a smoked salmon sandwich from the passing tray, then suddenly enlightened, nodded with a malicious grin, one eye opening many seconds later than the other. 'Ah, ah, *that* New York trip that forced poor Tristram to abandon his widowed mother and come running home! I never went, dear.'

'Goodness, it was just an excuse?'

'Goodness, yes, it was a variation on the theme of *King*

147

Lear, darling.' With a shrill laughter he minced off to greet one of the Opera House governors.

For the first part of the programme, Colin put us in a box with Lord and Lady Castleacre, young and to whom everything was 'su-pa', just 'su-pa'. After the interval Colin made us change box partners and we were put together with Mr and Mrs Baron, an American couple who had only a few days earlier landed at Southampton on the *S.S. France* and were leaving for Venice the following morning. Their itinerary included Spoleto, Bayreuth, Salzburg and Aix, ending with this gala and that gala with 'fireworks thrown in' in Monte Carlo.

'How exciting, what an itinerary!' I gasped.

'But wouldn't you find it rather tiring?' asked Tristram and I could hear him thinking: 'Can't think of a worse punishment than what you're about to undergo.'

'Oh, no, we'll just collapse and rest on the boat going home, so that's just fine,' said Mrs Baron, whose eyelashes were caked stiff in mascara and sprang upward like spiders' legs round her beautiful almond-shaped black eyes. She was far from being young, but without the definitive signs of old age either; only the tremendous strain of keeping old age at bay did show at odd moments. She was militantly culture-minded and very very interested in everything. Mr Baron, a silent bulk of a man with an all-purpose grin on his dimpled massive jaws, donated huge sums of money to museums and opera houses on the West Coast, which in return put his wife on their boards of trustees and committees. Mrs Baron whispered into my ear, 'I'd love to know more about you two. You make such a fascinating couple.'

At the supper which Colin gave at Trois Gros in a side street near the Opera House, I could tell Mrs Baron, seated between Tristram and Lord Castleacre, was intensely engaged in doing exactly what she had said she'd love to do.

'What's your name? Tristan? Trist-ram? Oh, how divine. I've never met anyone with a name like that. How divine. And your wife? A-sah-ko? You know, Tris, that's a lot easier than yours.'

148

How much Tristram loathed the barrage of personal questions from the suffocatingly sweet and inquisitive woman was shown in the way his upper trunk leant at a sharp angle away from her, his shoulder almost permanently crushed against Mrs Piccard-Smith on his right.

Mrs Baron must have started with the predictable: 'Where and how did you two meet?'; for I overheard Tokyo and the Blake exhibition mentioned, whilst I was eating my avocado with shrimp. As I had the good fortune of sitting next to a retired army colonel who regaled me with an engrossing account of his adventures in Aden and Oman, I paid little attention thereafter to my beleaguered husband, but when the plates with the scavenged lamb bones were taken away, I noted that Mrs Baron was now on to Tristram's parents and to my rising uneasiness her gushing enthusiasm overflowed to involve other guests as well in the subject.

'You mean you're not a Britisher through and through? I'll be darned. I'd have never guessed, Tris! Oh, how interesting, your father's American?'

Raspberry and blackcurrant sorbet arrived and I hoped this would cool her ardour but not at all: being so stoically careful about her figure, she was not one to touch an iced mass of carbohydrate. Having declined the sorbet, all her unencumbered attention now poured on Tristram.

'But, Tris, your father, Frank, what's his family name?'

Tristram put a spoonful of ruby-red sorbet in his mouth, let it melt, swallowed it, then gave the name.

'Oh, my *gyad!*' Mrs Baron clasped her hands over her heart, her eyes raised to the ceiling, her spidery eyelashes aflutter and kicking. This burlesque reaction naturally captured everyone's attention.

'What is it, Myriam?' Colin asked from the far end of the table. I looked at my husband and at this stage he was just as puzzled as we all were, only slightly nervous.

'You'd never believe this, Colin, but I was once almost engaged to the father of Tris here. A small world! Our parents were good friends and they thought, wouldn't it

149

be nice if those two . . . you know? Well, I never! How's Frank?'

'He is dead.'

Oh, how Tristram must have hated it all. Had he been still eating *carré d'agneau*, who could have blamed him for knifing Mrs Baron to silence. As it was, he had only a dainty dessert spoon. He scopped up another mouthful of raspberry sorbet.

'Dead? Frank, dead? Oh, I am so very very sorry!' Here, Mrs Baron swayed the upper part of her body in an ancient wailing manner. The next thing I saw was a red blob of sorbet trickling down on Tristram's white Lanvin scarf which he had not taken off, lest he should lose or leave it behind in the cloakroom. It was last year's Christmas present from Letti. From here, events accelerated in speed and violence.

'Oh, what have I done? Hot water! Stay still. Hot water!' Mrs Baron kicked back her chair, shot to her feet and swung round to get the attention of a waiter. By doing so, the exuberant woman made things far worse: her tiny square gold (*solid* gold, Mr Baron had told me earlier) evening bag hung from her shoulder on a gold chain flew round and caught Tristram on the temple. I have never been hit in the face by solid gold; I have no way of knowing how painful it is; but, judging from his reaction, it had to be a lethal agony. His evening-long resentment of Mrs Baron's inquisition made him an outraged ham. He staggered to his feet, covering his temple and eye with his right hand, his free left hand disdainfully throwing down his soiled scarf on to the floor. Replying to Mrs Baron's loud apologies with a wordless sizzle, he walked away. Colin, cool and dapper, accustomed to public scandals, followed him signalling me not to move. Perfect good manners reigned round the table: no one made too much or too little of the incident; and to do her justice, Mrs Baron was beside herself with repentance and being quite sincerely so; she went on telling me what to do with the bruise, witchhazel and cold compress. When everyone had finished coffee and with both Colin and Tristram still absent, I left the table and was speaking to the head waiter, when Colin walked back in from the street.

'He's gone home. Taken the car. Don't worry, I'll take you home. He's off his rocker.'

Colin looked out of temper and exhausted. 'I thought I knew him . . . Mind you, though, she is a trying cow.'

He turned me round and we walked back to the table. When I got home I found on the hall table a hardly legible note:

'Sorry I had to leave you like that. Took sleeping tablets. Pl. don't wake me till morning.'

The following morning, Friday, it was nearly ten o'clock when Mrs Apps told me that Doctor was up.

'I'll never accept an invitation to anything where American women like that are let loose!' Tristram, omitting the usual good morning, glared at me from the depth of four soft pillows. His churlishness was a relief; I had been dreading finding him being sorry for himself.

'How is the bruise?' I asked.

'Pounding with pain. Feel it, darling, it's hot.'

I could hardly see where it was that he had been hit, only a slight hint of redness. As I applied my finger tip against his temple and saw him put on a solemn, wounded look, I felt like simultaneously roaring with laughter and crying. My big husband, such a baby, so selfish, so unsteady, so inconsiderate, so greedy for attention: to think that through the rough seas of life I had no one else but him to sail with! I felt faint and at the same time thirty years older than the child I had been when I'd left Japan. I applied the cold compress and rubbed witchhazel ointment on his temple, which gave him the satisfaction of believing that he had indeed suffered a cruel aggression by an American monster and me the pleasure of looking after my big baby of a husband.

I was practising a Schubert waltz before Mr Goldberger's visit at five, when the telephone rang. It was Mrs Baron calling from Venice, person-to-person. Even on the blurring long-distance telephone line I felt her apologies wet and palpitating. She said she had given Tristram's scarf to the most efficient 'lovely person' at Claridge's front desk who would arrange to have it dry-cleaned at the best French cleaner in town and then mail it back to me as soon as it was returned.

'May I ring you next time I'm in London? I'd love you to lunch with me, if it's possible, just you and I. Would that be OK?'

I told Tristram about her call from Venice but not about the invitation to lunch.

11

As an unusual heat wave descended on England, the fact that Letti had not written nor called about our annual visit to Mortcerf gave Tristram the jitters, all the more because he did not want to go this summer.

Every morning, staring into the bottom of his tea cup, he asked me if during the night I had thought up a better excuse not to accept the invitation, should she even at this late stage decide to ask us. Letti was one step ahead, however; she rang from her rue de Grennelle flat. 'I've stayed too long, too north. Now, I need the sun and the vulgar southern food in tomato sauce. Off to Majorca this afternoon. If you want to, you're most welcome to stay at Mortcerf as usual, you know, darling; Madam Malenfant and Josiane would be delighted to have you.'

'No, Mother, there's no point in our coming to Mortcerf if you aren't there yourself,' said Tristram charmingly.

'I'll see if I can't come back through London so that I can see a bit of you both,' said Letti with a retaliating charm.

On the heel of Letti's call there was another from his publisher.

'No, I think you are mistaken,' I heard Tristram say. 'With regards to the paperback edition, you've suggested fifteen thousand copies yourself. You've never mentioned twelve thousand. Never. As to the advance, you said £3,000, no, I don't think I misunderstood you.'

Thereafter Tristram began tape-recording telephone conversations, business or personal, indiscriminately. Whether he was in the bath or hardly awake in bed, if the telephone rang, he dashed downstairs to his study where the infernal machine had been connected to the telephone. When one tape was finished he dated it, locked it in a steel cabinet and put a new tape into the recorder. I never saw him replay any of the tapes except once, when he replayed the conversation he had had with the vet. Sido Basta, aged fourteen, had been confined in the vet's surgery for over two weeks, following a sudden paralysis of his hind legs. After playing it twice, with tears streaming down his face, he rang the vet back and told him to put Sido to sleep.

As if all this were not enough, our neighbour on the crescent decided to repaint the façade of his house and erected massive scaffolding, making the outlook from Tristram's study gruesome. He had had a window air conditioner installed a few days after Letti's telephone call, preparing himself for a studious summer in London, but the humming roar of the machine was such that the volume of his record player had to be raised to distortion level. The rivalry between the percussive baroque harpschicord music and the noisy air conditioner made it well nigh impossible for him to concentrate on his current work, an extensively illustrated book on the life of Courbet. In the same week, a water pipe burst in the intricate depth of the plumbing system.

Tristram took all these minor domestic nuisances as a catastrophic personal tragedy. His usual reserve broke down and he told me that his maternal great-uncle, a manic depressive and glutton, who particularly loved cream puffs, on reaching the age of seventy, decided he'd had enough, locked himself up in his room with enough cream puffs to feed an army and when he had eaten them all, shot himself.

'I'm much too sensitive to cope with plumbing disasters or the brutalising roar of household gadgets,' he said and asked for his supper in bed. As he complained that the avocado pear was hard, 'Hard as a stone;' and banged it like a child a toy drum, I sat on the floor opposite his bed, munching Patata cheese-crackers, my eyes fixed on the *Evening Standard* hanging on the edge of the blue blanket; I could not have felt more detached and alien to my husband just at that moment, yet there was something stronger than temper or pride: collusion of habits after three and a half years of life together. I heard myself ask mildly:

'Shall I feed you?'

Tristram loved being spoon-fed in bed when he was not feeling well.

'Mmm, mm!' He nodded.

A molly-coddle-milksop, I rolled my mental eyes in despair but at the same time my heart swelled with such a protective, indulgent tenderness that it almost hurt. I spread the napkin like a bib round his neck and sitting on the edge of the bed, carefully scooped out a spoonful of what he insisted on calling '*Crème renversée*' and I called by its Japanese name *pu-rin*, after pudding but Mrs Apps wouldn't budge from custard and shoved it into the expectant mouth. When he finished *crème-renversée-purin-*custard he said, 'Tell me a story in Japanese to fall asleep on, will you, darling?' Tristram found a story told in unknown language most helpful to induce him to sleep. I sat on the spot which Sido used to occupy to radiate her doggy smell.

'Once upon a time, there was a little boy born out of a peach that had dropped into the river below . . .'

I am already twenty-six years old, childless, and telling a fairy tale in Japanese to my husband, Ph.D., D. Litt., critic, author and owner of a gallery. Doesn't add, I thought, then said so aloud in Japanese, but Tristram was already asleep, puffing regularly; so I left Sido's place and tiptoed to my bathroom and sat on the toilet seat, blank and disconsolate for heaven knows how long . . .

It was at this nadir of our London summer that, one airless evening, I answered the door bell.

'Who is it?'

'Me. I took a chance.'

As I yanked the door open, Ju, four inches taller than me, poured in and swallowed me up, blinding me inside her permeating hair, my mouth pressed against the base of her neck, which smelt numbingly of patchouli.

'Ju! Ju! Is this really you? Not so dry and bony as before.'

'I feel great. Curd and molasses and nuts, nuts, nuts. Hey, who's dry and bony? Your hip bone's drilling a hole in my thigh!'

With giggling fits of joy and intense awkwardness after a long separation, it was Ju who had the courage to gently push me away and create a distance between us to look at each other. She put her palms on my shoulders.

'What tension, honey, Relax. Ree-lah-x.'

If her Miss Sugarheim image had been albinic and desiccated, with a firm slim layer of flesh all over and a lusty chestnut glow on her skin, which almost camouflaged her freckles, her hippy ladyship, dressed in a printed cotton voile dress which hung in a copious light mass down to her feet in sandals with a matching headband straight across her forehead, had colour, sheen and sap. When she sighed 'Ree-lah-x' the third time, fixing me with a hypnotic stare, I felt the scaffolding of my defence collapse from head to toe. I blurted, snivelling, 'I've missed you, Ju! I don't think I've been very happy here.'

'Oh, poor Soo-kie!' She gathered both me and my slobbering inside her arms of seductive charity. 'How could you have been happy in this stinking sick society? There's no love, no humility, only greed and indifference and selfishness. Until the world learns a totally new set of values there'll be no happiness nor peace.' She went on as if she had rehearsed it all by rote. I was no longer sniffling.

The two-year brush with the Orient seemed to have freed her tongue and made her a voluble theoriser, first aid guru, kitchen-sink missionary, intensely self-righteous and didactic. Racked by the imperfection and misery of the world, she was no longer interested in herself. Pom had turned her vision inside out. She was no longer the girl who would seek refuge from the world in an empty bathtub.

Tristram was not yet home. I prepared verbena tea and took the tray into the sitting room. Ju sat cross-legged on one of Tristram's prize carpets and sipped her tea in an oriental manner, which I myself had taken two years to unlearn, that is, to ignore the handle of a tea cup, hold it inside one's palms and whistle up the tea.

'I got off a Cathay Pacific plane at eight this morning and in just under half a day I already feel like vomiting: materialism banging on my eardrums and scratching my eyeballs everywhere I go and look; the air is shaking with high-voltage competition and a bullshit misconception of human achievements: buy this, buy that; can't do without those; get to the top faster; read faster; earn more; pay less tax; look thirty at sixty! Can't they realise this life we're passing through is of no value?' Ju projected beyond me, as if I were in the front row of a huge auditorium.

Eastern philosophy is tricky behind its seemingly naive surface. It must be conveyed from one abdominal cavity to another, through the unheard vibrations. Ranted, it sounds silly. I looked away from the fine foam at the corner of her mouth.

'And, hey, since when, this cute little rubbish?'

She disdainfully lifted between her fingertips an embroidered tray cloth, Tristram's family heirloom. 'Frightfli-frightfli precious.' She chuckled, amused, but I heard a judgement in it. A narrow judgement at that. I did not like it. She looked at me looking at her, then inched forward on her knees till she could hold my face between her warm hands. She bent and kissed me on both cheeks and eyelids with an unhurried gravity. I held my breath at a whiff of her healthy glands mixed with salty perspiration and patchouli.

'You won't grudge me growing up, Suki, will you?' She whispered as if I were a baby in a cot making life difficult for the mother by not going to sleep at once. 'I love you, Suki you're my best friend. When Tarq died, Pom said "But, darling, you still have Suki." I'd love to help you change and be free. There's so much we can . . .'

'A gushing randy lot,' Tristram's words were echoing through my mind, when Tristram himself walked in and, not recognising Ju, said very politely with a stutter.

'O-oh, e-excuse me . . .'

Only after Ju sprang up and embraced him with a

157

succulently pronounced 'Good to see you, Tristram!' did he realise who it was.

'How's Pom? Where is he?' He blurted.

'As a matter of fact, I was just going to tell Suki, when you walked in. He's rented a car and driven straight down to Falaise Hall to see his brother, Edward. For various reasons we want to have a place in the country. You know Daddy. He believes in real estate as a long term investment. Edward's now sixty-six, rheumatic and finds Falaise too big and too cold in winter. See what I'm getting at?'

'But, what would you do with a mausole . . . ,museum of a place like that?' asked Tristram.

'A World Elsewhere!' replied Ju. 'We want to create a World Elsewhere.'

'*Coriolanus*,' mumbled Tristram with a strange air of vexation, then asked obligingly, 'Would you like to stay the night here?'

'Thanks, but I think I'd better rent a car myself and drive down to Falaise tonight.' She then asked Tristram to cash a cheque for ten pounds.

'Is that enough? How are you going to pay for the car rental?' asked Tristram.

'By an American Express card,' she winked at him.

After she left, Tristram stroked his chin. 'Hippy-dom suits her. She's sexier, livelier, and at last has something to say, although, mind you, what she says is as predictable as a toilet flushing. So, on the neurosis of the super-rich and the inarticulate frustration of the misfit aristocracy depends the alternative shape of our future society . . . What a depressing thought! Why don't they cut the cackle, just buy India and a few starving African nations with their American Express cards and forget about their bleeding consciences?' He downed his dry martini and sinking low in the armchair, rubbed his temples in slow circles.

'I should be feeling on top of the world. Manchester City Museum has commissioned me to mount a large exhibition on Redon next spring. I received the letter of confirmation this morning.'

'But Tristram, that is wonderful!'

He snorted a dry unpleasant laugh. 'Is it? I wonder. And what is more, I've been finally chosen as the next director of W Gallery,' said Tristram, almost grim.

'What? W Gallery? You become director, W Gallery!?'

So flabbergasted and thrilled, I could not put together a proper sentence. I knew Tristram had been shortlisted, but with other candidates being at least ten years older and far more experienced in running similar state institutions and his owning a half share in a commercial gallery, he had not been as optimistic as to his chances as many of his friends.

'But, Tristram, why didn't you tell me at once? Ee-mah-ginnne! W Gallery, and you the director. Aren't you glad? Excited?'

'Should I be? Is it really all that fantastic? There's a twenty-four-year-old rich girl planning our next world elsewhere, I'm planning a picture show which will last for three months, Tuesday to Saturday, ten to five. I land a directorship of a moth-eaten old museum; her husband who had never had to struggle or fight for anything in his entire life, builds his own utopia on his own thousand acres. You can't blame me if I feel like chucking it all up.'

'You shouldn't be so jealous of other people, especially when everyone else is envious of your success.' This was the first time I spoke in a 'you-shouldn't' way to my husband.

'But, darling, I am jealous. A very jealous person. It's the foundation of my success: it generates discipline, hard work, humility, and critical perspective . . .'

I groaned my deep Japanese groan and gave up. I was much too 'split bamboo', slap-dash-flexible and uncomplicated. For the sake of my own sleepability, I jammed down my *enryo* lid and thought only of a hot bath.

The following afternoon Letti telephoned from Madrid to say she was coming to London in four days' time for her annual check-up by various London doctors and to go shopping.

159

'I'd love to stay with you, Tristram, if I may, now that I'm all alone, I don't like hotels.'

Letti could not have expected Tristram to believe that she had been holidaying in Spain and Majorca alone for over a month, but what mattered here was that she had thrown him a ball of friendliness, he had to catch it.

'We'll be delighted if you come and stay with us, Mother,' replied Tristram, his thumb nail against his teeth.

She arrived looking younger and fitter in an electric-blue dress that exposed her arms and much of her slim back. The blue eye-shadow looked like silver crescent on her tanned skin which had the texture of well-done steak and when she embraced me I felt the warm sea salt on her bare shoulders.

On her first night in London, Tristram asked Colin to dinner and Letti was extremely affable to everyone, full of laughter and anecdotes. She drank much more schnapps than I had ever seen her consume at Mortcerf. Tristram opened one of his best bottles of wine, a Chateau Lafitte. Colin, being on yet another diet, drank little; Letti and Tristram finished the first bottle with Mrs Apps's excellent steak and kidney pie which Letti had particularly requested. Then that inevitable and awkward question had to be asked: how much more can you drink of the red?

'Cheese and cold lemon soufflé to follow. What would you like to drink, Mother?' In the way he asked, one could not fail to detect a negative encouragement.

Colin smiled. 'Count me out. I'll stick to Perrier.'

Tristram looked at his mother. Letti looked at him.

'Darling Tristram, you know I love being pampered. Let's have another Lafitte.'

Tristram left the dining room and presently we heard him slam drawers and shelf-doors one after another in the kitchen, obviously looking for a bottle opener, which I detected on the dresser. I got up and took it to the kitchen, glad to leave the atmosphere of amused complicity between Letti and Colin. Tristram was in a pale green rage, if rage could have a colour. He snatched the cork-screw and banged it into the new bottle of Chateau Lafitte.

Lettie, who declined cheese, drank only one more glass of the wine and Tristram tried hard but could not drink even half the bottle.

The mother and the son somehow managed not to find themselves tête-à-tête but both busied themselves in pursuing their own affairs. On her third day in London Tristram had to go to Manchester overnight. Letti lunched with some friends, saw her dentist and met me at the Bacon exhibition in the late afternoon. In the taxi coming home, Letti pressed her jaw as one would a slightly over-ripe avocado or a kiwi.

'Still a bit sore. I don't think I can face a long drinking dinner with the Conways. Can we have a quiet meal at home? A picnic in the kitchen will do.'

Mrs Apps was putting her coat on when we arrived home, but quickly provided smoked trout and savoury rice, fruit and cheese. After telephoning the Conways Letti came into the kitchen to ask whether there was a bottle of white wine in the refrigerator. Mrs Apps snapped shut her mouth like a fish that had swallowed a fly and her whole face reddened. When the silence and a curious stare from both Letti and myself became intolerable, she turned to me, shaking her little coin purse nervously.

'Now then, let me think!'

The poor woman was beside herself with embarrassment. She even began making some squirming sideways movements toward the service door behind her.

'Ooops!' It was Letti who broke the silence. 'I forgot! I must make one more telephone call.' She hurried out of the kitchen. The relief that her exit produced on Mrs Apps was touching. She tapped at her heart with her jangling purse and collapsed on a stool. 'You see, Mrs Harder, this morning before he left for Manchester Doctor took all the wines that had been brought up back to the cellar. There's no wine left in the pantry and you know Doctor keeps the cellar key.'

I went to face Letti who, I knew, had not made a telephone call. She was lying flat on her back on the length of the sofa, smoking a dark slim cigar, her high-heeled sandals dangling perilously near the porcelain lamp on the

161

table by the sofa. At random intervals she stretched her arm inaccurately in the direction of an ashtray on the coffee table, dropping ash on the clutter of magazines and knick-knacks. I was glad Tristram was not there to witness his mother being so carelessly at home amongst his cherished furniture.

I cleared my throat and sat on the pouffe facing her.

'Isn't it splendid, Mrs Har . . . Letti, that Tristram will be the next W Gallery director and also mounting an important exhibition of Odilon Redon at Manchester City Museum? Isn't it exciting?'

'No one can deny he's brilliant and hard-working.' She covered her eyes with her forearm, still holding the schnapps, 'And my dear girl, for his sake, I do hope *you* will be able to stick it out.'

She left for Paris the following morning without waiting for Tristram's return.

12

Everyone talked about the devaluation of the pound. Tristram assured me that I had no reason to worry as 'the purchasing power' of my nine-pounds-ten-shilling weekly allowance suffered no decrease so long as I spent it in England. He also urged Mrs Apps to buy English butter and cheese and biscuits. With the pound devalued by 14.3 per cent all imported goods would cost that much more, he explained with his customary patience when it came to household economy. Colin who had made it the gallery's policy to quote the price of the paintings only in US dollars was one of the few who did not worry. Tristram's half share in the gallery which he had to dispose of on his appointment as the new director of W Gallery became an attractive proposition and a buyer, a Californian friend of Lillian Sugarheim's, was rapidly found. The letter of intent was signed and exchanged before the month was up.

Tristram then arranged to go to Paris with Mr Hawkins to seek expert advice on French inheritance law and at the same time to visit prominent private collectors of Redon in Paris, Lyon, Bordeaux and Cannes.

'I'll be away nine days, seven nights,' said Tristram who did not travel casually. 'Whilst I'm away I'd like the whole of the ground floor painted. Mrs Apps can cope with the painters. Isn't this an opportune moment to visit your friends at their Hampshire commune?'

Ju met me at the station in a mud-splattered Range Rover, looking positively bizarre: a walking American Indian's tent. I was not surprised that the newspaper vendor, alerted by one of his customers, came out of his

163

stand to have a look at her. Her flaxen hair fanned out from under a green Tyrolean hat topped with some jaunty feathers and a colourfully woven cape enveloped the rest of her in an elongated triangle, barely showing her old cowboy boots.

'Can't get over you've got here at last, Suki!' She somehow managed to bring her arms out of the deep folds of her cape and bearhugged me. There was an intense look of happiness that made her face appear haggard. 'I've got something very special to tell you, Suki, just you. Now, listen, ready? OK. I'm pregnant, six months gone!'

I flew sideways at her neck and in tottering tight scrimmage we raised incoherent cries of wonder and joy.

'I was kind of hoping that you might give me the same news, you know, Suki?' said Ju when we breathlessly leant against the bumpers of the Range Rover.

The offhand way she introduced the subject made me drop my usual defence and speak frankly for the first time.

'Too bad. That's really too bad. His side, is it?' She asked as we sat inside the car, careful not to sound inquisitive.

'He's been to a specialist and wants me to have an artificial semi . . . ensemi . . .'

'Right, I know what you mean,' Ju cut my embarrassment short. 'That's tough, that's very tough.'

'He doesn't put pressure on me, but I can feel he thinks I'm selfish and mean not to want to do it. But, Ju, think! I'll be terrified for all those months, wondering what sort of a baby will come out of me. And, later on, if I find some quality I can't like or understand in my own child, how can I cope with it, not knowing where and how it came from?'

'I know, Suki, I understand, but don't cry like that. Your eyes will be swollen and red.'

Ju who used to bleed inwardly like an overripe mulberry at the slightest friction now sat next to me, a mother-to-be, solid as a rock, patting me on the lap with one hand and with the other driving the tank of a car down a winding country lane. . . . I groaned in wonder, blew my nose and went on softly groaning.

I had believed the Pommeroys to be poor, squatting on barren land, mismanaged and neglected by a succession of dishonest lazy agents, their Falaise Hall a majestic pile of rubbish with leaking roofs, an algae-green pond infested with mosquitoes, half the windows of cottages mere plywood. My astonishment, therefore, erupted in a sharp draw of breath when, suddenly coming out of the dank wooded drive, we entered an immense open space under a low pewter-grey sky, flat and oily green, at the centre of which stood a massive square four-storeyed building of muted rose and ochre stones with large tall windows framed with white flagstones. No visible sign of decay or neglect. All the windows, even of the smallest cottage, had glass and a kidney-shaped lake at the bottom of the hill looked clean. Ju narrowed her eyes, following my gaze, her nostrils inflated with possessive pride.

'Isn't she a magnificent old lady, the house? The more I get to know her, the more I love her. You know it's all mine now? Old Edward sold it to me. Mind you, if Pom had waited long enough he'd have succeeded to the title and to the whole lot in his own right when Edward went, but Pom wanted it this way, so that Edward could buy a nice flat in Poole large enough for himself and his major domo before he's too old and dilapidated to enjoy it. So, everyone's happy. That's the main thing. Even Daddy. He's not one to miss a bargain when he sees one. With the pound devalued, he paid relatively little. There are thirty-seven rooms in the main house, plus the stable apartments and some quite nice cottages where Pom lets his brother's old managers and their widows continue to live, and a dower house at the other end of the estate.'

Ju slid out of the car with the cautious, measured stiffness of a pregnant woman. I went over to her side of the car and pushed open her cape, put my palm gently on her tummy and sighed. Ju placed her palm next to mine, shut her eyes and we groaned in unison. Ju said she could feel it moving. I could not, but I did feel that there was something alive and glorious inside, not just an accumulation of fat and tissues.

'Suki! Great to see you after so long.' Pom's voice it had to be, slightly yankee in 'great'. I turned. A swarthy profile with a mass of long grey hair flew past me, then I was between his chest and his crossed arms. Ju, leaning against the Range Rover bumper, watched my discomfiture with a mischievous smile. Pom held me at arm's length.

'Ju is right, you've been pissophisticated by the West. Look at you, a willow, a weeping willow.'

When I had last seen him, over two years earlier, he had been a bundle of youthful, urgent muddle, running between the Worlds Elsewhere and body-building gyms; oscillating shamefacedly between huge steaks and a repentant week of nuts and honey; intense and elusive, fanatic and confused, laughing like a firework and talking provocative nonsense. Now I faced a man of dark resin. He may in fact have grown neither thinner nor taller, but I had a distinct feeling that some ferocious inner energy had whittled him down, leaving only a protein core. His hair, drawn back from the face, had turned greyish. His face had lost that young Anglo-Saxon pink. His eyes, those gentle fixing dark eyes, sunken in their deep sockets, were perhaps even more disturbing with that penetrating long gaze focused some way beyond me. He had never been one to dress coherently, but after his eastern sojourn he seemed to have gone haywire: baggy Indian trousers, not too clean but silk, tucked inside green rubber wellies and a turtle-neck sweater under a fringed colourful poncho made out of what must have been a South American rug, with a piece of printed cloth tied round his unruly splurge of hair.

I blushed and laughed nonsensically, so totally unprepared for the transformation. 'You have changed so much, Pom!'

'Of course, we all do. Look at Ju. Have you felt our baby?' He hugged Ju so tenderly that I felt obliged to look away.

'Darling, get Suki's suitcase,' said Ju, putting her arm

166

in mine; I squeezed her arm against my ribs but could not help staring at Pom. Despite the speed with which he walked and the weight of my suitcase, his body, balancing on the tough springs of his feet, seemed to glide placidly with a minimum of disturbance to his carriage.

'You don't walk, Pom, you float!' I exclaimed.

'Ah, you noticed that too, clever you,' Ju stopped, her hands on her tummy. 'Ever since we got back, he's been training every inch and ounce of his body. Hours and days on end. Craii-zy, but I agree with you, Suki, it does show, especially in his walk.'

'Doesn't make sense, though,' I said provocatively. 'Why should someone who wants so much to die young train his body night and day?'

'Ju, she's one of the rare Orientals who believe two and two make four. Suki, you've become westernised and predictable. If you want to exit between stale sheets with a bed pan under you any flabby old body will do, won't it?' With this mouthful Pom pranced ahead of us into the hall. Ju chortled and mumbled lovingly:

'Mad, mad, mad.'

The interior of the house was a bleak travesty of the exterior magnificence. It reminded me of a looted cathedral. Against the high, grandiose walls and ceilings of bas-relief and boiserie, unmatched chairs and benches and bursting cardboard boxes were put hugger-mugger. Up the central staircase worthy of a nightly descending ghost, Pom led me to a room with a worn-out dull-green carpet with the texture of sandpaper. A draught cut the shortest distance between the weather-shrunken sash window and the gaping mouth of the fireplace.

'Ju told me that you, being a lavatorial cleanliness fiend, should be allowed to share with us the best bathroom we've got.'

The best bathroom was at the end of a long musty corridor linoleum floored and overwhelmed by an electric hot water cylinder, complete with a jumble of spaghetti pipes.

'The towel warmers don't work, by the way, but Suki,

you have a soul-cleansing view of the fields and the sky as you sit there peeing.'

He turned to go, but stopped with a quizzical tilt to his head and came back to look at me. He raised his right hand several inches above my head, his eyes squinting as if he were adjusting his mental wavelength, then slowly let his hand come down the back of my neck. When his finger penetrated through the hair and touched the skin on my neck, I recoiled and the expression on my face made him wince, as if he had heard an inaudible scream.

'Such a tension, here, here, and here. Feel it?' He held my upper arm between his middle finger and thumb as if he were examining the ripeness of a peach.

'You have a lovely arm, quite lovely,' he said as I blushed uncontrollably. 'Won't last long, but whilst it does, it's exquisite. Teatime! Come down to the kitchen.'

He carelessly removed his fingers from my arm and walked out of the bathroom and I felt an obscure disappointment, physical as well as emotional, for the rest of the day, perhaps for the rest of my week there.

The kitchen was cavernous, the size of an average Japanese house. Ju put on a stained old apron and brewed an exotic herb tea, I buttered brown bread and cut the banana-and-walnut cake she had baked with the assistance of Claude, a nineteen-year-old French boy, son of an ex-Gaullist minister, whom Pom had rescued from a police station in Benares.

'Accused of attempted arson,' said Ju. 'High on heroin, he didn't know what he was doing.'

Ju called the narrow-shouldered gentle boy 'my boy Friday' and, taking advantage of the unwieldy dignity of her pregnancy, used him on errands and small chores all day long. Claude on his part adored Ju *comme le pain je mange*' and seemed totally devoted and in awe of the mistress of the house. Ju had no domestic help except for a few old farm labourers who gave some hours of slow work in return for their free cottages and two women from the village who came in five mornings a week, which, with the house so rambling and the grounds so extensive, was far from sufficient.

I volunteered to sweep, dust, polish, wash and where necessary scrape out hardened cakes of dirt; helped Claude bottle vegetables and fruit Pom brought in from the garden; and joined Pom and Claude for meditation and yoga in the empty ballroom. Life on this level was repetitious, restful and even tedious in a big dose and I could not honestly say I was more aware of the fleetingness of life or more in tune with the universe; only my appetite and complexion improved noticeably.

On my third day, Tuesday, Pom was absent from our morning meditation.

''ee goes up to London every Tuesday,' explained Claude at breakfast in the kitchen. ''ee won't be back till Thursday.'

'Where does he stay in London?'

'Sleeps where 'ee feels like. Crash pads and squats, everywhere.' With a floral nylon apron over his pullover and jeans, Claude busied himself in getting Ju's muesli.

'Let me take the tray up for Ju,' I said, 'so that you can get on with the spinach quiche for lunch.'

Much as I loved Pom and Ju, I found their indifference to dirt and chaos revolting: give them five minutes, and they'll turn any place into a pigsty. Gingerly selecting a space for my feet amongst the dense litter on the floor, I tiptoed into their bedroom.

'Another nightmare last night!' With a long groan Ju slithered off the mattress laid directly on the floor and wriggled on to a large Indian cushion. 'This time a baby with red round eyes with no lids. They never shut, like red buttons. Suki, it's Tarquin's revenge!'

'Tarquin? Nonsense!'

'I'm telling you, Suki, it's Tarquin. Whenever we made love, Pom and I, I made sure I got Tarq out of the room. But, occasionally things just happened and he was there, and I always felt horrible afterwards, just horrible. See what I mean?'

'Y-yes, to a degree, I felt the same way with Sido . . . but, I can't imagine Tarq being jealous or vindictive. He'd have been so sweet and good with your baby.'

I opened the curtains with a peremptory gaiety. 'Tell

169

me, Ju, is Pom happy here, living the life of a guru-Robinson-Crusoe?'

Ju looked far out on the foggy green and her eyes went liquid: Tristram would have said: 'dripping in excess schmaltz'.

'He doesn't care happy, happier or unhappy, that's not in his vocabulary. I'm telling you, there's much in him that, kick or yell, I can't even begin to understand. When I was a kid I couldn't believe there was air till Daddy whipped it with his riding whip and let me hear it whistle. I suspect Pom's like that with his life. He's got to pit himself against it with speed and violence till he can feel it shake, buckle and hurt. I now believe a part of the reason, maybe the whole reason, why he wanted to go to Saigon was to come eyeball to eyeball with death that really killed. In India and Japan he'd meditated and fussed about death rituals, but there was no immediate danger, no hot blood burping, no stench of decomposing corpse . . .

'We went, Pom in a safari jacket with its patch pockets filled with camera, transistor radio, traveller's cheques and sunglasses, and me with half a dozen insect-repellent aerosols. We arrived, and, wow! Pom said he had the sensation that the top half of his skull was sliced off, his old brain spewing out like whipped cream. He went to pieces. He couldn't walk straight, heard things, had fits of raving, vomiting, fainting, horrible, real horrible.

'I'm glad I can talk about it calmly to you like this, but it was tough then. You saw how grey his hair's turned. That happened then. But, thank God, after about two months there, he sort of came to, had this idea to create a preparatory school for accepting life and death in a world as god-damn-rotten as it is. Once begun, he worked like the Indian deity you see with a dozen arms and legs. You'd have had to see him to believe what I am saying. Incredible. Berserk high on a sense of mission, he worked flat out for every drop-out, misfit, and freaked-out nutcase who came into his sight. We had some real criminals as well, you know, like one soldier who had cut open the belly of a pregnant Vietnamese out of perverse curiosity

170

or the other one who had buried the captured Vietcong suspects up to their necks in dirt and sliced their heads off.

'How come I didn't go to pieces myself with all this going on round me? It's Pom. He was just everywhere and everything. So much compassion and energy and mad inspiration pouring out of him; he literally made everyone who came near him suspend disbelief. About eight to ten of us were there and we worked like lunatics, it was just Pom right or wrong. You could say we lived in a sort of tamed hell between the real killer war and our own fantasy war. It was great. Unbelievable, too, now that it's over, those thirteen months.'

Ju twirled a wisp of her hair and her pale eyes were, I could tell, focused way beyond the low grey-flannel sky of Hampshire.

'Why did you then suddenly abandon the sanctuary?'

'We were given twenty-four-hour notice to clear out of Vietnam. Just like that.'

After gravely picking out a sunflower seed left stuck on her muesli bowl and munching it, she sighed. 'I guess you are right, he can't sit here for long. But, after Saigon, what's on offer for him? Don no's the answer . . .'

Pom returned on Thursday evening, bringing with him a young man called Richard, a square tank of compressed muscle. With a cauliflower-shaped big head hammered into his torso with very little neck, he looked much shorter and squatter than Pom who was actually about the same height. During supper of Jerusalem artichoke soup and apple crumble, he hardly spoke and, when spoken to, just ducked his head with a grunting noise. He surveyed the world round him from under his low-hanging forehead, much of the whites of his eyes showing like fried egg without the yolk. Watching his table manners and a tattoo on his forearm, I was wondering what this uncouth crab-shaped man had in common with Pom, when Pom said proudly:

'Richard is a judo black-belt two-dan and probably one of the top five in karate in England today. Darling, he can have the chimney room, can't he, on the third floor?

171

He must sleep with his head pointing north and feet south.'

On this, Richard bobbed his head a few times to express his assent. Ju, exquisitely pastel and fuzzy against the swarthy crab-man, licked the rest of her nightly potion of wheatgerm and honey and said. 'Why not?'

Saturday, it was a windless opaque day with the damp cold climbing up our legs. I was busily scraping some obstinate dirt from the pedestal of a bust of one of Pom's ancestors in the entrance hall, when a white Mercedes arrived. A lean, middle-aged Indian in a smartly cut black fur jacket and an Aquascutum scarf wound round his short neck sauntered into the hall, accompanied by an English woman, natural blonde and blue-eyed, also in fur and with a matching Aquascutum scarf.

'Mr and Mrs Chandrakant Mashi,' said the Indian, glinting a row of gold capped teeth behind the rubbery orator's lips. 'Announce us to Lord Pommeroy. He knows me well.'

Indians to me are not Orientals; they strike me more as overbaked French. Noting that he did not add 'please', I ran to the greenhouses where Pom and Richard were applying winter tar wash. At the mention of the name, Mashi, Pom dropped everything with an unseemly haste and darted back to the house. Having run all the way to the greenhouses, I was too out of breath to keep up with him. I was not a little vexed to learn from Claude who was stirring vegetable curry in the kitchen that Mashi was a great guru, pioneer of a chain of communes throughout the United States and had probably come to advise Pom on how to set up and run his type of commune here at Falaise Hall.

Master Mashi stayed exactly three hours as his next appointment at the Clarendon Nature Cure Commune was at four. By nibbling a small but frequent mouthful of food with his rabbity front teeth, he managed to talk uninterruptedly throughout lunch. He stressed the importance of having on the premises a shop to sell naturally grown vegetables and fruit, jams and cakes and cosmetics fabricated by the communards in an old-fashioned manner, which, clumsily packaged and over-priced, would not fail to secure enthusiastic custom.

'In your case, you have an ideal spot beyond the lake where I believe seaside holiday traffic passes. One of our communes in Tennessee is doing a roaring trade selling their own brand of mashed avocado shampoo and oil of camelia hair pomade.' In order to illustrate, he touched his head with the palm of his hand. His wire-hard black hair was deep-fried in the sticky grease. Mrs Mashi, an extremely good-looking woman in her late thirties, seemed to stop breathing with a look of terror on her face every time her husband but looked at her. He treated her with open contempt. Whenever someone addressed her, he replied and if she drew a breath as if ready to say some-thing, he raised a bird-like noise of either disapproval or giggle, we were not sure which, and she immediately shut her mouth.

The guru with business acumen was nothing if not punctual: he and his persecuted wife left at three on the dot. As the white Mercedes disappeared round the corner of the drive, Ju said, 'My shrink would have said that Mashi is insecure and paranoiac about his wife. That's why he's constantly tyrannising her. He can't get over the fact that she is his. He loves her.'

''ee loves 'er?' Claude screamed incredulously, almost upset. ''ee 'ates 'er! 'ee 'ates 'er!'

For once Richard suddenly spoke up and everyone looked at him. 'He needs a kick in the ass, that guru so-and-so.'

Ju and I yelped like trodden puppies before bursting into a fit of convulsive laughter. Pom just grinned. I realised that at twenty-five and after Saigon he was seldom heard belly-laughing as he used to be.

As we washed up Ju and I could see Pom through the misted kitchen window, walking toward the stables, his right arm thrown carelessly on Richard's shoulder, his head hung low, but still with that floating gait of his.

'Poor Pom, it's so smug and staid here,' sighed Ju.

A week passed as if it were one sneeze. The house had become appreciably cleaner thanks to my hard work, everyone congratulated me. On my last night, we were sitting by the fire. Ju, no longer able to sit comfortably on Pom's lap, sat leaning against the armchair in which I sat with my legs tucked under me. Pom stretched himself on the floor with his head on Ju's lap. They looked good together, he so dark and steely, she so fair and fay. With slow strokes of fingers she combed his hair and traced the curve of his eyebrows, then his nose and the rims of his lips. His jaw shone bluish and rough by the evening. Her lips parted, Ju let her fingers travel upwards against the grain of his bristle. With a shudder of pleasurable disgust she chortled.

'Ough, a hairy ape!'

I raised a tepid soft laugh like a good family friend, but I could not help feeling goose-fleshed all over. As a child I had dreaded and at the same time adored the punishment Father alone in the family could inflict on me: to have my face rubbed against his unshaven cheek on Sundays when he did not shave till late in the morning. I used to run amuck screaming as I fled from him pursuing me with a playful but nonetheless terrifying grimaces. My hysterical shrieks, Big Brother said, used to shake the sliding screens like a minor earthquake.

My thoughts leapt and landed with a deadly precision on Tristram whose sleek alabaster cheeks did not need a second shave in the evening, who could not in all likelihood impregnate, and who was my successful, stylish husband.

Hold it, hold it! An alarmed voice rang inside me. Don't you compare your husband with your best friend's husband! How dare you, how could you?

The guilt I felt was an adultress's and mordant. Brusquely I had to cross my legs, then uncross them. The moment passed unnoticed but later when I kissed Ju good night I went up to her like a cowed dog and could only mutter good night in the direction of Pom before throwing myself out of the door.

Tristram came home just before lunch the day after my return from Hampshire, relaxed and cheerful. How much taller, more elegant my husband was. I blushed to myself as his smooth cheek rubbed mine as he kissed me.

'I think I've eaten and drunk probably some of the best food and wine available in Europe during the last week. The privately owned Redons were out of this world. And Hawkins for the first time justified his inflated fees by finding a first-rate adviser in Paris. Altogether most satisfying. How were they, your home-county gurus?'

I told him that Ju was expecting a baby.

'The little Honourable Pommeroy, and if it's a boy, Edward Hersingdon having never married, the brat'll be heir to the Earldom and the Patata fortune,' he quipped in his usual vein of 'Grrreat people of this world!' and later in the afternoon wanted me in his bedroom. I was horrified and protested under my breath.

'But, Mrs Apps is still here!'

'Don't be a ninny. We're a legally married couple.'

To this day can I recall the faint but pervasive chemical odour of aeroplane fuel in Tristram's hair and the struggle within me to obliterate the image of my best friend's husband. How I had to grind my teeth and eyelids till my head throbbed not to see him, and ultimately how useless it all was. I saw Pom, I felt Pom and since there was a plenty of room in me left cold by Tristram, Pom seeped in like warm milk into bread; my head reeled with the deafening echo of his forbidden name, till Tristram's voice whispered smugly in my ear:

'Darling, good girl, you liked it, didn't you?'

Only then did I open my eyes, which slowly filled up with stinging tears. Tristram, mistaken, caressed me with solicitude.

'Stay still. Very still, darling, in case . . .'

I wailed in unrestrained shudders. I had been married for over three years.

13

My sister Fumiko sent me a Christmas card printed by her husband's company, Mitsui Trading Corporation, announcing his appointment as chief of the Mitsui Düsseldorf office from January 1st 1968. On the front was a glossy reproduction of a snow-covered medieval German town and on the back Fumi had scribbled: 'As soon as I get to Dusseru – Papa has been there since October – I'll ring you. Have lost three kilos in the chaos and the farewell formalities of the move.'

'Dusseru' and 'Papa' made me smile with an excruciating delight as if someone had put in my mouth one of those uneatable, uniquely Japanese sweets. All Japanese businessmen and their families sent abroad had a way of blithely truncating the tongue-twisting names of European cities: Amsu for Amsterdam and Copen for Copenhagen, and as for calling her own husband 'Papa', it was so typical of her class and its affectation, considered to be urbane, *modan* and chic, it made me giggle, followed by a flood of tears. This homesickness had been made more intense by the exaggerated merriness of the festive season. While Tristram's black-tie dinners provoked a dull pain of boredom and sense of my own inadequacy, the smallest detail in a letter from home of a family meal – Father mistaking the first kiwi in his life for a burnt potato croquette or Kenji's family arriving for a visit with huge boxes of precious mushrooms and hairy crabs but themselves preferring Mother's Chinese dumplings – released in me a jet of joy from head to toe.

I longed for home, its reassurance, consolation and laughter but knowing Tristram's horror of losing, even temporarily, his belongings, I dared not mention my desire to go home. He was cordial but on the whole indifferent to my family. When I could not contain myself and read out some funny parts of a letter from Mother or conveyed my parents' greetings to him, he invariably said, 'How nice. Do give them my kindest regards, will you, when you next write to them.' That was all.

After the last piano lesson of the year, Mr Goldberger told Tristram that the progress I had been making was remarkable for someone who was a late starter, and Tristram was pleased. Ever since my undernourished childhood after the war, I have had a fiendish dislike of waste; squandering time, food, money, paper, friendship, anything. I worked from one Thursday afternoon to the next, whipped by the horror of wasting time and Mr Goldberger's tuition. Glad as I was to have pleased both my teacher and husband, I knew that behind my conspicuous progress in piano playing was not so much my love of music as unhappiness. Here I use the word, unhappiness, as an inexperienced dermatologist would diagnose an itchy spot as 'an allergy', a sweeping oversimplification, disregarding the immense store of complex subterranean causes, and I did so with a pang of guilty conscience as well, for I could never completely convince myself that a young and ordinary Japanese woman, married to a wealthy, handsome, brilliant English gentleman, living the way I did with starched napkins and solid silver cutlery, should be allowed to blame anyone but herself for her unhappiness, if indeed she was unhappy. Being diffident and apologetic about my unhappiness, whenever I got into a certain familiar mood, I invariably made a dash to the piano and there as I played a Mozart or a Schubert piece, I managed not only to banish such a self-important and indulgent vapour-like thing as unhappiness but also to hoard up enough joy and humility to see me through the coming days.

In mid January Fumiko telephoned.

'After Singapore it's perishingly cold here in Dusseru,' she whined. Being the wife of the Mitsui Düsseldorf manager, she had her own Honda and a chauffeur driven

Mercedes 4000 at her disposal whilst her husband was in his office or at lunch. She had 'a very *modan* de luxe *apato* with two bathrooms and a maid from nine to six.' She lowered her voice conspiratorially and added: 'Mother wants me to come and see you in London. I'll try as soon as we are settled in. But, tell me, how are you?'

Her commiserative searching tone made me bristle. Typical of her generation, Fumiko was convinced that mixed marriages of all kinds, from a prostitute to a GI to an Imperial bastard to a Manchurian princess, were bound to be disastrous.

I declared loud and cheerful, 'Fine, excellent. Couldn't be happier!'

Thereafter, Fumiko telephoned me regularly with her usual worry-aloud whining manner, which had a curative effect on me, like a long lukewarm bath. She was never in a hurry to terminate her calls, as obviously not only her *apato*, her Mercedes, her golf club membership, but also her telephone bill were paid by her husband's almighty firm. Tristram, coming home in the middle of those long international calls, questioned me each time to make sure that it was my sister not I who had made the call.

One afternoon in February, Fumiko rang to say she could arrange for the childless wife of one of her husband's subordinates to look after her eldest son, aged eleven, and come to London the following weekend with her seven-year-old daughter, Tomoko.

'My sister Fumiko, remember her? Well, she's arriving on Friday with my niece.'

'Where are they staying?' asked Tristram.

'Oh?' I looked like a dog when it hears a bee nearby, blank but tense. My vanity and pride prohibited me from asking, but, we have guest rooms, can't they stay here?

'I don't know how old your niece is,' he resumed in a conciliatory tone, 'but this house is really not suited for children. So many fragile antiques. Children love fiddling with chess sets and tend to get up frightfully early in the morning.' He then added with charming affability, 'But, do ask them both to lunch on Sunday.'

178

She rang me that evening, Tuesday, to say that she had arranged it all and that she would arrive on Friday afternoon and return by the first flight to Düsseldorf on Monday.

'Now, I'd like to talk to you about your hotel,' I began in a breathless hurry to beat her on the subject. 'What I think is . . . Tomo-chan being so young . . .' I felt the silence on the other end of the line as absorbent as a vacuum cleaner nozzle.

'Tomoko would love to be near Hyde Park,' Fumiko said after clearing her throat. 'Can you book us a twin-bed room with a bath somewhere near both the Park and your house?'

'About how much would you like to spend?' I asked, so embarrassed was I that I felt a film of perspiration form at once above my lips.

'With the pound cheaper, Asa-chan, let us not worry about the price too much. I think Mrs Harder's sister should stay at one of London's best, don't you agree?' There was something slightly sickly sweet in her warble but I was in no position to take offence.

'Up to thirty or forty pounds, all right?'

'Don't worry how many pounds, Asa-chan, you don't know Papa. He's generous to a fault.'

I got the message and kept silent.

My sister and her moon-faced daughter, Tomoko, stood out amongst the arriving crowd of passengers at Heathrow airport. Whilst I was writing to Mother for kimonos and dresses made by Mrs Ikushima, in Tokyo and Singapore, Fumiko must have been busy buying Dior and Celine clothes, Gucci shoes and a Royal Danish astrakhan jacket. She looked so expensively and elegantly turned out, complete with Louis Vuitton suitcases, that I even held back the familiar cry of her name till she recognised me. Her small feet in exquisite burgundy-red leather boots made a dash toward me. When I saw them trot and totter in our incorrigibly Japanese way, toes turned in and the weight of the body on the outside of the feet, I yelled, tears descending like a curtain, 'Sister Fumi!'

She leant over the railing that separated the arriving

passengers from the awaiting crowd and screwing up her very expertly made-up eyes and brows in an effort not to wet her eye lines; not knowing whether to bow or to shake hands, she nodded and nodded with a choked high-pitched croon, her gloved right hand patting my shoulder to make sure I was real.

'Auntie Asako, how do you do?' said the youngest, most level-headed of the three, her black lustrous hair cut straight and square like a Paris mannequin, dressed in a Scottish tartan ensemble of coat and skirt and shawl together with a matching little beret with a green pompom.

Mother and daughter, looking straight out of a fashion illustration, were extremely conscious, almost apologetic about being foreigners. My little niece kept whispering to her mother, 'Mama, don't hold Auntie's hand. People'd think you're children' or 'Mama, Papa said if you tip too much, English porters will think we are Japanese' and so on. She smiled queenlily and said 'Thank you' in English to a porter who complimented her on her Scottish outfit. At first I felt like pulling the ridiculous pompom cap down to her chin and dropping her into one of the litter bins, but after a while I found her so cheeky and entertaining that I gave up resisting and smiled at her precocious sallies as indulgently as her mother did.

When the porter turned back to ask, bus or taxi, I raised myself taller, about to say 'Taxi!' wanting at least to pay for the taxi.

'Oh, I forgot in the excitement!' Fumiko shot a bird-like cry. 'Our London office is sending a car for us.'

'Papa arranged it. When our London or Paris manager comes to Dusseru Papa sends a car for him,' said my niece.

Dogs don't eat dogs, I thought but was impressed to find 'Our London Office's chauffeur' waiting patiently with a cardboard sign with Okada written on it; but of course there was a price to be paid for the comfort and convenience that she enjoyed at her husband's company's expense: in public – a foreign public – my sister seemed to stiffen under the weight of representing Mitsui and Japan. In the presence of the Mitsui chauffeur and the

Hyde Park Hotel clerk who took us to her room she spoke to me in a curious mixture of our Kansai dialect and the affected TV-drama Tokyoese. But as soon as three of us were alone, she zipped off her boots, pottered about the hotel room in slippers like an over-energetic hamster in a cage, emitting high-pitched squeaks and croons at everything she saw and touched, and reverted completely to our Kansai dialect.

'I'll write and tell Father and Mother you're in good health and looking pretty and happy. *Aren't* you?'

'What?'

'Happy?'

'Oh, very!'

'Good. This dress you're wearing, isn't this by Mrs Ikushima? I thought I recognised the fabric. I helped Mother in choosing it.'

As I mentally dry-ran my retort: 'Can't I be happy in a made-in-Japan dress?' my niece piped up.

'Grandma can't understand why you don't buy Diors and Chanels. They are much cheaper here than in Japan and you live here, Auntie.'

'Grandmother never said anything of the sort!' Fumiko glared at her daughter, then as if it were on a natural extension of thought, asked. 'How is Harda-san?'

The child looked at me closely.

'Tristram? Oh, he is fine, working hard, and looking forward to seeing you both at lunch tomorrow, no, sorry, the day after tomorrow, Sunday. Unfortunately, tomorrow we have an official engagement in the evening, but I can be with you all day.'

Fumiko looked at me with her head a psychological angle tilted to the side. 'He does take you out to dinners and receptions, doesn't he?'

I heard in her voice the bewildered incomprehension of many a Japanese businessman's wife who spends most evenings at home alone. Since the announcement of Tristram's appointment as the next head of W Gallery, our social life had become more charged than ever; drawing much more thrill and enjoyment than he would like to admit from the kudos and the accompanying brouhaha of his new position, he now accepted many more invitations, even to a stand-up buffet party at the Royal Academy as on this particular Saturday evening. Luckily, the Mitsui London office manager would be away on a North African business trip and his wife was to take my sister and niece to see *La Fille Mal Gardée* at Covent Garden.

Tristram, who declared himself allergic to soya sauce since his William Blake visit to Tokyo, had suggested his favourite Sunday dish, kedgeree. 'Don't give them Japanese food. They can have that in Dusseldorf. Kedgeree has fish and rice: the Japanese ought to like it.'

Fumiko and Tomoko had been asked to come early as Tristram had arranged a chess party at two thirty. They arrived at noon on the dot. Tristram was still in the bathroom. Tomoko in her Scottish outfit carried a large bouquet of roses and my sister, an oblong gift-wrapped box from Solingen, Koenings Allees, Düsseldorf. Overcome by the amount of decorative items they spied in the house, the mother and the daughter stood immobile at the entrance hall and did not relax till I said Tristram was not ready yet. Tomoko at once set out inspecting chess sets.

'Like a museum, Mama!'

'Who dusts and cleans all this?' whispered Fumiko.

'Mrs Apps, the char.'

'He's not poor, your husband, you know?' She sighed, looking round. 'He's what we call a "have-lots", isn't he? Imagine, and I thought London had been badly bombed during the war. I guess it was not as bad as it was in Japan.'

'I guess not,' I listened but heard no water being emptied out of Tristram's bathroom upstairs, so I showed them his study, dining room and finally the kitchen, where we stayed whilst I prepared the salad. At one o'clock I went upstairs, knocked once and went inside. He was in a blue bath robe, lying on top of his bed, reading a Sunday colour supplement.

'They've been here for an hour. We are all waiting for you,' I said, a strange hot lump rising to my throat and I judged my pulse to be beating faster.

'Oh, darling, I didn't know. Why didn't you warn me?' I picked up his breakfast tray and walked out.

'He's washed his hair. He'll be down in a minute,' I lied to Fumiko and Tomoko, who had seated themselves at the kitchen table. When at last we heard him come down the stairs, they jumped to their feet and stood at attention.

'Where are you?' Tristram was heard.

'We're all here, in the kitchen,' I blared. Tristram came in, sporting a wine-coloured cravat, looking very Sunday and with a whiff of aftershave lotion. My sister dived to bow, Tomoko stared. In passable English after four years in Singapore Fumiko thanked Tristram for looking after me and for the luncheon invitation. Tristram with a good colour and a plummy animation in his voice, like Duke of Edinburgh amongst friendly Commonwealth pigmies, raised my sister, shook hands with and patted Tomoko and altogether made them feel welcome in the kitchen. We moved to the dining room where my sister presented Tristram with the huge Solingen box.

'I gather in Japan you don't open a present in front of the person who gives it. Very civilised. I shall open it later. Thank you,' said Tristram, putting the box on an empty chair. With the chess party to follow, he was anxious to get on with the lunch.

As I had suspected kedgeree was too rich a concoction for my Japanese visitors. They nibbled it as if it were rice pudding with cod-liver oil. Tristram ate heartily, was affable and charming and asked after my parents and brothers.

'Father is fine and very busy. Mother is suffering from stomach ulcer, not serious, but she's lost weight and wants very much to see Asako.'

'She's lost weight therefore wants to see Asako?' Tristram smiled wickedly and lifted the wine glass to my sister who, like me, drank only water. I saw my sister and niece melting in the glow of his charm.

'You see,' I said to him, 'for my parents' generation who knew starvation, to lose weight is a frightening sign of declining health. She's not getting younger, I haven't

183

been to Japan now for nearly four years, I'd love to go home and see my parents.'

'But, Asako, your home is here.'

. Fumiko understood and blushed like a child caught in a mischief. Turning to me, she said in Japanese with a touching honesty. 'You know, it's so true what Harda-san says. Papa scolds me often, Won't you ever grow up? When you married me, you left your family for good! But, I can't stop being a Katagiri daughter, although I know it's wrong.'

'In English, please,' Tristram said, winking at Tomoko, who could not take her eyes off him.

'So sorry,' Fumiko inclined her head. 'I said I understand well what you say, Harda-san.'

'Good, I'm glad you agree with me. What's next? Cheese? Fruit? Pudding?'

I took away the visitors' plates full of cold kedgeree and brought the cheese board and biscuits, which no one except Tristram ate. Spoken to, Fumiko did her best to respond, but she had no conversation of her own. As soon as we finished Mrs Apps's gooseberry fool which the sweet-toothed Japanese guests greatly appreciated, Tristram stood up, jolly and snappy, 'Coffee in the sitting room, Mrs Okada?'

'O, *sank* you!' My sister made a small bow toward the dining table. We all stood up.

I was alone in the kitchen, staring at the Italian coffee machine as if my watching would quicken its percolating action, when Tristram opened the kitchen door.

'Peter and Thadé are here. They say they'd love some coffee too.'

When I came out with a tray of coffee for five, Tristram, Peter and Thadé were seated on the sofa and the armchair in one part of the room, Fumiko and Tomoko silently on a bench in front of the closed piano. Peter and Thadé kissed me on the cheek and complimented me on my lovely sister and niece.

'D-d-darling,' Tristram stammered, rubbing the area between his chin and his lower lip with his right index finger. I knew this gesture and the stammering. 'Asako, why don't you show your sister and the little one your four-poster bed?'

'Yes, I will.' I poured the men coffee, poured for ourselves and said, 'Let's go upstairs,' in slow articulated English. My sister and Tomoko jumped off the piano bench with the alacrity of dogs going out for a walk. We went upstairs, carefully balancing our coffee cups.

'He is not very proud of us,' Sister Fumi said in English and drank her coffee in slow measured sips, as Tomoko began inspecting my four-poster bed.

'I want to go home,' I said in English.

Fumiko nodded and when she lifted her eyes they were blown large like fish-eyes with crystal balls of tears. She pointed inquiringly at my closet door. I shook my head and pointed at the bathroom door, toward which she hurried. While my sister was in the bathroom Tomoko, having removed her shoes, sat on the edge of my bed.

'When we came to Dusseru, Grandma said to me, I don't want to live too long if I have to see you marry a foreigner too.'

'Did she? What did you say to that?' I tried to sound as unaffected as I could manage.

'I said, Don't worry, I'll marry Koshino-san and live near Grandma in Japan.'

'Who is Koshino-san?'

'My brother's best friend.'

At four o'clock Tristram rang through on the internal phone asking for tea and cinnamon toast, which my visitors helped me prepare but refused to go out and serve. The three of us had tea in the kitchen. Then, Fumiko said, looking out at the already dark street, 'We must go.'

'Why, you don't have to go yet. Stay a little longer.'

'Harda-san asked us for lunch, we mustn't overstay our welcome.' She was once again very much a lady on Mitsui stilts. They left through the back door so as not to disturb the chess players. The chess party did not break up till after eight, everyone having had drinks.

'Tell me,' Tristram said as we were having poached eggs on toast in the kitchen. 'Why does your sister have to have so many gold capped teeth? At her age it's terrible. Considered in rather bad taste here, you know?'

'Not in Japan. We think it's nice to have gold invested in your own mouth. After the cremation your family pick up the gold with long chopsticks from the warm ashes.'

'No inheritance tax on the gold teeth in the ashes either, I presume,' said he wistfully.

An inexplicable bout of rage and depression wracked me throughout the night and I felt quite exhausted when I woke from a fitful sleep at six thirty the following morning. I took a bus to the Hyde Park Hotel, had breakfast with Fumiko and Tomoko before the Mitsui chauffeur arrived. Before going through passport control my sister handed me an envelope in which she said was a tip for the chauffeur.

Within less than a week I received a telegram from Father, insisting on my returning to Japan, giving Mother's poor health as a reason. 'Telephone collect as soon as possible.'

When I rang, Mother accepted the charge in a bouncing cheerful voice. 'Don't worry, I am as fit as a salmon leaping upstream. It's just that we want you to have a holiday at home.' Father then came on the line and said he had arranged to send me an open return air ticket London-Tokyo-London. 'It's valid for one year, but don't make us wait too long. As soon as you choose the date and the flight, telephone Fumiko in Dusseru and she'll let us know.'

'What did Sister Fumi tell you about me and . . . ?'

'Too long to go into it on the phone,' said Father.

Not a word was mentioned about Tristram and that was message enough. I waited till seven o'clock when Tristram began preparing his double dry martini. He listened and glanced at my father's telegram. After a long stare at the frosted edge of his glass and a heavy gulp of drink, he said, 'I wish you hadn't broken this till the morning, when I could have coped better. I hate hearing disagreeable news at night. Very bad for my sleep.'

It was, I admitted, inconsiderate of me. A tactical error as well. I had no one to blame but myself when, several hours later, in the deepest rut of sleep I was suddenly woken up by an intense spot of torch light on my face. Tristram always kept a powerful torch by his bedside: if there was a power cut he could, he maintained, read by his torch for some hours.

'If you must go home,' a voice behind a deranged disc of light said, 'let me get used to it first. I have an idea. We'll talk about it in the morning,' then after an imperceptible pause of hesitation, 'you do care for me a little, don't you?'

I remained silent, stunned. The spotlight flew up, wildly danced along the ceiling, and I heard the door shut.

The following afternoon he came home early and spoke for a long time with his travel agent before he came out of the study and called me.

'You said that a return ticket London-Tokyo was arriving here shortly and naturally I wouldn't like to stop you from taking advantage of it,' he began. 'If you are not entirely heartless, however, I'd like you to concede this much: I hate staying alone in the house. I'd go bonkers. I have been meaning to visit museums in New York, Washington and other East Coast cities before I take up my post at W Gallery. Could you leave for Japan the day before I leave for America, i.e., February 9th? I'll be back around the 23rd, but you, having gone all the way to Japan, might as well spend two weeks with your family to make it worthwhile. What would you say to coming back on the 25th? February is a short month.'

I made a wild cry of joy and gratitude, throwing myself on his neck.

I rang my sister in Düsseldorf from the Fulham Street post office. My worry-aloud sister raised a long diphthong of satisfaction, but instantly began whining: 'Now I feel terrible! I wish I hadn't made him out so, so, you know, egotistical in my letter to Mother as I did. The fact that he can't bear staying in the house alone shows how sensitive and loving he can be. And, let me say this, he is a very handsome gentleman. Tomoko is mad about him.'

'Don't worry, Sister Fumi, Tristram is all of those: gentleman, charming, sensitive, very egocentric,' I said

187

cheerfully but as I spoke I felt my tongue thicken from the grave importance I attached in my heart of hearts to this homecoming. A chance to examine my nearly four-year-old marriage.

Till the aeroplane arrived at Anchorage I suffered a strange sensation of haste and peril, as if I were being chased, the end of my hair being pulled back. The long stopover at Anchorage was an agony. I stood by the huge glass windows gazing impatiently at the aircraft being refuelled and checked. Had I been allowed to run out and help expedite the procedure I'd have gladly done so. Only after leaving Anchorage did I feel I was securely on my way home and nothing could stop me. After the captain made an announcement about the weather conditions in Tokyo, I found it hard to breathe at a regular rhythm; every so often I had to heave a great sigh to lighten my emotion.

I emerged from the customs into a dense sea of waiting people. I heard a piercing loud yell:

'Asako!' My brother Kenji.

I ran like a dog jumping on four paws. In keeping with our national undemonstrativeness we did not kiss or hug but simply devoured each other through tear-swollen hot eyelids, everyone touching me tentatively here and there or in Kenji's case, knocking me on the back with incoherent little grunts.

Both Father and Mother were remarkably unchanged: Mother looked very much an affluent city lady in her bouffant hair style with a black velvet coat over a silvery mauve kimono. Kenji, on the contrary, had changed unrecognizably. The last time I had seen him, he had been a gangling youth utterly devoid of social weight and purpose. Now, for someone only twenty-nine he carried with him an unmistakable air of 'having arrived': tall, solid, visibly a man who ate and drank excellently, wearing expensive-looking clothes, shoes and tie with a welcome amount of sloppy indifference. Had it not been for his simple boyish manners, people who did not know him

188

would have thought him an insufferably spoilt young man for whom life had been too soon too kind and too easy.

Mother noticed it first. 'Where is your overcoat?'

'Overcoat?' I looked down at my Liberty wool dress I had bought in an after-Christmas sale. 'Oh, dear, I forgot it! I was in such a hurry that I must have left it in the hall cupboard.'

'You must have a coat, it's a cold winter this year,' said Father sensibly, while Mother and Kenji burst out laughing, She hasn't changed!

I tried but could not join in their hilarious laughter, for I was seeing inwardly the pitch-dark interior of Tristram's house at six o'clock in the morning. As there had been no direct flight to Tokyo from London on the day Tristram had specified for me to leave, I had to fly by the first plane to Paris to catch a direct Japan Airline flight for Tokyo at noon. Tristram had been lingeringly affectionate with me ever since the date of my departure had been set. The night before my departure he carried me to his bedroom, and afterwards he took a stronger dose of Seconal and handed me a torch.

'Please, darling, try and be quiet as you go. I must sleep. I'm depressed enough as I am about your going; can't afford to be a physical wreck as well.'

Being married to him, I was a past master in noiseless manoeuvre in the dark; after sliding the suitcase and shoes and handbag and a carry-all out of the front door, I left on the hall table my house keys which Tristram had requested me not to take with me, fearing, quite rightly, that I might lose them on the journey. Not until I was seated in a radio taxi with the freezing morning air hurtling back from the driver's lowered window did I realise that I had left my overcoat behind the locked door. I had hung it on a chair by the door the night before, a solid woollen coat, not the Harvey Nichols mink, and I had missed seeing it in the limited scope of the torch light. Tristram had taken two or three Seconals and there was no question of returning to wake him for the sake of a mere overcoat.

'Ring your husband as soon as you get to the Maru-nouchi Hotel. In the meantime your only chance of not

189

catching your death of cold is to borrow one of my wife's. When I get home I'll send it to you in Mikage,' said my brother, which prompted me to ask after his adoptive parents, his wife and his children.

'Fine,' said he. 'You'll see my family at Arima hot spa next weekend. Big Brother may be able to come with his family. Depends on his work.' He then slapped me on the back. 'Cheer up, before you leave we'll put four kilos on you!'

In his chauffeur-driven Toyota Crown Deluxe he delivered us to the Marunouchi Hotel where Father, Mother and I spent the night, as the Imperial was being pulled down for reconstruction.

It was eight o'clock in the morning in London when I rang Tristram and he was already up.

'How sweet of you to ring, darling. Tell me, can you remember where my astrakhan cap might be? You know the one I mean, black, Russian style, I think I'll need it in New York.'

I told him where to look, then spoke about my forgotten overcoat. When I asked him to send it by air cargo he said he would get to the airport half an hour earlier and send it from there directly. I thanked him effusively and he replied like a governess: 'You really must be more careful.'

'I'm catching your disease, aren't I?'

I could hear him laugh despite himself. 'I miss you and I just can't wait to be together and all being normal in our own house. I hate *déplacement* and it's particularly horrid to leave home when it's sunny like today.'

Next morning we left for Osaka by the 'bullet train'. Mother offered me the window seat, bought me a dozen *mikan* oranges in a nylon mesh bag, a pot of green tea, some of the famous fish paste of Odawara, fermented soya beans of Shizuoka, mustard pickles of Isé, and so on, stopping every ambulant vendor as they wended their way down the train corridor.

'Poor girl, you haven't eaten these delicacies for goodness knows how long,' she said, blithely ignoring the fact that I had never liked any of those highly spiced foods.

190

After eating *mikan* oranges till I felt my fingers would turn yellow, I ate a boxed lunch and bits of the esoteric condiments to please Mother.

The train was speeding at over two hundred kilometres an hour; I sat back, shut my eyes and inhaled in long slow gulps the smell of a Tokyo-Osaka super-express train, so, so familiar, I could recognise almost every component odour in it: men's hair pomade, Lion toothpaste, soya sauce, Kao soap, Mentholatum, Tokuhon anti-rheumatic plaster, Jintan anti-halitosis pastilles . . . Outside the windows too, matchbox houses with black tiles, school children in uniforms running along the train, a forest of neon signs and billboards and TV antennae, fresh-cut thatch, bowing businessmen on the Nagoya station platform . . . every single image helped to take me home, like removing artichoke leaves one by one to get at the succulent *fond*.

It was therefore all the more disconcerting that, hardly had I taken off my shoes at the door of my parents' house in Mikage than the telephone rang and the nineteen-year-old maid, new to me, came out running in a state of panic.

'*Gaijin*, madam, *gaijin!*'

I put on slippers and walked reluctantly toward the telephone.

'It's a boy, Suki! Named him Nicholas. Nine pounds. Two weeks premature and I almost died.'

'Oh, Ju . . .'

With my eyes skulking from the paper sliding screens to my gentle parents then to the young maid agog at hearing English for the first time, I felt so muzzled and inadequate in reciprocating Ju's overflowing joy. 'Oh, Ju . . .' I repeated lamely.

That some 14,000 miles away, nine hours behind us, there existed a world which I had neither quite absorbed nor been accepted into, where blonde babies were being born, smoked salmon being sliced, the Royal Ballet dancing to Elgar's music, and Harrods being only a brisk ten minutes' walk away . . . seemed too, too fantastic at that moment.

Notwithstanding my tongue-tied response, with the strident and one-sided hurry of a long-distance caller Ju went on: 'Pom stayed with me throughout the delivery. Just great. I don't know how otherwise I'd have pulled through. No, I'm still at the London Clinic. Daddy put his foot down, yelling, "No village vet to deliver my first grandson!" He's gone back to the States yesterday, absolutely thrilled. Hey, when you get back, you'll see us living in the dower house down the lake. It's being entirely renovated. Daddy doesn't want us to go on living in the spooky crumbling big house, full of weirdos coming and going, carrying God knows what bugs. A big white bathroom with a big window, three bedrooms and a modern kitchen, that's all I asked. The World Elsewhere? Doing great. That guru Mashi, remember, with a pretty English wife? He's been sending Pom people, ideas, teachers, vegetable and fruit seeds and cuttings, books on this and that, all written and published by himself. Crai – zeey, but there you are!'

A nurse seemed to have walked in. Ju covered the telephone receiver. 'Darling Suki-pookie, must hang up, my lunch's arrived. I must eat; I'm breast-feeding. I love you. Pom and Nicholas send you their love. And, hey, give my love to your folks.'

The line went dead. I held on and then with a paralytic slowness put down the receiver, wondering how on earth do I give Ju's *love* to my *folks* in Japanese.

'Your husband?' asked Father.

'No, my girl friend. She's just had a baby.'

'A boy or a girl?' asked Mother instantly.

'A boy.'

'Good for her!' said Mother. 'Come, I'll show you what we've done to the house. Father's done many *modan* things.'

He had gone *modan* indeed. The house was now equipped with central heating and split-level air conditioning; the bathroom had kept the wooden square bathtub but on the tiled wall a central heating panel had been installed; the kitchen-dining room was Western style with chairs and spot lights and every possible electric gadget. While Father took a bath, Mother and I drank roasted oat tea.

It was extraordinary how little curiosity she showed about my life in Europe: once I was back in the radius of her maternal possession, she paid no attention to the three years and a half I had spent in a staggeringly different world from hers as a married woman and mistress of the house. The time that had passed meant to her just so many deaths amongst our relatives and friends, which she reported to me with gory medical details. Listening to her, I could hardly believe that London, Mortcerf and Falaise Hall had ever existed in my life; my marriage, husband, household account books, and pounds and shillings and the No. 21 buses all seemed like scenes from foreign films.

The following morning I was already having breakfast with Father, when Mother came down.

'Oh!' she stopped at the door, her hand over her heart. 'I can't get over this. Asako is back with us . . .' and began weeping. It was the first moment when I realised that Mother was four years older since I had last seen her.

'Mother, Mother,' said Father.

'How could you bear getting old in a foreign country?' She asked me in a way that made me believe she had been thinking about the question for a long time.

'Come, come, Mother, one gets old regardless of who or what might surround you,' put in Father.

'Surely, when you're old you should be amongst your own kind,' Mother insisted, staring at some tea leaves that floated standing upright, reputedly a sign of a good day ahead.

Days passed with no sign of my overcoat, but in the much coveted Inland Sea climate of ours, I seldom needed to wear my sister-in-law's cashmere coat which Kenji had so promptly sent me. The joy of my being home and the youngest daughter again was made all the more delicious and poignant by the fact that everyone knew it was a fluke bonus and short-lived. The sense of unreality made our family get-together in Arima hot spa a desperately happy occasion and all of us worked hard to make it so. Big

Brother's wife, whom he had married shortly after my departure for Europe, a marriage arranged by one of Father's influential patients, was an *interri*, an intellectual, a graduate of Tokyo Women's University. 'Very correct,' Mother said, 'sends me cards for the heat of summer, for the cold of winter, for New Year and a card with a pink heart in February, but somehow I feel that her own heart behind all these cards doesn't weigh more than the postage stamps she puts on them.'

This *interri* sister-in-law of mine telephoned to say Big Brother could not get away from his work for the weekend. And later Big Brother himself rang to speak to me. He was invited to attend a medical conference on endocrinology in Athens next summer, he said. 'London's a bit out of the way, but I'll certainly go to Dusseru to see Fumiko. Why don't you come and join us in Dusseru?'

Recalling the strong *avant* tie between him and Fumiko, I tried to accept that on his map of Europe Düsseldorf was less out of the way from Athens than London, but secretly wondered if Fumiko had not warned him that his reception in London would be far from the kind of welcome he could expect in Düsseldorf.

As for Kenji, no question of letting work or distance or wife interfere with our Arima rendezvous. He made his son, now aged four, play truant at his kindergarten and travelled over six hours by train to join us. My sister-in-law, Taneko, whom I had remembered as a frail colourless creature had put on some weight in the most attractive way imaginable: bouncy, juicy, extremely fair and fine-pored, dimples on her plump hands. She laughed with a noise like a choked dove at almost anything my brother said and whenever he called her 'Fatso' or 'Pudding Face' she pouted a half second before puffing out the merriest of laughter. So simple and uncomplicated, yet not a fool, I loved her after one meal together and called her Sister Tané.

'I knew you'd like her,' Mother gloated. 'She doesn't bear our family name, yet I feel she is more our daughter than Kentaro's *interri* who does.'

And, I saw the proof of her statement when we three

194

women and the little boy, Taro, took a bath together in a large hole carved inside a rock into which hot spa water poured in and overflowed constantly. Before getting into the water, Sister Tané nimbly squatted behind Mother and scrubbed her back. Mother, seated on a small wooden stool, with her eyes shut, had a beatific smile. Sister Tané, her cheeks flushed red and her eyes only on the soaped face cloth that skated all over Mother's back, chewed her lips in utter concentration. I watched them, soaked up to my chin in hot water and a strange chill reached down to my belly: once you leave home, you can't come back, not in the happiest harmony of things. Between Mother and Sister Tané there was the serenity of their natural relationship, the daughter-in-law doing what the daughter, I, used to do for Mother. Now, if I insisted on washing Mother's back, it would have to be a special one-off gesture, too loaded with meaning for Mother to relax and wear that serene deep smile. And if I had been 'returned goods', a divorcee or a middle-aged unmarried daughter of the family, the picture would have been a gloomy one. That in everyday reality I was already excluded from the inmost family circle dawned on me so irretrievably that had it not been for a commotion created over my nephew slipping on the tiled floor, made treacherous by a rushing overflow of hot water, I would have fainted from a stunned heart.

Morning and evening, Tané rang home for news of her one-year old daughter and afterwards rushed to my brother to recount all the small new adventures of the baby. Kenji listened with rapt attention, grunting now and again to punctuate her twitter. After such a telephone call my parents and my brother and his wife, otherwise all meticulously discreet and almost reticent about my life with Tristram, turned on me with a primitive tribal vehemence, exhorting me to have babies, three at least: one girl, two boys. 'Yours would have longer straighter legs and a high nose and big sunken eyes. If they should not do well at school, never mind, they could always become fashion models or movie stars and make a fortune, think of it!'

195

I blushed, smiled and kept silent, but at times felt an onrush of tears and began seriously wondering if it wouldn't be worthwhile getting pregnant by artificial means if only to make my tribe happy.

The effort on my part to keep up with the bubbling domestic gaiety was immense. I was outwardly as jolly and tomboyish as before but heaven knows at what cost; I was worn out and limp by the end of each day. Even with Kenji with whom I used to feel as close as if we were two bars of butter melted into one, I had to be on my guard, simply because he was so happy and whole, and I knew I was not.

Weather perfect, food fresh and digestible, blind masseurs of the spa exquisitely to the point, and Kenji as always wielding his charm over the inn servants and getting so much extra service and goodwill out of them, the two days in Arima became, as Mother declared on leaving, 'such memories as I'll take to warm my grave.'

Going home, Father drove his white Nissan saloon car with Kenji sitting next to him, and we three women and Taro on Tané's lap sat in the back. As we were driving through a little mountain village with a faded red Fox Shrine and a scatter of thatched farmhouses with drying persimmons hung from the eaves, I was suddenly seized by the desire to remain a child and scramble back into the small congenial hole of my Japanese family life: without reflecting I heard myself say: 'Suppose, Mother, suppose I stayed with you and Father and lived a happy little meek sort of life here? I mean, nothing exhausting and grand like London or being rich and famous? I could teach English or work for an airline company?'

Mother made an impetuous, leaping movement with her hands as if to say, yes, yes, do! But immediately she dropped her hands on her lap, giving a quick shake to her head. Kenji stretched his neck to have a look at me in the mirror. Tané went on placidly stroking Taro on the head, keeping a judicious distance from her in-laws' affairs. It was Father who broke the silence.

'If, Asako, if everything else failed, of course, come

back, what are we here for? But, that's the last, very last resort and you know it. You have a husband, maybe soon children. I hope so. That's where your home is.'

'But, for heavens' sake, Asako,' said Kenji, wringing his neck to a breaking point to look me in the face, 'if you are unhappy or unwell, don't drag it out, come back. I'll build you a house in the Japanese Alps. I've started a new branch in my company, "prefabu" housing.'

I yelped with laughter at 'prefabu' housing.

'What's wrong? What's the matter?'

Everyone gazed at me with fright: has she gone mad? Tears streaming down my cheeks, I shook my head. 'Nothing, nothing, it's just that . . . "prefabu" housing, "prefabu", Brother Kenji is a scream!'

'Oh, thanks, I'm a comic, am I?' Kenji grimaced and slapped his own forehead. Everyone laughed. The car was just passing a small village school with its playground empty, it being a Sunday. Just a fast passing image, but to this day I recall that empty dilapidated old school as vividly as if I had seen it a minute ago, and at once there comes over me a sensation of so much yearning and tenderness.

Mother began talking about my departure with a daily deepening urgency: 'Four more days.' 'Think, only three more days to go!' 'It's passed so quickly . . .' The morning on which she greeted me with 'Asako, the day after tomorrow!' there was a telephone call from Tokyo International Airport customs department. My overcoat had finally arrived.

'But, why to Tokyo? Doesn't your husband know where we live?' asked Father with an asperity rare for him. It was indeed a bore that Tristram had sent my coat to Tokyo and not to Osaka, as it meant a night less to be spent at home, having to fly to Tokyo the day before my departure for London. My parents saw me off at Itami airport with just as many tears and misgivings as at my departure four years earlier. At Tokyo Airport I was met by Kenji who had driven into Tokyo solely to look after me till my departure. He made a contemptuous little grimace at my navy-blue British passport when he took it

197

with him into the freight customs office, leaving me to man his car; but presently he hurried back.

'That worthless swine oughtn't be allowed to call himself a man! Asako, what's wrong with your husband? He's sent your blasted coat by collect charge. I've become so used to having my secretary or chauffeur pay for everything that I don't have enough cash on me. How much do you have?'

Luckily, I had a large sum Father had given me to pay for the hotel that night. When he finally returned with a cardboard box my brother was calm and grave.

'I'll start looking for a husband for you. A Japanese and real man. This one won't do.'

I laughed hilariously, which made him aggressive.

'Aren't you shattered? Aren't you sickened? How can you laugh? It's your husband!'

'I'm used to it,' I said, no longer laughing.

'Why bother going back to him tomorrow? Stay, You'll be much better off alone.'

'It's been a holiday and it's been wonderful but if I stayed as "returned goods" at home, I don't think Father and Mother would be happy in the long run. They wouldn't be proud of me. There's a saying in England, She's made her bed and she must lie on it.'

'A slothful, unprincipled, sluttish way of coping with bad luck.'

'Nonetheless, looks like the only way of coping.'

Kenji, incapable of retaliating further in words, made a low grumbling noise in the chest and banged me on the head, not to hurt, but to make sure I understood his affection, concern and fury. His careful fist banged and banged my head. I held my head rigid with an obstinate half smile.

The following morning at Haneda Airport, as soon as he put my suitcase on the scales, he said.

'Right, then, I say goodbye.'

After a quick wave of his hand he walked away into the crowd and I joined a long queue for passport control. Occidental passengers who had watched us would have never guessed in a thousand years how much affection and regret there were crammed into our perfunctory goodbye. It was like that, between Kenji and me.

14

It was past eight o'clock in the morning when I arrived home, and indeed home it was that I felt I had come back to. Tristram's home, of course, but to a small degree mine too for this lease of marriage or even life and I was strangely moved. Surprised that in a mere fortnight I had lost the feeling for shillings and pence, I fumbled for the right change and told the taxi driver not to bother carrying my suitcase into the house. I stood for a while outside the door, looking at the polished brass door knob, listening to the milk van that rattled along the crescent. Remembering that I did not have the frontdoor key, I went down the steep stairs and rang the basement door bell.

Mrs Apps clasped her hands in front of her wide open mouth, out of which came a voiceless yell of joy. She squeezed me in both arms and thanked me for my postcards from Japan which now adorned her kitchen wall.

'Doctor's not up yet, but it's about time, I say. Go on, surprise him. He'll be so pleased.'

I took Tristram's breakfast tray upstairs with *The Times* and the *Guardian*.

'What a lot of noise you two make, yak-yak-yakking away!' said Tristram, pouting like a sick and neglected child, then kissed me with a night-stale breath. He asked if I had received the overcoat. The ingratiating way in which he mentioned the coat made me wonder if he hadn't in fact in his absent-mindedness genuinely forgotten to pay for the transport. He had that unfocused morning innocence about him in his striped blue pyjamas in his mildewy blue room. I said, Yes, it had arrived and kept me warm, thank you so much. Tristram said how he'd missed me.

'Can't bear being alone in the house. America was fun and interesting, but not as a lasting pleasure. Slept so appallingly badly that in the end I played chess with an old friend of mine also a confirmed insomniac, on the phone, usually from two to four in the morning. Since I got back two days ago, I've slept rather better.'

His 'rather' like 'lather' made me warm inside and I smiled.

'Glad to be home?' He took my hand in his, a tea cup in another.

I nodded with a big grin. I was, truthfully. Very glad to be home where I was a woman, mistress of the house, instead of being a daughter, still a girl. After asking after my parents and my journey, he suddenly said with facetious sarcasm:

'Oh, how very sweet of you to ask! Yes, my Redon exhibition *is* coming along very nicely. I think it will be a beautiful show.'

'Oh, good! Sorry, I meant to ask earlier, but . . .'

'April 16th, Tuesday,' he said, his chest blowing out a little. 'Everyone who passes as a big noise in the art world will be there. And, have you heard that your friends have turned Falaise Hall, the seat of the Pomme Rois since William the Conqueror, into what is called "a free-for-all, fluid, multi-purpose non-institutional commune" where I gather at any given moment two to three dozen hippies are installed, chanting, meditating, fornicating, smoking hashish, inhaling cocaine, popping acid and blithely living on free Patata-chips and Popkiss drink from the Sugarheim Foundation?'

'I'm sure Ju has nothing to do with all that. She told me she was moving to the dower house.'

'The poor girl had no choice, I'd have thought. Some Seventh Day Adventists or Christian Science freaks staying there had to be deloused by the local health authority. I can just imagine how your Lady Pommeroy, née Sugarheim, with a month-old baby must have reacted to that.'

201

'How do you know all this?'

'One way or the other. Apparently, just a few days ago Ju rang up Colin asking him to stand surety for bailing out a young American who was found in possession of cocaine. I gather he was there to teach the hippies how to manufacture some hair pomade.'

'Oh, dear, I thought everything was going so well for them!'

'Oh, yes, it is. What I've told you only confirms how well the commune is operating within its fluid, free-for-all multi-purpose framework. But, enough of the Pommeroy shenanigans,' Tristram drew me closer to him. 'I'm so thrilled to have you back.' He kissed me suggestively on the earlobe, but that night, after a supper just two of us, with my parents' gift, a beautifully illustrated book of Ukiyoe, on his lap, listening to Alfred Deller sing Purcell in that centreless, yawning castrato soprano, he fell into a deep sleep.

'Mu-see-c, wha-a-ai-le, wha-a-a-ai-le . . .'

I covered him with a blanket and tiptoed upstairs and slept with a dizzying intensity till after ten the following morning, by which time Tristram had gone out. As soon as I finished unpacking I called Ju.

'The baby's divine! Can't wait to have another. A girl next time. I'm just mother all the way. I want at least a dozen kids. With a dozen we could run a commune all in the family, no outsiders and that'll be terrific.'

'How's the dower house?'

'Love it. Just what I wanted. The Aga stove is divine, keeps hot water boiling all day and bakes the best bread in the world.'

'Lots of people staying at Falaise Hall?'

'Sixteen, eighteen, something like that in the main house. Some weirdos and freaks, OK, but they cut me wood, bring me vegetables, bake me Alice Toklas biscuit, and some arty-crafty ones sell me scented candles and herb pillows at a discount,' Ju enumerated in a defensive hurry, then in a low assertive tone which prohibited any further prying questions from me, 'Who knows? It may be a fiasco, it may not work; the larger the commune gets, the more bureaucracy, admin aggro, bumph, hierarchy, and so on. Even Pom says he'll go berserk unless he can get away to London for violent karate exercise twice a week. But, he's a doer, not a quitter, he's got to do it before he can take stock. Give him a chance . . .'

Mrs Baron, the gushy American lady, telephoned me from Claridges and asked me to lunch, which I accepted without first asking Tristram. I felt sufficient strength in me to do so after my visit home.

As soon as we were seated side by side on a velvet-covered banquette at L'Ecu de France, Mrs Baron put her jewel-laden moist hand over mine and with a soulful look from behind her thick mascara asked me how my husband was. I laughed out of context before replying with an idiotic vehemence: 'Fine, fine, thank you!'

She did not mention Tristram again till we finished eating. Then, with a determined twist she turned her bottom forty-five degrees and fixed me with an even more soulful look. 'Suki, may I talk to you like my own daughter?' She seemed so very kind and was paying for my sumptuous meal, so I said, of course, please do.

'You're married to Tristram Harder, so you know *all* about him and his family.'

While I cogitated over whether it was a statement of fact or an inquiry, she shut her eyes and shook her head. 'I don't think so.' I gave up and raised an effete laugh: I was never good at coping with a bossy, high-handed woman.

'You're a doll, Suki,' she declared. 'No need to blush, you're a doll. But, Sweetheart, you're a young woman over twenty-one and young women don't go on calling a dog a bow-wow, a cat a miow-miow, see what I'm trying to say?'

I neither saw her point nor was I in the habit of calling a dog a bow-bow, but it mattered little, for she went ahead on her planned route without waiting for my reaction.

'When we first met I liked you immediately,' Mrs Baron smiled as much as her tightly stretched skin would allow. 'I knew we'd be friends. Honey, aren't we going to be friends?'

Here, I had to agree with Tristram: they are gushy, the Americans.

'I felt sorry for you too. Here's an innocent little soul who loves her husband yet knows nothing about him. So, I thought I'd better give you a full picture of your husband's background, since no one over here seems to know much about it. When you know, you'll probably begin to understand him better and sympathise with him. I've been analysed for years, oh for years! I know what I'm talking about and I'm telling you, that husband of yours is a walking warehouse of insecurity and repressed aggression; and God, what tension there is in that boy! Why? Because, sweetie, he's got so much to hide from you, from us, from the whole world, especially from himself.'

'What is he hiding, Mrs Baron?'

'That he's a dispossessed character, he belongs to no one, nowhere, nothing. He has no identity. He wants to wash himself clean of his own heritage.'

I made the blank laugh of a Japanese tourist caught in a situation out of his depth.

'Yes, he does!' Mrs Baron shook her raven-black hard-set head resolutely from left to right. 'Has he ever told you that his father, Frank, was a Jew? His great-grandfather, a Russian Jew from Kiev? I bet all he ever told you was that his mother's an Austrian baroness or something, eh?'

'I knew Mr Harder was American.'

'Sweetheart! I'm American; but, what's *that* next to the fact that I am Jewish?' Her fingers, capped with perilously long red nails, made a contemptuous gesture of flicking a breadcrumb or a dead fly off the table.

'When his great-grandfather arrived in Maine, he went in for what he had known best in Russia, fur and leather. By the time he had expanded his business into a mammoth retail chain store business, his fortune was colossal. He had no son, so left half of it to his only daughter, Dorothy, and the rest to a charity foundation in Michigan. Dorothy married a Mr Samuel Harder, a sweet man, once gave me a jewelled music box on my birthday. They adored their only son, Frank. When Frank graduated from Harvard and went to Europe he got involved with a penniless Mid-

European countess or baroness and poor Dorothy was worried sick, but what could she do, the boy was infatuated. They got married and had a child, your husband, Tris. So far, not good but not disastrous, right? Later, when Frank's wife eloped with a French painter, Dorothy was kind of hoping that this would be the end of their marriage. So you can imagine how furious she was when the adultress turned up after the war as if nothing had happened and Frank like a perfect ass took her back. Dorothy told my mother she felt like disinheriting Frank altogether. In the end she didn't go that far: Frank was after all her only child and was always very sweet with her.

'Then, guess what Frank did next? Brain-washed by his communist wife, he got himself mixed up with a bunch of red writers and film-makers. Finally, when he was put on Senator McCarthy's blacklist, Dorothy changed her will. In leaving her fabulous collection of jewels, furniture and paintings, she skipped one generation and left them all to her grandson, your Tris, and locked her liquid assets up in a discretionary trust. She was paranoid about some graspy outsiders marrying into the family and getting away with murder *and* a fortune. She decreed that only her direct descendants were to enjoy a capital payment and annual allowance and that if and when there ceased to be a direct descendant of hers then the entire trust was to be wound up and the proceeds donated to her father's foundation in Michigan. I never met Frank's wife, but, honey, I'm telling you, she messed up Tris's life as no one could.'

'How?'

'How? I tell you. First, by forcing on him, out of all context, a British nationality. Why, the boy's no more British than I or you. Secondly, by giving him that ridiculous tongue-twister name. Treees-traaam! Now, where did she pick that up? Can you imagine what that must have done to the boy's psyche? Dorothy always referred to him as Manny. Don't ask me why. So, till I met him at the ballet, I'd known him as Manny. Thirdly, she deserted

Frank and the kid, as you know, for God knows how many years. Then, lastly, the law suit.'

'What law suit?'

'Frank, egged on by his wife, contested Dorothy's will. They couldn't bear watching Dorothy's superb collection drop into Tris's hands. Think of it, Suki, they're supposed to be commies, right? What about the classless society and egalitarian principles and all that jazz they trumpet? In the end, they settled out of court.'

'The tiara..?' I began but did not know how to end the sentence.

'So, you do know something. That's right, there was this famous Russian tiara which Frank's wife claimed was a present from Dorothy on her marriage to Frank. A number of Dorothy's old friends had to testify that she had never given it to her daughter-in-law but had only allowed her to wear it at one of the balls she'd given. Manny got it, in the end, I think.'

'I don't know. I've never seen it.'

'I bet you haven't, dear. Judging from what I've seen of him, your husband is as close and careful as his grandmother. Ah, well, poor Frank, now he's gone, the claws are out, isn't that so?'

I did not reply. I poured more Vichy water and drank a glassful in one breath. It tasted as disgusting as ever. Mrs Baron did not miss a thing.

'I'm sorry, dear, I've upset you by trying to be helpful.'

'No, please, don't worry. I'm fine. It needs time to settle down.' I didn't quite know what needed time to settle where and how, but I felt a strong urge to appear more coherent than I felt; not an over-twenty-one calling a dog a bow-wow. I scrubbed my forehead with vigorous strokes, dropped my hand on the banquette, then, feeling even less coherent, with a groan collapsed against the velvet-covered wall. Our eyes met. Mrs Baron burst out laughing. A second later I did too.

'Good girl, if we could all laugh! You know, you'll be OK. Take time, you'll be just fine.'

I was fine, continued to be fine, amazingly, just fine. Had Mrs Baron spoken to me before my visit to my family, I'm not sure if I could have reacted with the same equanimity; my hold on our marriage had already been tenuous enough, and having always regretted my husband's lack of generosity, to find him also lacking in candour, might have greatly upset me. But, it was extraordinary how much surer of myself I felt after having been home to Japan. Both my severance from and belonging to my family had been brought home with such force. I myself had wilfully chosen and executed the severance; except as a last resort there was no turning the clock backwards; as to my belonging to them, it was something so whole and beyond my control that it remained unscathed by mere phenomenal changes in my life: where and with whom I happened to live, what I did or how often I saw them. It was a bondage rooted in the centre of the universe, beyond the time limit of our short lives. Once assured of this, I felt fearless and generous. The new confidence grew in me till I felt I could cope with Tristram and all his neuroses, and yes, why not, even manage a child and enjoy it with him.

For the first time I felt in me a fierce desire to make the marriage work. I was too loyal a wife not to want to give it a try and too proud an optimist to balk at the challenge.

An overcast, dull Sunday, the sky hanging low over our heads like a greasy frying pan, and the friends who were supposed to dine with us had been detained in Oxford by a car accident. With a feeling of being stranded in one's own house, we found the afternoon drag on interminably. After tea we sat in the sitting room, listening to the sash windows clatter with occasional gusts of wind, Tristram surrounded by a confusion of Sunday papers, and I, staring at a Royal Copenhagen plate on which strawberry jam had congealed hard like a ruby.

I looked up and saw his thumb jammed between his rigid teeth, his eyes closed and his jaws set stiff with efforts to contain something he might not be proud of if it did come out.

'Tristram?' I said quickly, but very gently. He froze, did not break down further, did not utter the dreaded 'I can't bear it any longer!'

I advanced on my knees toward him and removed the jumble of newspapers and put my hand on his lap. 'Tristram, I will have a baby and we'll be cosy and calm and very together.'

The words came out with a solemn conviction. He grabbed hold of my neck as it happened to be the nearest thing to his hands. The clumsiness of his caress touched me immensely. I believed that I loved him, that he needed me, that together we could build something which singly we could not, something akin to happiness that was durable and solacing.

'You'll be kind to me, won't you, darling?' he asked timidly.

That he could not bring himself to finish his question 'even if I shan't be your child's father' and that he dared not use 'love me' but felt safer with 'be kind to me' made me feel even more protective of him. I put my cheek on his knee, crying.

That night in his bed I said simply: 'I'll spare you the unappetising clinical details on the way. I'll tell you only when I am pregnant.' Tristram with an irresolute groan of gratitude and embarrassment buried his face in my hair.

A few days before Tristram's Redon opening, well past midnight, the telephone rang with a scalding clamour. Tristram's bedside telephone was disconnected at night. I dashed downstairs and picked up the phone on the kitchen wall.

'Hello?'

'Bewitched, bloated, a bit queasy,' Ju was singing a vaguely familiar tune with an aggressive joy. I could imagine her hot breath clouding the surface of her telephone.

'Ju, where on earth . . . I thought you'd gone to New York to show Nicholas..'

'I *am* in New York, dummy,' she giggled exultantly.

'What is it, then, crazy girl? You scared me calling at

208

this time of night. I thought something'd happened to my parents. Now, what is it?'

'I'm pregnant again! Yes, Sir, we've done it again! I've seen the top gynies here. Daddy didn't like the wishy-washy ones in London and insisted that I should have a thorough check-up here. I'm just deeleereeous! And everyone here is bowled over by Nicholas. It's too bad he's not a hundred per cent Jew boy, Daddy grumbles, but anyone can see Pom and I are good stock to make terrific kids. We can soon man the whole World Else-where, given time and a hard bed.' She shrieked with laughter.

Before hanging up, she showered me with Honey-bun and Lovie and other cute little expressions of affection, the facility and fecundity of which I always envied in her. After I had crawled back to my bed, I could not get back to sleep; worse, I could not help seeing Pom's bluish afternoon jaws. A good stock . . . could man the whole World Elsewhere . . . every implication of every word Ju had uttered rang with savage echoes.

A randy pair! I bit the edge of my sheet and pinched myself in the thigh but to no avail, I still saw and resaw Pom.

The reviews of Tristram's Redon exhibition came out in the press in one deluge and they were unanimously good. There were queues outside the museum every day and two magazines and a Sunday colour supplement carried elaborately illustrated and commented articles on Redon, his work and Tristram's exhibition. Tristram was asked to give his opinion on BBC 2's late night programme on art.

What I admired most in Tristram was his tenacity of purpose. No crisis in his personal life, no physical complaint, let alone the agreeable assaults of success could distract him from the rigid discipline he applied to himself. His study door shut and Rameau and Schütz being played non-stop for at least three hours daily, precisely two weeks after the opening of his Redon exhibition he delivered to his publisher the two hundred-page manuscript of *Redon, his tragic life and work*, which I found gripping throughout despite my having to consult the English-Japanese dictionary frequently.

With my husband's rising fame, people whom I used to gawk at, mostly at their cavernous nostrils from my low stature, took more notice of me, even sought me out and several music lovers amongst them invited me to concerts and suppers with famous musicians when Tristram was occupied elsewhere. I worked harder on the piano and Mr Goldberger was pleased, grunting like a little piglet when I played to his liking. Tristram and I led an enviably full and interesting life; if we had a private moment at home it was either when we were dressing in a hurry to get to somewhere or when, having returned from a late evening out, we were removing clothes in numbed silence in order to collapse into bed as quickly as possible. I was not happier, but certainly not unhappy. As for Tristram, his professional and social success almost convinced him that he was happier.

Nothing succeeds like success, it was Tristram who taught me the expression and it seemed that at this particular moment in his life he himself exemplifed the proverb: unexpectedly from Maître Rosenthal came a word that his client would not be unwilling to settle. But Paris just then was paralysed by the so-called May Revolution with students occupying Nanterres and unions threatening a general strike; and Tristram and his solicitor Mr Hawkins, waited for the volatile French to calm down a little before they undertook their visit to the Maître.

On May 30th de Gaulle delivered a speech which fell on overheated French heads like an ice-bag of common sense; there were immediate signs of the collapse of the Event of May and air travel to France became possible again. I drove Tristram and Mr Hawkins to Heathrow Airport, my first long drive after passing my driving test. With his bulging black attaché case in his left hand, the Gucci bag and *The Times* under his right arm, and the passport, the pipe and the ticket in his right hand Tristram kissed me clumsily goodbye. I asked Mr Hawkins to hold on to Tristram's umbrella and make sure he would not leave the aeroplane without his impedimenta. When I shook Mr Hawkins' hand, his sweaty hot hand reminded me that it was almost summer and I felt suddenly terribly thirsty. Hunger and thirst often attacked me with virulence. Mother had explained it was due to low blood pressure to which our family was subject. So, after parking the car I walked back to the terminal building, hopped upstairs and entered a dimly lit restaurant with round formica tables. Too early for lunch, there were not many customers and few waitresses. Making my way for a better-lit table, I passed a large head planted on a straight back. The posture caught my attention but it went instantly out of my sight as I hurried for the table I had set my mind on.

A dry rough hand gripped hold of my arm and yanked me backwards.

'Pom.' I said in a matter-of-fact affirmative, which, recalling the scene later, struck me as being odd, even funny ludicrous.

Pom said nothing; as if it were the most natural thing to do, bending his head low and lifting my left arm slightly outward, he bit the inside of my upper arm. If a desperate drug-addict accosted you, offer ten pounds at once, the approximate cost of a minimum supply of hashish, I had been warned. This advice was certainly passing through my mind as Pom's lips and teeth unhurriedly chewed the area where I had once had an allergy test. A waitress carrying two full plates of fried eggs and chips swerved smartly round us and hurried off. Hot with pins and needles of embarrassment, I stood perfectly immobile. Finally Pom lifted his reddened face.

'I am neither mad nor drugged. Far from it. I told you before, you have lovely arms. Irresistible. It's like biting into a kumquat not too long in syrup. Come, have tea with me.'

I guffawed at 'Have tea.' So incongruous after what he had just done; besides, so English and polite a suggestion coming from someone who looked like a bandit from the Caucasus or an Afgan desert. He wore an ochre-coloured garment of which I was not sure where it all began and ended. It billowed and gathered round him in an over-all shape of a bat on the wing, over which he had a saddle-like loose leather jacket, spangled with metal studs and staples. A tinsel-studded leather band was tied straight round his head, giving his wild mass of hair the shape of a Hiroshima atom bomb. A well-worn pair of gym shoes gave his fantastical get-up the contemporary air of an urban guerilla.

Pom ordered two hot teas. The unexpectedness of our encounter, his appearance, hot tea in the stifling heat, and his having bitten me inside the armpit in the middle of an airport restaurant all somehow contributed to make me feel irresponsible and dislocated. By some contortion of logic, I persuaded myself that it was not really happening, therefore quite all right for me not to ask after Ju, his wife and my best friend and for him after my husband.

'What are you doing here?' I asked.

'Up to no good,' came his reply.

I burst out laughing: I could not deny I liked men with a 'split bamboo' temperament.

'Killing time, you could say,' Pom grinned, waiting for me to stop giggling.

'Why kill time? It passes fast enough.'

'Wasteful, I agree, but the Orly this morning was a frantic mess. I got on, they couldn't. I'm waiting for my boys.'

'Because you were a first class passenger and your World Elsewhere disciples on economy class?' I winked at the BEA first class tag on his well-worn fisherman's bag out of which I had once seen Tarquin emerge.

'I was on economy class too, slut, till a smarmy VIP officer upgraded me by a twist of his biro. One first class passenger flying in from Sydney didn't turn up; economy class was overbooked. That's all, you malicious little bitch!'

'Colin sent us the cuttings about your visit to Paris: you and your disciples joining the students inside the liberated Sorbonne and squatting round the ten-foot-high barricades on the boulevard St Michel. Ah, yes, and the photo of you being booed out of the Renault factory at Birancourt too.' I chose not to mention that another article sent by Colin had openly suggested that Pom was trying to create a private army of soldier-monks.

'God hasn't put me on earth to justify what gossip hacks write about me,' he made small bullets by rolling the torn wet bits of his paper napkin and flicked them at me.

'Bored?' I asked.

'Sort of, yes, you could say that,' he said without mirth. 'No one dies for an ideal or a worthwhile cause any more. Only traffic accidents and botched-up crimes and the like leave meaningless corpses on the pavement. There'll be no revolution in Europe, only degeneration from all-devouring materialism. Yes, you could say I'm bored and dispirited.' He stared vacantly at the row of spotlights buried inside the smooth ceiling.

'You have, Pom, what we call *sanpaku* eyes, three whites: the white of the eye showing on right, left and below of the iris.'

'And what is that supposed to mean?'

'It's supposed to mean that the nerve cells of the brain are expanded, causing abnormal thinking, which leads to a fatal destiny. Criminals on wanted posters, for example, and those who were assassinated: Caesar, Lincoln, Ghandi, Kennedy . . . And Hitler, of course. Mad, obsessed, in a rage, unbalanced; and occasionally a sign of genius.'

'That's a consolation,' he said flatly. I missed his old volcanic laugh. I felt myself inadequate.

'Have you known, Suki, or can you describe to me what perfect bliss is?' Pom asked out of the blue.

'Bliss? No, not offhand . . .'

'I can. I tell you.' What he was about to tell must have meant much to him, for his voice went hoarse, throttled. 'I'm running. Alone. It's hot and dry. About six in the evening, summer. Sweat stinging my eyes; lungs wheezing, painful; my feet are light and OK; only my gym shoes feel like boiled chewing gum; my shirt and cotton trousers smell of sharp washing powder, lemony. There's no thought in me. I'm just running, running, very gently pushing down the grass. A good steady rhythm. Suddenly, a whip of wind, phew! The blast of fresh air

213

comes under the cotton, perspiration cooling like peppermint ice on my skin. Jee-zuss!' Pom shut his eyes. A long silence before he spoke again. 'At long last, at twenty-five I'm beginning to understand. The way of life is to die. At any moment if there's a choice, choose an earlier death. First come, first served. Nothing complicated. Simple, straight, calm!'

'Say you, aged twenty-five; but I bet you'll die between sheets like the *Hagakure* author himself.'

'God forbid! No, mine will have to be appalling bad taste, instant, grotesquely physical – bones splintering, blood spurting and not a vestige of an everyday routine.'

'Fussy.'

'Of course, I am fussy! The drawback is that we live in the age of non-heroism, non-credo and in the world run by the strutting weak, the unproud, the sneaky, the underhanded and the unshamable. Today, even if I died for a spiritual revolution or from too much compassion and love for humanity, the media would make it look as stupid and banal as if I slipped on a banana skin and cracked my skull. Think of it, Suki, wouldn't that be a waste? Wouldn't that be a shame?'

He banteringly hit me on the knuckle of my hand and looked at me, half smile, half grimace. 'Well, we've talked enough about myself,' said Pom after a while. 'And you, Suki, what about you? Are you all right?'

I nodded, thinking, am I all right? Me? All right! Why not all left? A stupid question, he's an ass, no *interri* like Tristram, this one; just a *sanpaku*-eyed, split-bamboo simpleton, like Kenji. A hairy ape, a father of a son, no, shortly of two sons . . . I picked up my tea cup, lifted it to my mouth, to find it was empty. I put it down, infuriated. All that talk on death had left me as exposed as a chrysalis unsheathed!

'Suki, goodness, what's the matter?' I could not speak, jaws had gone cement-hard. I licked my lips and they tasted salty. I gave up. I knew I was going to be grotesquely truthful.

'I need ahn . . . I want ahn . . . baby.' Picking up the paper napkin, I blew my nose and wiped my tears.

'Asako, you poor child.' Pom took my hand and pressed it between the thick balls of his palms. 'Ju told me. I know. I'll give you one.'

I did not take in at once what he meant, nor was I sure if I had heard him correctly; only from the way he looked at me I knew whatever he had said he would do for me, he meant it and out of the pure goodness of his soul. My embarrassment then was such that it burnt me in the face, neck and between my breasts; but, oh! how relieved I was too to have finally said what I had for so long yearned to say, *and* to the very person to whom I had yearned to say it.

'I will, if that'll make you happy. You know I will. A baby.' He spoke in a measured, grave tone like a kind doctor preparing his patient for the worst, his eyes almost turning *sanpaku* again. Then, he smiled that most cheering, cocky smile of his, as if to slap me on the back, 'Come on, old girl, have everything you want, life's so short!'

I could not help myself: like a thick soup on a slow fire my whole body shook with a soft bubbling giggle. So inappropriate and ungrateful a reaction in the circumstance; I tried to blow my nose again but the paper napkin flew away as I exploded into a loud guffaw. 'It's craii-zeey, absolutely craii-zeey!'

'Behave yourself, Mrs Harder.'

Pom stretched halfway over the table, drew me closer with his hand on my nape, kissed me on the mouth. I shut my eyes and opened my lips. Fire spread and singed me to unknown depths. If Pom had said, come with me, I'd have followed him to an airport hotel, to one of Notting Hill Gate crash pads, behind a park bench, anywhere.

A young voice, hardly a man's, was heard at a startling proximity.

'Lord Pom!'

Pom spun round and without an intimation of embarrassment or surprise, beaming broadly, yelled back, 'Oh, hoy!'

His lips hardly cooled from our kiss, he burst into a laughter of pure masculine hilarity. The four young men in worn jeans, T-shirts and gym shoes with rucksacks slung on their right shoulders, stood to attention, their eyes on Pom with the same intensity as police dogs' on their handlers. No one paid the slightest attention to me. Pom asked them a series of short rapid questions as to how they had managed to fly out of Paris. He was forcible and peremptory with them, but from the way his eyes lingeringly surveyed them I spied a fierce and committed affection, the kind which I had not witnessed even between him and Ju.

'You've met Mrs Harder, Richard, haven't you?' Pom opened his wide chest toward me, reclining his head casually in my direction. 'Suki, this is Jim and this is Chris. And, Karl, Mrs Harder.'

They each bowed with a stiff punctuation, adding no sociable smile or word. It was not hard to guess where Jim and Chris had been picked up: a West End karate club or a Hampshire stable, but as for Karl, I did not know where to place him. Sandy-blond, piercingly blue-eyed with a deep cleft in his jutting arrogant chin, he was so upright that he could have been kept in a narrow box throughout his growing years. Judging from the neck as spare as a flute, he must have been even younger than Richard, probably not yet eighteen.

'Suki.' Pom took a small step toward me. Before he uttered a word I knew I had been dismissed. Vanity made me speak before he did.

'Well, Pom, I say goodbye now!'

'Lovely to have met you like this, Suki.' He took my hand; I thought he was going to shake it, but he kissed me on both cheeks.

As I turned to go, from the corner of my eye I saw Pom gesture to the boys to sit down, himself yanking a chair and dropping on to it with an impatient childlike alacrity. I felt a steel door being slapped shut in my face, sealing off a world of taut fraternity into which I could not have stuck a pin.

Kenji used to imitate a *yakuza* gangster he had seen in films. 'It's a man's world. Get lost, woman!' he would say, then with a cruel frown kick away an imaginary woman, presumed to be hanging on to his foot like a wet rag.

It's a man's world, get lost, woman! Every step I walked away from Pom and his soldier-disciples became faster; by the time I reached the stairs I was running, panting. As I waited in a slow-moving queue of cars to pay the parking charge, I recalled what Kenji had so often told me: 'Nothing nobler than a friendship of men sworn to die together, Asako, believe me. That's why a samurai would not spend the night before a mortal battle in the company of women, mother or wife. Always with men, equally doomed. Nothing to do with who's more important and such like. That is the way of manhood.'

Pom's breezy indifference toward me the moment his four gangsters turned up hurt me, outraged me, humiliated me; so much so that it was not till I stood outside our house that with a sudden shock I realised that I had kissed, on the mouth, my best friend's husband and had not outright declined his offer to plant a baby in me. More astounding still, Tristram did not enter my thoughts till after this, nor was I racked by as great a sense of guilt as I had been by merely dreaming of his bluish afternoon jaw. I was appalled. An unprincipled slut, a dirty she-dog.

For the first time in my life I swallowed half of one of Tristram's Seconals, took a long hot bath, slept dreamlessly and woke up with a huge, nameless hope, feeling as new and innocent as a runner on the starting line, convinced – heaven knows why – that whatever I could possibly do with or to Pom, one kiss, one night, one week with him, even one baby by him, would not come between him and Ju, or, more importantly, between Ju and me.

Japanese may have just as fierce a sense of honour and as good manners as other races, but, I must admit, possessing none of the absolute and exacting religious integrity, we do turn shockingly elastic when it comes to interpreting Gods' laws for men. Adultery it was that I was to commit, no other word for it, I knew, for I had learnt the ten commandments at the Japanese Sacred Heart. By precepts of any religion, be it Christian,

217

Moslem, Confucian or Buddhist, it was bad and forbidden. Yet, and yet, there I was, exultantly inspired to give my husband the serene, lasting security of a happy family life by adultery, having selfishly put down my *enryo* dustbin cover on such embarrassing side-issues as carnal pleasure and deceitfulness which would inevitably be involved in any such enterprise.

Shortly after her return from New York, Ju came up to London to see her gynaecologist and spent the night with us, having left Nicholas at Falaise Hall with an Irish nurse she had brought back from New York. Pom was, she explained, in Blackpool.

'With his army?' I asked, obscurely disgusted by my own lack of trepidation as I pronounced 'his'.

'His army!?' Ju raised a brilliant aggressive laugh. 'I hear you met all of his four knights.'

'Yes, at the airport, when I took Tristram to . . .'

'Yeah, Pom told me. What's this boy, Karl, like?'

'Haven't you met him?'

'No, he doesn't live with us in Hampshire. He's Pom's London boy, sort of.'

'He's striking looking, whitish blond, blue eyes, tall, slim, a little unreal, frightening too, so intense . . . like a dog that chooses only one master.'

'Yeah, that's what I hear. Claude, you remember my boy Friday? Poor Claude is terrorised by Pom's new soldier-monks thingummy. He says there's nothing more dangerous than religious fanatics, and make no mistake these are just that. While I was away, Jim, Chris and Richard moved out of the main house and installed themselves in the old coach house, calling it the barracks.'

'Spooky,' I used the word I had learnt from Ju. 'Pom is going too far. Can't you do something about it?'

'Are you kiddin'?' Ju smiled inwardly and looked like a bronze Bodhistava, implacable in her mercifulness. 'It may be that I've been analysed out of my wits, but I can't, I just can't judge people and try to change them. My shrink would have said, at root, it's his father and brother complex, both over six foot and military giants. Or, as Edward insists, it's his mother's mad Irishness coming out. Who knows? I just can't look at Pom in separate logical details; I swallow him whole, period! If one day he had yellow eyes, next week, green; or one night he's Catholic and weighs ten stones and next night, a Moslem and weighs eighteen stones, it would make no difference to me. That's what's so beautiful about us two. Even if I should walk into a room and find him in bed with another girl, it wouldn't change things one iota. Well,' she giggled a little-girl giggle, 'call it love.'

I held my breath, body and soul agape at this declaration. I had often been teased by Ju for being non-demonstrative, but on this sole occasion it was I who pounced on her, hugging her tight in my arms, with tears of God knows what denomination pouring down my cheeks.

15

It was a very hot summer; at lunchtime I resignedly watched the prosciuto ham sweat and curl at the edges and found the cooing doves, retired deeper into the woods, singing half an octave lower than I remembered in previous summers.

Letti, fifty-seven years and a widow this summer, was at first sight as slim and caustically elegant as I had first found her; but on closer inspection too much green eye-shadow was smeared over her eyelids and for the first time I saw food stains on her blouse. Undoubtedly there was the absence or rather departure of Toma the dago behind these trivial signs of carelessness, not yet of neglect, on the part of Letti, or so Tristram and I deduced from the fact that she never uttered the T of Toma. Letti, who had obliterated from her life and memory her own and only sister, because she had gone horse-riding with the occupying German officers, was attempting to do the same with Toma, but with infinitely greater suffering, which showed when she talked of next winter, next year, where to go, what to do, and I saw her expression harden as if slapped by a blast of cold air. She also talked about her late husband with a gutteral emphasis of emotion unknown when he had been alive. 'What I miss most after darling Frank died is that now I have no one to look after and waste time on and believe me each day seems all too long.'

Being nothing if not stonily disciplined, Letti filled the blank hours of her life with work. She got up earlier and worked at least three hours before lunch in her studio, then despite the crushing languor of the hot afternoon I would see her disappear through the rose tunnel, impatiently tying a cotton scarf round her head, her jaws set and combative; and I would not see her till seven when she re-emerged to join Tristram for drinks in the library. It was on our third day that she surprised us with an invitation to visit her studio. Tristram, who had never out of his *enryo* asked to see his mother's work nor attended any of her exhibitions, held his breath. But, Letti was a step ahead and chic: when we reached her studio door she lifted the left index-finger to her lips.

'Children, you don't utter a word about my work. Easier that way all round.'

I am no judge of ultra-modern painting but what I saw, geometric juxtapositions of grey, lemon yellow and green on endless large canvases, all shot with tendril-like lines of neon-sign pink did not grip me. There was nothing that reflected Letti's personality, her dash, her temper, or her innate chic. I felt my mouth dehydrate, so depressed and so disappointed was I for her: all those solitary hours of stoic endurance, for *this?*

Tristram, no doubt cursing himself for having left his pipe in his room and thus being unable to cover his embarrassment and horror, walked in stiff measured steps, and grunted vacuously as he read the critiques of Letti's past exhibitions in Antibes, Deauville, Brighton and Lausanne, neatly framed and hung on the immaculate white walls.

That night, Tristram took a heavier dose of Seconal and whimpered as he lay spread-eagled on his stomach, his usual position of lying in wait for the pills' effect.

'There should be a special police branch in the Ministry of Education to curb citizens' creative urge. It's a crime to encourage mediocre talent. Oh, God, it's a crime, a cruel crime!'

'But, she is doing very well: a one-woman show in Munich, then a group exhibition in Geneva this winter?'

'I don't accuse her of lacking in contacts and rich friends to whom her paintings mean just a break in their wall-paper. But, to see a lonely woman carrying on hysterically as if her art meant everything to her, and as if hers were art . . .'

'What should she be doing instead then?'

'What comes naturally. Find another husband, a decent widower of her own age, go on a Swan lecture cruise down the Nile, go to Abano for a cure or buy presents for her grandchildren . . .' There, he paused and, rolling over, added: 'That sort of thing . . .'

Came Sunday and I was dismayed to see that, of the twenty guests Letti had asked, many were those whom she had tried to discourage Frank from inviting: 'Frank, not *them!* There's a limit to how low one can descend.'

New faces belonged to those whose acquaintance she had made during the fervidly hopeful weeks in May 68: a generation or two younger than Frank's APWAV hangers-on, her new friends were radical, argumentative with their rubbery intense French lips never at rest, and spent their holidays at a far-off Club Mediterranee or at their parents' villas on the Côte d'Azur. Amongst them Letti played a role of a rich, elderly, indulgent *patronne*, did not disappear upstairs during the meal but remained a solicitous hostess till the end. Then, ashen faced, her lipstick licked away, the rouge on her cheeks rubbed off by so much embracing, she went upstairs with a thermos of camomile infusion and we did not see her till the following morning on her way to the studio.

Did the widow Letti terrorise me less this summer? No, oh, no! Every morning my heart still leapt like a frightened yoyo as I tiptoed down the corridor outside her bedroom, and I was still as alert and cautious as a pin cushion in her presence, trying not to stand in her light or to cause a draught on her shoulder. But after having gone home to my family, not only did I feel I could cope with my mother-in-law but I actively wanted to be an 'added pleasure' to her.

One morning she came down earlier when I was alone in the breakfast room. Without a trace of make-up, her face shone like an oiled paper but her square-cut fiery eyes and the fine bone structure were a solid diamond that neither age nor use could erode.

'Go ahead, read your book,' she ordered me and ate her breakfast, taking her time, in total silence. Knowing how weak she liked her tea, I boiled more water for her as noiselessly as I could. She nodded in acknowledgement and after having emptied the third cup began quietly:

'You are considerate, Soukie, a rare gift and I compliment your mother for it. When Tristram first wrote us about you, he praised your special quality as being bulkless and pliable. At the time Frank and I laughed: our son has found a little rubber balloon of a wife. After four years I know he was not deceiving us. Don't blush, young lady, it's not entirely a compliment, not if you want a vital, working marriage. Of course, you could say it's none of my business and I ought to be peeling my own onion as the Frogs say, but I tell you, you are a tough nut to crack. Your reticence, your withdrawal and your ungrippable surface poise, all make it a hell of a hard job for your husband to realise that he's not making you happy. He may in fact suspect it in his heart of hearts and who knows he may be even miserable about it, and don't forget, here we have a very selfish and insecure husband. Unless you come out of yourself and make him see it, it'll be more convenient for him not to do anything about it.

'Dear girl, there are times when you must put your foot down, shake your head and scream. Marital rancour grows like mushroom in confinement. It can grow to monstrous proportions. I've seen mushrooms lift up thick asphalt. Then, it's too late. I saved my marriage by abandoning it. That was drastic. It suited my temperament, suited Frank's. I'm not advising you to do the same. I'm Tristram's mother, not yours; naturally, I think of him first. I want you to stick by him, but I can't expect you to do so unless you can make your life with him reasonably happy and worthwhile. A-a-ah, I can see the question you're asking!'

Letti passed her pointed finger from left to right of her own forehead.

'Why settle for being *reasonably* happy? Why not a total happiness elsewhere? I'm still young and pretty. That's what you're asking. *Ma petite*, I've lived more than twice as long as you have; although you may find what I'm going to tell you disgustingly pragmatic, even cynical, you'll have to give me the benefit of the doubt. Believe me, you can't forever run after the wilder shores of love, and there's very little joy and a great deal of pain to follow.

'You are . . . what? Twenty-five? Twenty-seven! Not old but not young enough to start all over again. Look, Soukie, no one's perfect. I know my son as well as you probably do. I admit you could have had an easier man, a less neurotic man, a less selfish and more cuddly husband; but then he could have been ugly, smelly-footed, stupid, boring, tasteless . . .' Letti raised then dropped her shoulders with weary resignation. 'Bah, what's the difference? Very little. You loved Tristram enough to follow him all the way here. He too must have been quite smitten by you: a self-conscious sceptical man like him marrying you, *une étrangère extrême orientale*, on the spot. So, Soukie, can't you build on what you two already have that works and that's good? I've never liked nor trusted women alone. There's something hungry and hysterical and rancid about them . . .

'At the end of my very free and self-indulgent life I confess I've been lucky or, to put it crudely, smart to have had Frank. Like a pillowcase over a pillow, a man in a woman's life is the natural complement, it completes the picture. Don't you quote me to my Parisian friends; they'll howl with laughter; but I am talking to my daughter-in-law and I'm duty bound to tell her facts, not idealistic fiction, even at the risk of sounding like a suburban old hag.' She paused, wincing imperceptibly at the horror of her last words. She flapped her eyelashes resolutely once, then, fixing me with her pupils which seemed to me to flare open like green sunflowers:

'Has Tristram ever suggested to you to have an . . .'

I cut her short by putting my hand on her wrist below the tall honey jar. 'I am trying.'

I blushed like a furnace, furious at my inadequate English expression, embarrassed to boiling point by the subject, also at a loss how to retrieve my hand from hers.

'Good girl,' Letti squeezed my hand once and shut her eyes, suddenly bashful and prudish, and added quickly.

'On n'en parle plus.'

224

Indeed, Letti never broached the subject again. That she became neither demonstratively more affectionate nor confiding with me after our breakfast tête-à-tête appealed to me. We never became friends, and I preferred it that way.

16

'Pom wants to hide and die. It's that bad, that ugly,' whined Ju and, rolling over on her back on the white lace bedcover, lifted Nicholas, plump and blond like an ill-shaped peach, who with a big grin began stirring the air with his four short limbs. 'Gosh, you're getting heavy!' Ju dropped the seven-month old on the bed. Nicholas quickly turned round on all fours, crawled to the edge and with an intense look of indecision peered down at the carpeted floor. He was a beautiful baby with Ju's fair skin and hair, with Pom's dreamy dark eyes and chiselled lips and chin. I encouraged him to jump into my arms. He began giggling, more and more excited, then with a tearing, high shriek tumbled down. When his precious wriggling weight was against my breast, I squeezed him, devoured his sour-milk baby odour and as he stood on my lap, stamping his ludicrous little feet like blunt forks into my thighs and pulling at my hair, I could not help kissing him all over his head.

'I'm taking him to my room so that you can sleep, Ju. Shall I wake you for tea?'

'Yeah, sweetie, lots of brown toast, quince jelly and honey and those coconut cookies you always have. Spoil me, I'd love it. I need it . . . spoil me . . .' She was half asleep, her hand gently spread on her now noticeably swollen tummy.

She had rung the night before. 'Can you put me up with Nicholas? Leaving for New York the morning after.'

'New York?'

'Having my baby there.'

'I suppose it's better to be in New York than . . .'

226

'Yep, it's Daddy's idea, the Trustees' idea. Wasn't mine.'

'And Pom's?'

'Poor Pom, he had to agree. What else could he do? He's just too overwhelmed with Falaise Hall and the police and all that shit. The place is in a mess.'

About Pom and the weird goings-on at Falaise Hall, I had heard from various sources since returning to London. During the summer, apparently, migrating hippies and communards of various nationalities and degrees of hideousness had arrived and used the place as a 'one night crash pad'. Quite a few stayed on more or less indefinitely and the house had been repeatedly raided by the local police looking for drugs and undesirable aliens. On one occasion, the villagers had petitioned the police to stop what they described as 'indecency and perversion committed in groups'. The day after the sensational news of the Czech youth self-immolating in the centre of Prague in protest against the Russian invasion, a forty-four-year-old school teacher from Glasgow, engaged in honey making and greenhouse maintenance, had set fire to his own prayer rug, causing himself first-degree burns and extensive damage to Falaise Hall's fine late 18th-century wood panelling in the drawing room, now their meditation room.

Colin, always on the side of the rich and their valuable antiques, immediately alerted Lillian in New York. Daddy Sugarheim acted with speed: he ordered a lorry-load of Patata tins and snack food to be distributed amongst the resident hippies, then had every single one of them promptly escorted off the premises. A well-known firm of land agents and surveyors were engaged to manage the estate and a security guard occupied the lodge at the main gate. A team of Mayfair decorators and builders began arriving to repair and refurbish the house from top to bottom to its original glory. Ju and Pom were consulted only about their own rooms and the nursery; the treatment of the rest of the building, the trustees with professional advice would decide upon.

After consuming toast and coconut cookies and a quan-

227

tity of quince jelly and honey, Ju revived. 'If I didn't have Nicholas and a baby on its way, I'd have done *that* to all my shit-brained Trustees,' she struck a furious obscene gesture with her hand. 'People think I'm personally rich. Jesus, tell that to my Trustees!'

The following morning, as she laboriously crawled into the Rolls Royce that the Sugarheim UK president had sent to take her and Nicholas to the airport, she handed me a small light packet in an old Selfridge's plastic bag.

'For Colin on his fiftieth birthday. A pair of mittens I've knitted. Don't imagine he'll ever wear them, but it's the thought behind. He's been meddlesome but loyal. Give him my love.'

Pom was not coming to see her off, she said. 'Easier that way. He'll join us when the time comes for delivery; he knows I'm scared. Honey, if you see Pom, be nice to him, will you?'

I cried torrents of tears as I watched the liveried chauffeur shut the door on her and Nicholas's little palms marked star-shaped smears on the car window.

Colin's fiftieth birthday party was held on September 11th, Friday. What was just a light drizzle at noon developed into a downpour in clamorous thick sheets by the time Tristram and I began dressing. After three dry martinis he stood limply by the curtains and gazed out of the rain-drenched window, his suntanned face in attractive contrast to the austere chic of his midnight-blue dinner jacket and white evening shirt. When he turned to me he said with bitter self-pity:

'It raineth, raineth and who's gonna get the bloody car?'

I let out a short laugh at this and just looked down at my ornate kimono and my feet in *tabi* stocks resting on flimsy silk-covered slippers.

'Oh, what a bore, what a bloody awful bore!' He snarled and, collecting his Gucci bag and an umbrella, went to the garage and picked me up in front of our house. As always there was no parking space in Chester Square. We went up and down the side streets in the vicinity. Knowing Tristram, I was prepared for the worst; so I just drew in a hissing breath and nodded when he threw up his arms and wailed: 'I'm leaving the bloody thing right here and risk the ticket. We'll have to walk from here. Sorry, but it's the best I can do.'

It was raining harder than ever as I hobbled inside the restriction of my kimono skirt and tottered into puddles precisely because I tried too hard to avoid them. By the time we reached Colin's door my *tabi* socks were drenched, *zori* slippers were two scoops of water and in spite of my umbrella the kimono hems were wet through.

To arrive at Colin's particularly brilliant party looking like an unwrung floorcloth! As I squeezed and sponged my clothes in Colin's Pre-Raphaelite bathroom, all I wished was to throw down the stiff wet mass of silk and lie like a corpse wrapped in dry towels inside the very bathtub where I had so long ago discovered Ju. Colin was kindness incarnate: he promised to let me use an iron after dinner and added before departing into the pantry to attend to a reported minor catastrophe: 'Here, keep these handkerchiefs. One mustn't iron silk direct.'

Father would have praised this as a shining example of 'As-as-as'. I was touched to tears, and I felt I understood why a man reputed to be such a grotesque social climber enjoyed the lasting devotion of so many friends.

After coffee cups and brandy glasses were removed, the sedentary were chased from the tables; the two large reception rooms were cleared for Flamenco dancers and musicians. Colin came looking for me to say that he had left the iron in the top-floor guest room. A few days earlier when I had brought him Ju's present together with ours, Colin had not yet heard from Pom and had presumed that the errant guru-soldier was not coming. My surprise, therefore, was violent at sighting Pom on the first-floor landing, engaged in an animated discussion with three or four people, in a well-cut evening suit and with a proper black tie, not a ribbon. I heard Czechoslovakia mentioned. Putting on an I'm-not-really-here distant look and twisting my body away from his direction I began stealing up the stairs.

'Excuse me,' I heard Pom stop the conversation. 'Suki, where are you off to?'

I pointed at the bottom of my kimono like a perfect imbecile, then, recovering my voice, said, 'To iron.' Pom nodded and turned to his Czechoslovakia.

As soon as I locked the top-floor guest room door, I squealed and shuddered from the sheer joy of being alone and able finally to peel the clammy garment off my skin. Naked, humming and tiptoeing, I took time in laying wet *tabis* and pants neatly on top of a hot radiator. I ironed the undergarment first and wore it untied, whilst it was still warm, and began ironing the bottom of the kimono carefully through Colin's fine linen handkerchief. I was calm and relaxed, so happy, working in the familiarity of household activities. The kimono finished, I ironed Colin's handkerchief. There was a knock on the door.

'Suki. Me.'

I heard my pulse beat hard against my temples. I bent down as deliberately as if I had a dizzy spell and pulled out the plug from the wall under the ironing board. The white silk undergarment opened out and I saw my naked body beneath it.

One more knock, unflustered and confident. I went to the door, unlocked it and took a few flying steps backward. Pom walked in, looking straight before him. He registered no visible alarm or embarrassment when he saw me barefoot and undressed.

'I say you do look comfortable,' he said and as if it were the most natural expected thing to do, turned and locked the door. I clutched at a handful of silk at the waist and sneezed, a bursting loud sneeze, with hardly time to cover my mouth. Pom laughed. Such split-bamboo laughter that I could not help laughing myself. With the raucous thudding of the over-amplified dance music right under our feet, the laughing together demolished from the scene any underhandedness, if there were any.

Before I finished brushing my nose with the back of my hand he took me in his arms. Through the gossamer silk I felt the energy and desire in his palm glued on to the small of my back; I could almost visualise his fingerprints against my cold flesh, like red-hot rings of an electric cooker. He did not force me, no, he did not rape me, but

230

like two hands clapping I went to him, he came to me. His lips did not search mine, mine met his, open, avid, and grateful. He did not seduce me, we seduced each other, with all the voracity and rapture we possessed, or rather on my part, I had not known I had in me.

Later, when I thought of the time we spent together I felt as if I had swallowed a long flame, not entirely of shame or of guilt. It stunned me immediately and left no space nor time for judgement to enter. Just an excruciatingly intense sensation of paralysis and burn. In front of it I lost *enryo*, could not reason, could not postpone, could not stop. I took and gloried savagely in that inevitable power and I only felt spent and purified afterwards.

He dressed himself, wordless, looking at me in the mirror from time to time, then took my hand and kissed it.

'When we meet again downstairs, probably for breakfast, don't shrink away from me. Come and sit with me. Of course, we'll have to talk about omelettes and the weather, not about your skin, your neck, your arm, otherwise . . .'

His square armour-like chest rose up and he kissed me on the mouth, a long spell, till I felt drowned and my neck unhinged backwards. Before I caught my breath he had unlocked the door and was gone.

The thought of Tristram did not come to my mind till I took a hot bath, with Ju lurking in and out of my mind's sight, smiling askance, curious, mocking, poo-poohing, amused, scandalised, and loving. I could not empathise anger or jealousy in her. As a sneeze built up in the back of my head I tried to throw both Tristram and Ju into my *enryo* dustbin, and with a loud sneeze banged the lid down on it. Soaked to my chin in the hot water that encouraged me to indulge in an arbitrary and wishful egoism – I'll be a good wife, Tristram. I love you, Ju, more than anyone! – I began counting the days since my last period. Not quite the ideal timing, but not without hope either . . . I counted again, crooking the fingers, then smelled my palm. Yes, though wet, I smelt Pom on my hand. I was frightened for the first time that night. I soaped and scrubbed myself with the flannel till my fingernails scratched my skin. After abundant rinsing I arranged my hair, ironed my crumpled undergarment again and put on kimono and obi with meticulous care. As layers of silk covered me, crepe strings biting into my abdomen, I felt myself prepared to face the world outside. Before unlocking the door I shook my head vigorously to see if I could still smell Pom. About this, I was fastidious, even if my husband with his Occidental lack of olfactory vigilance could not have possibly detected it. After being convinced that I smelt only of sandalwood soap and Mother's camphor soaked into the kimono, I tidied the room, turned off all the lights and went downstairs, where, to my grateful relief, I was quickly accosted by two ladies whom Tristram would have called culture-vulture Orientalists who bombarded me with questions on Japan from Shintoism, haiku poetry to raw fish and communal bathing. Thanks to them, without contriving, I did not come face to face with Tristram till breakfast was served.

'I love the smell of singed bacon fat, but not enough to eat it,' said Tristram, carefully pushing bacon strips to the far side of his plate. 'Not in the morning anyway.'

'I had to iron not just the kimono but the undergarment as well. I was so cold, I took a hot bath,' I said and thought with gratitude that none of what I had said was untrue.

'I won £170 at backgammon, not bad.' Tristram yawned and I saw delicate greenish veins stand on the marble of his temples, his eyes dark with fatigue and his jaws as fleshless as a boy's. I felt my gullet down to the stomach contract with such tenderness as I had never felt for him. I shan't, I won't make comparisons; he is my husband, he is no fire, he won't burn me, but he is mine, and I his.

'I hope it didn't leave nasty stains,' he said, eyeing my kimono with proprietary interest.

'Nothing serious, but the kimono will have to be mailed back to Mother for complete fulling.' I picked up a strip of bacon from his plate and as I ate it thought of what he invariably said whenever he spotted an aged couple in a hotel restaurant:

232

'Asako, look at them, wouldn't it be cosy for us to reach that age when we each of us carry a book to meals and read it between courses?'

I thought of Letti who had one morning failed to turn up for breakfast and thirteen years later reappeared to resume her married life and breakfast with Frank with newspapers propped up against jam jars between them. I also ruminated on the genius painter, R. H., who must be by now indistinguishable from molten hot lava inside a Hawaiian volcano; and on Frank, just cold ashes at the roots of his aspens. I blushed and choked on the strong tea. How dared I? How dared I ever judge others? How could I have?

'May I sit with you?' Pom was standing with his plate of eggs and toast.

'Of course, do!' Hardly out of my reverie, I jauntily yelled.

'Why, it's you, Pom!' Tristram swallowed a hot gulp of tea and with an agonised grimace fluttered his napkin over his mouth as if to fan his burning gorge. 'I wouldn't have recognised you. You look so dramatically different every time I see you. The last time you were a guru-Messiah in cheesecloth. Don't you look smart tonight,' said Tristram with an indulgent smile of an elder teasing a junior.

Seated next to my husband whose cold flesh had subdued the devlish glow inside mine, I turned to face Pom.

'How is your scrambled egg?' I asked; and to think that it was only a few hours ago!

'A little too much pepper, otherwise, fine.'

He ate slowly but with keen appetite, his eyes on the edge of his plate, his mind far off, without speaking further to anyone. Tristram dismissed him as a morose ill-mannered lout and jovially greeted Kevin Collington-Meade, a gossip columnist, whom Tristram had 'been to school with'. He and his companion, a tall, emaciated mannequin on red high heels, sat on the two remaining chairs at our table.

'Pom!' yelled Kevin whose unabashed flippancy was

233

his professional advantage. 'So, you have deserted your Hampshire World Elsewhere! Is it true that Colefax-Fowler's doing the interior decoration for Falaise Hall? The ballroom like the one with Rex Whistler's *trompe l'oeil*, you know, with painted ermine curtains and that kind of thing?'

If I had considered Pom merely as my sperm bank, I could not have shared the pain that Pom must have felt but did not outwardly show. He froze, then brought back his hand that he had extended toward the tea cup and touched his forehead. When he did pick up his tea cup he was invincible.

'You know Daddy Sugarheim, Kevin,' he smiled. 'He'll always get the best at the cheapest price.'

Kevin looked momentarily glazed-eyed as he made a mental record of Pom's reply, but perked up instantly.

'The World Elsewhere, Saigon Sanctuary, Falaise Hall Commune, now that that jaunt's over, what's next, Pom?'

'I wish I knew.'

'When's the baby due?'

'I'm reading your column daily to find out.'

'Still a vegetarian?'

'You vegetarian? Me, too!' piped up Kevin's mannequin. 'Don't you think it's about time there should be a comfortable vegetarian restaurant with waiter service in a smart convenient street in London?'

I recalled Ju saying: 'Pom wants to hide and die. It's that bad, that ugly.'

If Pom had strangled Kevin and his vegetarian model then and there, I'd have considered they deserved it.

In his column Kevin duly reported on Colin's party: 'a glut of caviar, titles and Flamenco Olé!' and digressing from it, he pounced on Pom, 'otherwise known as Centurion of the World's Smallest Army.' Accurately putting the number of his army at five, Kevin went on: 'I received this confidential information from the charming young Frenchman whom his illustrious father, an ex-Gaullist minister, had recently pried home from Lord Mad-Bad-Dangerous Pom's commune in Hampshire. With the Mayfair decorators and plumbing engineers stomping about the place, Lord Pom is leading a nomadic life, surfacing at most unlikely places, ranging from an East End squat above a massage parlour in the company of a South African black singer with pierced nose to a suffocatingly snobbish candle-lit party thrown by a hedonist duke in Gloucestershire. He was recently sighted parachuting on to a Hare Krishna commune in Wales and rumours are rife that Viscountess Patata Pom left for New York in a huff over her husband's marked preference for male company to hers.'

I threw down the newspaper as the innuendo rose like a stench in my nostrils and, recalling Pom and his boys at Heathrow Airport, my head swelled with revolting flights of the imagination; but I also did recall the night at Colin's and a sturdier organ than eyes or brain protested disbelief. My body memory was so potent that I lay on my bed like a fish enjoying a slow death on hot sand.

When Pom rang me I had a feeling that I was receiving a call from a conscientious doctor with my case history under his eyes, reminding me that another shot was due.

'A week since Colin's party,' he said simply. 'Swan and Edgar's this afternoon. Piccadilly side entrance. Say, three?' which meant, I knew, he was slotting me into a vacancy between his aikido and judo lessons.

After Tristram had left for the gallery, I scurried about the house like a cockroach, panicked and furtive, getting in the way of Mrs Apps's Hoover. I could hardly swallow her omelette at lunch. At one thirty I began dressing. I stood naked in my bathroom in a descending cloud of L'Heure Bleue talcum powder, Letti's gift this summer, and I could almost hear my heart thumping against the confinement of my ribs. By the time I was fully dressed I was as reluctant an adultress as a cow going to the slaughterhouse; it all seemed such a production. Why go out of this cosy sunlit houst into the gust and germs and smelly crowd, having lied to Mrs Apps: 'I'm going to a matinée of *The Prime of Miss Jean Brodie*'? Too complicated, too nerve-wracking, not to mention immoral, and to think, to have put on so much clothing just to remove it all in an hour's time to lie and shake like an over-turned beetle!

As I passed the mirror in the hall I dared not look at myself, lest what I saw there should turn my stomach; but I did steal a side-glance and almost felt like kneeling down and crying: I looked neither a tart nor a liar. I looked in fact prettier than usual, eyes sparkling and lips moist. The thought that within less than an hour Pom would be covering them with his kisses turned my whole inside liquid, hot and thick as a flambé sauce. For decency's sake I hurriedly removed my wicked thoughts and body outside my husband's threshold.

When I got off a train at Piccadilly Circus station I felt suddenly faint. I bought a Cadbury's milk chocolate bar and ate it ravenously. When he stood before me, eyeing my chocolate, I was astonished to hear myself ask quite casually, almost bluntly.

'Want some?'

'Yes, please.' He snapped a large half of the chocolate. 'Let's take a tube.'

From the Westbourne Park tube station we walked to a basement room devoid of lock or door knob but equipped with a grimy bolt on the inner side of the door. Just a room with a rain-and-soot streaked window, a bed with a sheet and a green acrylic blanket, two bentwood chairs and a slab of mirror hang on a nail on the wall. The most ecstatic lovers in novels were found in greater discomfort, a forest clearing or an insect-infested hay stack, I told myself and, facing the wall, began removing my clothes in an uncouth hurry, as I feared that if I left undressing to Pom he might just toss my clothes no matter where and how on to the filthy floor. I piled each item of my clothing on a chair after having vigorously blown at its surface. Pom snorted an impatient laugh at my *hausfrau* fastidiousness and like a bat into the dark hurtled his nakedness at mine.

He was quite movingly concerned for my pleasure, for my relaxing and opening and receiving. He gave and gave and seemed to soar all the higher in ecstacy, the more he gave. Afterwards, however, he was quite utterly finished and free of me and love. I would have had to be a blind and unfeeling moron if I did not realise that just as I had no exclusive right to the bed or the room I shared with him, so could I claim no emotional or sexual exclusivity from him, of which he possessed none and in which he saw no point.

I perched on a chair in my underwear and combed my hair, my bare toes recoiling from contact with the stained, unswept carpet and my eyes blankly set on last year's calendar pinned askew on the wall. A nylon stocking caught the frayed edge of a chair and tore, but having no choice, I put it on. I wanted to put the bed in some sort of order but my fingers revolted at the grimy, used feel of the synthetic fibre blanket, so I left it in as disgusting a mess as it had been. By the time I was dressed and shod, I felt myself cheap and sleazy, the type of woman who sits in a bus with her knees wide apart.

How ultimately unproud and futile 'an affair in the afternoon' is, I was beginning to think, when I caught Pom's eyes set on me as he strode about the room barefoot, picking up his scattered clothes and I blushed guiltily. I wanted to say to him, thank you, you've loved me again this afternoon and I do so want your baby; but all that I could do was to cross my fingers, lift them before my face and say:

'I hope, I hope . . .'

He nodded, smiling, looking distantly beyond me.

'I'm leaving the day after tomorrow, to see Ju and Nicholas. Just a week or so. Now, darling Suki!'

The way he said 'Darling Suki' was exactly that of Ju's whenever she wanted something. 'Would you be an angel and buy these things for Ju?'

'Oh, Ju!' I gasped with such a fierce longing that I felt obliged to cover my mouth with both my fists. 'I miss her. I miss her terribly. If only I could tell her that I might have a baby!'

Pom watched me, *sanpaku*-eyed, with a smile that could only be described as beatific.

As we hurried out of the squat door, in the passage where half a dozen grey plastic bags bursting with old rubbish were piled against the wall, we came face to face with an unsteadily lurching drunkard in long trousers with their hems eaten away by friction and a mucky greatcoat at least three sizes too large for his emaciated body. His thin red eyes flashed at seeing us and his filthy black hands leapt up and grasped the elbow of Pom's orange anorak.

'Bewdifl! Just bewdifl, wow, pow, bewdifl!'

He muttered again and again, bringing his eyeballs to an almost scraping closeness with the shiny orange skin of Pom's anorak. A warm stench came closer and I dashed past him toward the exit door. Pom stood still and spoke gently to the man either drugged or drunken to stupefaction.

'Let go, please. I must dash. I am late. Listen, I must go, please, let go!'

With a revolting unfocused tenacity the man clung to Pom's sleeve, drivelling frothily from the corner of his uncoordinated mouth. Pom cajoled and pleaded and begged, then threatened to knock him down in a minute, *unless* . . . To my surprise, I noticed Pom had turned quite pale, *sanpaku*-eyed, and his voice quivering. He wiped his mouth or perhaps perspiration over his lips with his clenched fist; then, dropping his shoulder bag to the ground, savagely pulled at the shoulder seam of his own sleeve with the man still derangedly tugging at it. As his anorak was worn and had been frequently machine-washed, the sleeve came off like a fig skin. The man fell to the ground and with a neighing screech of joy or pain, clutched at the torn sleeve. Pom, breathing heavily from the shoulders, said: 'Enjoy it. It's yours!'

'I haven't got a staying discipline. I can't cope with trench warfare or siege. I just can't hold on. I just . . . you know, let go.' He muttered as we hurried our way toward the tube station.

He still wore the same one-sleeved anorak when he dropped in at the house the following afternoon to collect various homeopathic preparations and pots of acqueous BP cream I had bought for Ju.

'What a frightful mess he looks,' said Tristram after Pom had left.

The following morning my period started. I leant against the bathroom sink and for long minutes gazed into the smoky wet September morning. Disappointment in dull slow steps climbed up on me; by the time I went to bed with a Panadol it was a stinging disappointment deep inside me, for which I had not been prepared. The cramps, unusual with me, continued the next day, a Saturday. I stayed in bed and Tristram went out alone to luncheon.

I was looking up in the medical book on ovulation and cycle, when the telephone rang in the hollow silence of the empty house. I took the receiver and from the echoing metalic sizzles in the background I knew it was Ju from America.

'Pom's here and I'm so goddamn pregnant. Oh, Suki, I feel like drinking a gallon of paraffin oil to let the damn thing slither out of me! And I'm having those horrible nightmares again. A mongrel baby with thirteen fingers or another with Tarquin's hair, that sort, you know?' She wailed and I wailed back that I had the worst cramps in my whole memory and as usual we settled comfortably down on our lavatorial level. When we reluctantly ended our lengthy conversation, both of us rolling on our beds, chortling nonsensically and cursing our tiresome female physiology, I had a queer sensation that if I should have a baby by Pom and one day she should come to know about it, she would accept with joy that my baby had the same father as hers.

After my period was over, for the first time in my married life, I seduced my husband. Tristram, in a mild fluster, kept muttering: 'Oh dear, darling, what does this mean? What is this?' and let slide the Harold Nicolson diary over the blue satin eiderdown cover.

'I have many little nagging thoughts racing in my head,' he said and I understood with tender amusement that this was his way of excusing the inadequacy he felt in face of my determined and dexterous ardour to get satisfaction for myself as well as for him. Afterwards he whispered with a proprietary smugness: 'At last I've succeeded in getting rid of your Japanese inhibition, haven't I?'

I replied with a groan somewhere between yes and thank you; how I adored my husband then, my darling pompous silly ass Ph.D., D. Litt. I stayed limp and adorable in his arms till I heard him fast asleep, returned to my bed and read Dr Fowler's *Modern English Usage* which Tristram had assigned me to read, following H. G. Wells' *Outline of History*.

It was Ju who telephoned me from New York to say that Pom had just left for London as he wanted to attend the Labour Party Conference in Blackpool due to open in a few days' time.

'It's been just heaven, just bliss, Pom and I, in spite of my being Mrs Bloated Pumpkin,' she said. 'He'll show you some divine photos of me and Nicholas. Do ask him over to your house, otherwise he'll eat junk food with those acne-faced boys.'

Pom rang at home on the 26th in the afternoon.

'Pom here. Are you alone?' He said as soon as a taxiphone beep ended and I heard traffic noise behind his voice.

'Yes.'

'Come and see me tomorrow afternoon. At two. Great Northern Hotel, King's Cross station. Room 63.'

'Yes.'

He hung up.

Exactly at two I knocked on the door 63, which was opened. I walked in and walked straight up to the window which gave on to a sunlit crowded car park below. I heard him shut and lock the door but took time in removing my gloves, finger by finger, remembering the insolent look the hotel clerk had given me downstairs. When I did turn round I found Pom contemplating me from some distance, naked. He wiped me clean of any thoughts, words and cobwebs. He prowled round me, once, twice, and thrice, making the orbit closer till finally, coming right behind me, stuck the length of his body against the back of my body. He being not very much taller than I, our bodies fitted like two palms and his mouth was hot against my temple.

'There's two hours before I must get dressed and catch a train. Love me.'

He made me turn and in his *sanpaku* eyes I saw raw desire. When he threw away my last clothing and held my waist delicately between his fingers, a shudder of impatience leapt through both of us. I opened myself to his caress and made no waste of it.

If I was so meek in subjugation, extravagant in giving, I was also voracious in taking. I want your child, if I had said it, I did not hear it, but he heard it. Once, twice, we loved and died and stayed still together, his generosity permeating me. When he rose again in manifest desire, he lifted me in his arms as lightly as if I were a yard of silk and, returning me to the centre of the bed, slowly fell over me. When he slid out of me, I whimpered and clasped a handful of sheet. I listened as he dressed, like a sick child to a circus leaving the town. Only once did I open my eyes in thin slits and saw the room two hours darker and found him huddled up on the floor by the sunless window, in prayer, his palms opened on his folded knees. His palms, scooping up what little daylight was left over, shone like two lotus blossoms. The image had a saintliness. I shut my eyes quickly.

'Good bye, Suki.' I heard him whisper. I think I nodded. He went out of the room and I did not stir for some time. When I did get up, hot rivulets ran down my already cold and dry legs. I hugged myself and for a few seconds I was happy again in the vigorous scent, green and mint-fresh. Pom's life radiated in me for these few moments.

'You look lovely and soft, darling,' said Tristram after supper in a voice which turned hoarse in mid sentence. I scrubbed myself thoroughly for the second time that day in a heavily scented hot bath and staggered into my husband's bed, my head rattling like a boiling kettle.

'How you Japanese live to a ripe old age, taking those insanely hot baths every night, I'll never know.' Tristram dropped Malraux's *Antimemoirs* to the carpet and switched off the bedside lamp.

– never turned off the light with . . . – I clung to

Tristram's chest, Don't compare! Don't refer, don't regret . . . I did all I could to please Tristram; for the first time I felt him outside his own skin. Exhausted, we both fell into a deep sleep. Being in a strange narrower bed, I awoke before dawn. I brushed my teeth, came back to his bed and we made love again. As I kissed him on the forehead good morning and left, I said, like a conjurer.

'I may have a baby. I feel, maybe a baby . . .'

'I hope so, darling,' Tristram yawned, pulling armfuls of blanket and sheet up to his chin, happy to recover the whole space of the bed to himself. 'We'll be so happy . . .'

Yes, cosy, I thought. Lapsang Souchong steaming; hot scones wrapped inside the linen stiff with his grand-mother's initials and me, mother, plump and doting, by the cot. The picture was complete, the style inpeccable. And the rest, what of it? It'll follow, filling up cavities and voids like butter melting into toasted scones. Before too long we'd be settled and middle-aged, reading books at table between courses, gliding enviably on to a placid ga-gadom.

At twenty-seven, I asked myself, isn't it about time to reach *satori*, the emancipation from material, spiritual and physical turmoils and temptations of this world? And be elevated to a state where one will 'live as one already dead', the sublime state of bliss and wisdom?

17

There was a television set in the house, but it was put away facing the wall in what used to be Sido's room where now each morning Mrs Apps hung her coat and put on her slippers. The only time I saw the set working had been four years earlier on the night of the general election. So, at least I was spared the embarrassment of seeing in action Pom's demented carryings-on with his four soldier-monks outside the Labour Party Conference Hall in Blackpool. Mercifully, too, *The Times* and the *Guardian* delivered at the house carried only a few cursory lines, dismissing them as 'para-military keep-fit Hare Krishna chanters lead by Lord Pommeroy in the guise of Isabel Burton.'

October 3rd, Tristram came home exhausted after a lengthy meeting with the governors and trustees of the gallery, changed into pyjamas and went to bed.

'I'm afraid your friend Pom has finally gone round the bend.' Tristram gave a harsh rap at the *Evening Standard* with his tapered finger. The coarse-grained photograph showed Pom and his men in flowing robes, presumably of cheesecloth and of saffron yellow, over baggy trousers, gaiters, and headbands with two soft sacks slung across their shoulders, squatting outside the conference hall, holding up a large banner stretched between two poles. Only the bold headline of their manifesto was legible:

THE LAST WARNING FROM THE WORLD ELSEWHERE!

'Why the *last*, I wonder,' I said.

'Just the kind of infantile grandiloquence they go in for. It's pathetic. Darling, I have a sore throat, talked much too much in the airless smoky room. Would you make me a hot lemon and honey with some whisky in it?'

Mumbling to myself, grandirokenss, grandilo-maybe-cance, I made the hot drink; then, too lazy to look up the word in the dictionary at once, I sat below Tristram's bed with the *Evening Standard*. It was my habit, dropping my head to one shoulder, to first read the stop press column on the back page, in case the Chinese or an earthquake or yet another typhoon had attacked Japan in the last several hours.

I tilted my head and read.

'What does this m . . . ?!' I shook the paper in front of Tristram.

'What?'

'Here! This! Self . . . self-immolation!'

'Lord Pommeroy tried to attack the Prime Minister at a Blackpool cinema, then set fire to himself. In the confusion a security guard shot dead one of his followers . . .' Tristram lifted his hand toward his ear as if to shield it from a draught. 'The phone is ringing.'

I ran downstairs and switched the telephone on to his bedroom. When I flew back to his room, he was shouting, 'hello, hello!'

'A long distance call. Must be Juliet. Rather you talked to her,' he threw the receiver at me.

Daddy Sugarheim was on the line without being preceded as was usually the case by his secretary and a personal assistant or two.

'No she doesn't know yet. She's on her way to Centre Island with the baby and nurse. So far we've been unable to track her down. She's due there in about an hour and a half.'

'But, Pom, is he really dead, really?'

'Yep, that he is.'

I removed the receiver from my ear and looked at it with a confused but intense feeling, almost an anger: dead, dead? What does that mean, dead? Tristram snatched the receiver and continued the conversation. Apparently, the UK Sugarheim's managing director had received in the late morning an express registered letter from Blackpool addressed to Mr Sugarheim, marked personal and strictly confidential. Only after Pom's death was reported to his office by one of the garage attendants who had heard the news on his radio did the director telephone Mr Sugarheim in New York and tell him about the letter. Mr Sugarheim told his English employee to open and read the letter to him. Pom gave no explanation whatsoever for his contemplated action but simply and earnestly pleaded with his father-in-law to look after the legal defence of the four boys should they be arrested and tried after his death.

Mother had often praised my 'screw-top stomach' for always keeping what it received. But, for a few days following the October 3rd, I retched every time I saw photographs or read articles on Pom's death or even thought about it. What I managed to reconstruct from various reports of the eye witnesses was a scene whose goriness and appalling slapdashness made my hair stand on end, but it was unmistakably Pom's kind of exit.

On the night of October 2nd, Pom and his gang hid themselves inside the ABC Cinema after an evening performance by Engelbert Humperdinck. The following day there was tight security for the PM's twenty-eight-minute interview with three journalists scheduled for transmission the same evening. Only the PM's own staff and the Thames Television crew were allowed in. About two minutes after the interview had commenced, two doors into the stalls and another into the dress circle were flung open and three men in jeans and T-shirts darted in, brandishing pistols and screaming, 'Keep calm! Hold up your hands and don't stop the cameras. Keep rolling whatever happens. Don't stop the cameras!'

One of them, a blond, tall Adonis of a young man, leapt on to the stage and taking a hand grenade out of his shoulder-sack, held it above his head for all the security guards and plain-clothes men to see, then menacingly aimed it at the Prime Minister, who cowered behind the armchair in which he had been sitting. Meanwhile, the two other aggressors positioned themselves at strategically chosen exit doors holding their pistols tight against their chests. The Adonis, that is, Karl, repeatedly urged the two cameramen to go on filming as he anxiously eyed the stage-left wing, from whence a few moments later strode Pom, wrapped up in multitudinous layers of cheesecloth, drenched and dripping as if he had just taken a shower, barefoot and apparently empty-handed. Hardly had he made his splashy entrance when the lights went out.

'Christ! What the hell..!' One of the crouching journalists heard Karl hiss in panic.

'Don't move, or..!' Another voice shouted from the back of the stalls. No one moved. The two cameramen desperately hugged the cameras that had gone dead and silent. It was the wizened old chief electrician of the cinema, a veritable hero the following morning in the press, who had wrecked Pom's design for a spectacularly public death, his burning body branding a lasting memory on millions of television-watching eyeballs. How was the man to know that the intruders in fact had no interest, murderous or otherwise, in the PM's person? With the presence of mind common amongst workaday technicians he did not hesitate to throw the main switches, plunging the whole house into total darkness.

'I'll still do it,' said Pom, matter-of-factly. Everyone heard a wet thud on the front of the stage, followed by a firm low voice reciting:

'I die not as a challenge but in a spirit of atonement . . .'

Suddenly, in the pitch dark of the cinema a flame flared open as if by a magic and engulfed a sitting statue of a man, straight-backed, head held high on calm shoulders. As he went on reciting what the journalists later described as 'quite banal and sophomoric pacifist stuff' he casually tossed away a small cigarette lighter and put both hands on his lap. They said that the flames were so intense, billowing higher and higher in spirals, that the burning man's speech soon began faltering. The last words heard from his live lips were:

'Reach out . . . for a world elsewhere . . .'

Those near the quickly charring human flesh were

blinded by stinging fumes and coughing violently in the heat and dry stench. One of the security guards told the press that the inflamed body diminished in size at an alarming speed, but not once did it waver or bend. As the burning man lost his speech, the blond Adonis staggered a few steps forward, handling his pistol in such a way as to appear to shoot the Prime Minister. As the eerie eye-stinging flames were the only source of light in the house, standing behind it, he was an easy target. One of the plain-clothes men, ducking between the empty rows of seats in the stalls, fired. The young man fell dead.

The hand grenade, it was discovered later, was not real and the autopsy showed that in Karl's corpse were buried two bullets: one in the chest, the other through the neck and lodged in the head, which incontestably proved that he had shot himself a split second before the detective's bullet felled him. This gave rise to an ugly rumour that he had joined Pom in a double suicide, that he was a part of Pom's pagan fantasy, that it confirmed Pom's homosexuality, or that it was a symbolic gesture inviting other youths to follow his example, die and atone for the world's sins, so on. All this, however, in my opinion was utter nonsense. For example, in the case of Karl's death, either Karl had lost his head and acted outside the synopsis laid down by Pom or he had his own muddled reason for following Pom in death. In Pom's original scenario, as clearly attested by his own letter to his father-in-law, the four boys, including Karl, were to survive him.

'I thought the Japanese were a sentimental race and loved weeping, although, I know your people have very little religious feeling. Still, you amaze me,' at one point during that weekend Tristram came near reproving my lack of any show of lamentation.

Mine was a dry, dry reaction: he's done it! He's done it! was the only recurrent thought that played in my mind. I could not think of anything else. I sat up through the whole of the first night after the news in a comatose calm, beyond thoughts and beyond feeling. His death was his personal statement and its gory, chuck-it-away violence seized me up like throwing meat into sizzling hot oil, it left me no room to bleed or to wallow in the sentimental luxury of mourning.

Naturally, I was disconsolate that never again would I touch him, never again see his afternoon jaws shine blue, never again watch his eyes go *sanpaku*, this accumulation of nevers, what people would call loss, was painful, painful because I was thinking of oh, unhappy me, me, me! Grief is unromantically selfish. For his own sake, I was happier that he had done it than if he had not. Even Ju had once raised a long wail: 'Kick or yell, there's a lot in him that I simply can't understand.' So who am I to try to make sense of his life, let alone his death?

After the first sleepless dry-eyed night, I felt ravenously hungry, ate well and slept soundly the next night. I felt stronger and in harmony with his death. If the black fumes of his death had incinerated the wet of my grief, so it did others' who had much more right than I to lament. Daddy Sugarheim was impressive. 'Asked nicely by a friend, there're very few things I won't do,' he said and, stoically ignoring media harassment, diligently carried out his late son-in-law's request and appointed solicitors and counsel in London, regardless of cost, to defend Richard, Chris and Jim.

As for Ju, she was heroic. She heard the news on the car radio somewhere between Lakeville and Manhasset on the Long Island Expressway. The nurse, an Irish girl of twenty-two, could not drive, and Nicholas was in a cot next to her. Ju turned off the radio, drove on another twenty odd miles, fainted the moment she put the handbrake on inside the gate of her father's country house on Centre Island.

As soon as the British police released Pom's remains – scoops of ashes and a charred cigarette lighter – they were sent to Ju by a Sugarheim courier. As pregnant as a watermelon as she was, she drove herself up to the Atlantic Ocean, not, as she later told me, into the stagnant water of the Long Island Sound, and sprinkled the ashes into it.

'I'm coping fine, but more like just hanging on, just,' she said. 'If he had to do it, he had to do it, right, Suki?

248

Isn't that so? Sh! Don't say anything now. I've got to keep the baby. You love me, loved Pom, so help me keep his baby. I'm not going to be too goddamn sensitive and razzled. Are you kiddin', I'm not taking no tranquilliser, none. I wouldn't dare, with his baby inside me. I'm grateful you listen. It helps. I told Daddy I wanted no memorial service. Pom has done it himself. I know now he had been preparing for it for a long time: Jim sent me his pocket calendar he had managed to hide from the police. All the appointments he'd made for the period after September 27th, the day he left for Blackpool, were meticulously crossed out, either moved up earlier or cancelled. Lillian bugs me by asking real stupid questions: "But, honey, aren't you humiliated, aren't you resentful that he never but never told you anything? If he'd loved you, how could he have done this to you and to darling Nicholas?" and so on, you can just hear her! Well, I tell you and only to you, Suki, there *are* times when I'm seduced into asking such questions myself, but that's when I'm harassed and tired and feeling sorry for myself.'

'I'm so relieved,' I told Tristram at once. 'Ju's much calmer and more controlled than I ever imagined possible.'

'A widow of an exceptional man, whether a martyr or a criminal or a saint, often throws herself with maniacal energy into shrine-building to her late remarkable husband's memory and can lead a perfectly rewarding and even interesting life,' said Tristram.

I thought his comment cynical and unkind at the time and gave him a slinky-eyed glance of disapproval; then, several days later, Ju rang again.

'Guru Mashi came to see me yesterday. He has over four hundred volunteers wanting to come to Falaise Hall to continue Pom's work and help me restart the World Elsewhere. I'm telling you, Suki, it's not in my power to stop it now. I've told Daddy and my Trustees so. The World Eslewhere will go on, and go on big. It's really exciting. I'll come back to Falaise Hall as soon as I have had the baby and we'll organise an annual festival on the anniversary of Pom's burning. He'll live on in the memory of millions.'

I understood what Tristram had meant by a hero's widow thriving on the shrine-building. Ju had the Sugarheim non-as-as-as callousness, the quality indispensable to making a successful executive. She would make a super-efficient manager, probably far tougher and better organised than Pom would ever have been, and for inspiration and charisma she had only to turn to the October 3rd martyrdom.

The expected date of my October period passed without a sign of it. I drew a deep breath and held it as I counted and recounted the number of days that had passed. A few days later I went for a pregnancy test. Too early, come back in a week's time, I was told. On the morning of my second visit, Mrs Apps asked me: 'Are you feeling all right, Mrs Harder? You've lost some weight, haven't you, dear?'

It was Tuesday. On Thursday I rang the laboratory from Tristram's study after he had left the house, and my heart was beating so wildly that I heard its echo against the earpiece.

'Congratulations, it's positive.' A cheery indifferent voice announced.

'Thank you very much,' I bowed ceremoniously to the telephone and put the receiver down; then impulsively I began dialling 010–1–212 for New York City. Only after completing Ju's number did I consider that it would still be only three in the morning for her and disconnected the call; besides, how would I have explained to her my baby? MY baby? Where does it come from, YOUR baby? she might ask. From your late husband, would I have replied? I might have . . . No, oh, no! It's got to be Tristram's! It's Tristram's!

In a single moment I became a plural-responsible person: like the lioness hovering mistrustingly over her cub I had seen in Walt Disney nature films, I was on my guard. I had two cubs to protect: Tristram and the baby. That I was the mother of the baby, there could be no question or doubt and as such the father had to be Tristram. As for the truth, except for the expert who had examined Tristram many years ago, there were only Letti,

250

Ju, Tristram himself and I who knew of the possibility that my child's father could be either some potent sperms in a sterilised tube or another man. And even *that* remained only a possibility, for Tristram could have successfully undergone treatment or an operation unknown to them.

I dialled Tristram's office. I wanted him to confirm to me that I had been a good girl, done a good job, and that he would be my child's father, and together we'd be stronger.

'Dr Harder is in a meeting. Can I help you?' replied Philippa, his secretary, sing-song. I stared at my cold white fist that clutched the receiver, then laughed.

'No, no, it's all right. Not important . . .'

I was next dialling Paris. Letti answered.

'I'm going to have a baby!'

I heard Letti gulp a small ball of air. 'Darling girl . . . what . . . ah . . .' She began slowly as if swallowing very cold icecream, then with her characteristic chic decided to accept, love and rejoice. 'Soukie, oh, I am so glad!' she said with total conviction. 'Dear girl, I can't think of anything better to say. I can just repeat how happy I am.'

I believed in and was moved by the mature warmth behind the banal words of congratulation. Perhaps she felt redeemed in a vicarious way that her son was to have a family life she had never bothered to give him.

'It's rather ironical, really. When Tristram and I struck a bargain over Frank's estate in June, I agreed to leave my share of Mortcerf in the first instance to his child or children in equal shares. So, my poor Third World artists have had it. When I go, Soukie, you'll be the mistress of Mortcerf and you know, frankly, I can't think of anyone I'd rather have to own and cherish it than you.'

After I hung up, I sat numb with joy for a long while. I was so impressed by Letti and myself. I felt so grown-up, not tougher, nor wiser, but hardier. Really, there is no justice in this world: an adultress solving so many tangled-up problems at one stroke *and* being congratulated! I was still cogitating confusedly, when Tristram opened the front door.

'I'm pregnant!' I spoke whilst he was still trying to pull his key out of the keyhole. He stood bolt upright, leaving his bunch of keys to jangle against the door. His gaze on me at first was blurred, then a rush of blood like tipsiness spread round his eyes. He clasped me in his arms, dropping his cane, the Gucci bag, and the evening paper to the floor. I had read him correctly: neither then nor later did he ever bring up the question how the pregnancy had been made possible. Not even the 'a' of artificial insemination broke his lips. That night, although we returned home long after midnight from a dinner, he took me into his bedroom and afterwards he said as softly as a wind through a cluster of mimosa, 'It was in September we made love in the morning and you said, didn't you . . . ?'

'Yes,' I said. That was the morning after I had last seen Pom. True to his style and nature, this was the closest and the last time Tristram went near the question of the paternity of the baby.

From then onwards it was quite convincingly our baby and as I held on to this conviction like a talisman, so did he. The next day he bought me at an Old Bond Street jeweller a superb eternity ring, told me never to remove it from my finger and taught me how to clean it with a toothbrush and a bit of toothpaste. That night with the ring on my finger for eternity I asked him if I might telephone Ju in New York.

'Can't you write, darling?' Tristram, being Tristram, asked.

'I have. I mean I have sent a telegram, but . . .' I had been uncomfortable, knowing the telegram was somewhat cowardly.

'You know her; the minute she gets your telegram, she'll ring you.'

She did, shattering the midnight silence. She did not shriek, did not gush, she spoke in a gentlest nasal voice: if a healing ointment had a voice, it should have sounded like Ju's voice then.

'Suki, I don't have to tell you, do I, how happy I am, how I love you and how Pom would have gone berserk with joy with the news,' she said. 'Just incredible, you and I, how one we are. It's in our karma. How else could you explain? Sweetiepie, I'll come back to England when your day comes. I want to make a fuss of you, hold your hand and share.'

I could hardly speak, pearls of tears rolling down my gorge. I was moved, I was undone. I did not panic at her last word and ask 'Share what?' I held on to the telephone receiver for life, for honour, for the future, for Tristram's and my child's sake. I'd have otherwise slobbered into an unnecessary, undignified confession, which would have spoilt everything. I hung up, convinced that she knew my baby's father, if not by fact or disclosure, by the sheer intuition of a truly loving soul and the most astonishing part of it all, it changed nothing whatsoever between us.

Ju had her second son on January 14th and named him Arthur. By then I carried a discreet sign of pregnancy myself and Tristram was busy obtaining estimates for turning the second guest room into a nursery and redecorating Sido's old room for a nurse and later a nanny. He also began enquiring about the French Lycée and the choice of a suitable nanny already obsessed him. Whenever he met anyone who had had anything to do with children and nannies he interrogated them down to the last detail. Colin rolled his eyes in mock despair.

'Darling, unless you put your foot down and exercise some Japanese discipline, you'll end up having the most spoilt brat and the most boring father in the whole of the British Isles.'

My parents' letter was a calligraphy of undiluted bliss. For them the baby meant the final and irrevocable cementing of my marriage, which, so far, had seemed to them a dubious enterprise, even a potential disaster and loss of face. Fumiko from Dusseldorf rang me to say she would come to London and look after me when the moment came.

'Of course, I'll stay at Hyde Park Hotel,' said my sister kindly. 'Don't worry.'

I made a face, recalling her last visit to London, then giggled like oatmeal just before burning. 'I'm not worried. It's you who worry ahead, Sister Fumi.'

Fumiko must have made a sort of mental and facial adjustment to my sally: there was a pause before she said, 'A tough little nut.'

'Not at all, Sister Fumi,' I retaliated with a militant gaiety. 'If you saw me now, in a throne-like bed, drapes and laces, you'd have said I'm a fairy-tale princess.'

Fumiko either snorted or laughed, I could not tell which, and added tartly: 'Well, my kindest regards to your prince charming!'

After hanging up I subsided into my pillows and thoughts: my life, from the rainy night in Tokyo when a perfectly ordinary Japanese girl shared a taxi with a foreigner, up to five o'clock this afternoon when she, a mother-to-be, cossetted by plenty of inessential luxury and fuss, sips weak Lapsang souchong out of a Flora Danica tea cup, would to an outsider sound like a fairy tale indeed. But a fairy tale ends as a shepherdess swoons in a prince's arms, never telling us what happens thereafter; it never tells how much determination, endurance, optimism and humility so fierce as to almost amount to pride, what art of timing and strategy worthy of the best of generals a girl must mobilise to keep alive her marriage contract with an intimate stranger; and above all, what courage, what insane courage she must have to enter into such a contract at all.

What I know today, I will not tell my own daughter. I want her to plunge if she must with all her absurd courage intact. The rest will follow, for worse, for better.